About this book

Abolish border controls? Let in large numbers of Third World or Eastern European immigrants? Can this author be serious? That may be the first response of some readers to this remarkable argument in favour of scrapping the costly, often inhumane and only partially effective barriers that the United States has set up along its lengthy border with Mexico, and with which Europe and Australia have surrounded themselves.

Yet, as Jonathon W. Moses argues, the whole apparatus of passports and visas, with borders fenced off and patrolled, is a relatively new phenomenon. Historically, it was never regarded as necessary. Nor were immigrants seen as threatening. Indeed, the United States, Canada and Latin America were built on migration. Europe itself, facing a falling population, has over the past fifty years actively encouraged large-scale immigration. What is more, the widespread agreement, particularly on the right, that the free movement of goods and capital is beneficial to economies begs the question: why not free movement of people too?

Moses cogently marshals the historical, moral, political and economic arguments in favour of the free mobility of people across national borders. He discusses and counters the most significant obstacles to increasing international migration, including public opinion in the developed world and the conventional wisdom that free migration is too difficult, too costly, too dangerous or too unrealistic to consider.

This book's argument may not be popular in the North, but it is sufficiently compelling not to be dismissed without serious debate. And its implications are clear and profound: free international migration can lessen the huge material inequalities and human injustices that many associate with today's globalizing world.

About the author

Professor Jonathon W. Moses has been at the Norwegian University of Science and Technology (NTNU) since 1993. Educated at the University of Washington and the University of California at Los Angeles, he has taught and carried out research at these universities as well as at the North–South University in Dhaka, Bangladesh, and the University of Durban–Westville (now the University of Kwazulu-Natal) in South Africa. Migration has long been a special interest, and he has published many journal articles and book chapters on the subject. He is the author of *Open States in the Global Economy: The Political Economy of Small State Macroeconomic Management* (2000), *Norwegian Catch-Up: Globalization and Development before WWII* (2005) and co-editor (with Robert Geyer and Christine Ingebritsen) of *Globalization, Europeanization and the End of Scandinavian Social Democracy?* (2000). He is currently completing a book on methodology in the social sciences.

Praise for this book

'The free movement of goods and capital across borders has been hotly debated for decades, with phalanxes of scholars, activists, and politicians arrayed on all sides of the debates. But the free international movement of people is widely regarded as undesirable or impossible, or both. In this courageous book, Jonathon W. Moses presents a sustained argument for free international immigration. Moses surveys the history and morality of immigration, as well as social-scientific analyses of its political and economic impact. He finds no compelling reasons for immigration restrictions, and addresses virtually every possible objection to his argument. The political realism of Moses's radical proposals may be questioned, but his logic and evidence are impeccable. *International Migration* is carefully reasoned, forcefully presented, and passionately argued. Intellectual opponents of free international migration have their work cut out for them.'

Jeffry Frieden, Professor of Government, Harvard University

'An excellent book – cogent, well-argued and comprehensive. Right on target for a world that is not fully reconciled to the logic of globalization.'

Nigel Harris, Professor Emeritus, University College London

'*International Migration* stands out in the vast literature on globalization. It speaks with clarity and moral force on an aspect of globalization about which relatively little has been written. There has been almost an academic conspiracy of silence on the question of international migration. In this book Jonathon W. Moses weaves together political, economic and moral arguments to make a persuasive case for his vision of a world without borders. This book is refreshingly provocative for the boldness of its ideas, and provides a counterpoint to the one-sided view that all we need in the name of globalization is freer trade and mobility of capital, but not the mobility of labour.'

Amit Bhaduri, Professor Emeritus, Jawaharlal Nehru University

International Migration

Globalization's Last Frontier

_____

Jonathon W. Moses

WITHDRAWN
UTSA Libraries

White Lotus
Bangkok

Fernwood Publishing
Nova Scotia

Books for Change
Bangalore

SIRD
Kuala Lumpur

David Philip
Cape Town

ZED BOOKS
London & New York

International Migration was published in 2006 by

In Burma, Cambodia, Laos, Thailand and Vietnam:
White Lotus Co. Ltd, GPO Box 1141, Bangkok 10501, Thailand

In Canada: Fernwood Publishing Ltd, 8422 St Margaret's Bay Road (Hwy 3)
Site 2A, Box 5, Black Point, Nova Scotia, B0J 1B0

In India: Books for Change, 139 Richmond Road, Bangalore 560 025

In Malaysia: Strategic Information Research Development (SIRD),
No. 11/4E, Petaling Jaya, 46200 Selangor

In Southern Africa: David Philip (an imprint of New Africa Books),
99 Garfield Road, Claremont 7700, South Africa

In the rest of the world: Zed Books Ltd, 7 Cynthia Street, London N1 9JF, UK,
and Room 400, 175 Fifth Avenue, New York, NY 10010, USA
www.zedbooks.co.uk

Copyright © Jonathon W. Moses 2006

No part of this publication may be reproduced, stored in a retrieval system or
transmitted, in any form or by any means, electronic or otherwise, without the
prior permission of the publisher.

The right of Jonathon W. Moses to be identified as the author of this
work has been asserted by him in accordance with the Copyright, Designs
and Patents Act, 1988

Designed and typeset in Monotype Bembo
by illuminati, Grosmont, www.illuminatibooks.co.uk
Cover designed by Andrew Corbett
Printed and bound in Malta by Gutenberg Ltd

Distributed in the USA exclusively by Palgrave Macmillan, a division of
St Martin's Press, LLC, 175 Fifth Avenue, New York, NY 10010

All rights reserved

A catalogue record for this book is available from the British Library
Library of Congress Cataloging-in-Publication Data available
Library and Archives Canada Cataloguing in Publication
Moses, Jonathon Wayne, 1962–
    International migration: globalization's last frontier / Jonathon
W. Moses.
ISBN 1-55266-194-6
    1. Emigration and immigration. I. Title.
JV6035.M67 2006a 325 C2005-907268-7

ISBN 1 84277 658 4 Hb (Zed Books)
ISBN 1 84277 659 2 Pb (Zed Books)
ISBN 978 1 84277 658 2 Hb (Zed Books)
ISBN 978 1 84277 659 9 Pb (Zed Books)
ISBN 1 55266 194 6 (Canada)

Contents

For Thandeka, Aurora and children everywhere
— for whom borders don't exist

Preface

> Perhaps the sentiments contained in the following pages, are
> not *yet* sufficiently fashionable to procure them general favor;
> a long habit of not thinking a thing *wrong*, gives it a super-
> ficial appearance of being *right*, and raises at first a formidable
> outcry in defence of custom. But the tumult soon subsides.
> Time makes more converts than reason.
>
> Thomas Paine[1]

I believe that free migration offers the potential and hope to
better an unjust world. If this potential is not immediately obvious, it may be because so much of it is hidden beneath layers of
political rhetoric, xenophobia and historical amnesia. This book
is an attempt to raise the migration debate to a level where we
might again recognize the potential it offers.

The political, social and economic consequences of global
capital, goods and service flows are enormous, and yet these
flows have been gradually liberated in the face of remarkably
little public resistance. There was hardly a whimper of defiance
when capital controls and autonomous domestic monetary policies
– the keystones of national economic management policies in the
postwar period – were jettisoned by most states. In the name of

economic efficiency and consumer freedom, we have granted international investors and producers free mobility.

By contrast, advocating free migration is akin to political leprosy. While the modern legislature is filled with promoters of free trade, foreign investment and more general forms of economic liberalization, there are astonishingly few representatives for the party of migrants. Remarkably, the academic community is only marginally more open to the idea. This book is an attempt to understand why there is so much resistance to liberalizing national controls on human mobility.

My journey began by collecting and evaluating what had been written on international migration. At the most general level, I found the academic terrain to be remarkably barren: not many scholars are willing to consider such radical measures as the liberalization of national border controls. Still, it is possible to discern some variation in willingness to broach the subject. Moral philosophers, for example, tend to be more willing to consider the moral benefits of a freer migration regime (and/or the moral costs of our own control-based regime). Political scientists, by contrast, are remarkably (and rather uncharacteristically) silent on the subject. Their focus is limited mostly to explaining variations in control regimes used to isolate the world's wealthiest states. Nestled in between these two types of literature I found a number of economists and economic historians who are interested in different aspects of international migration, if leery of embracing the idea of a world without borders.

As I became familiar with the most significant landmarks in this terrain, my concern grew along with my puzzlement: I could find little justification for the negative tone of today's migration debate. There is little reason to expect an enormous flood of immigrants into the developed world; little evidence that Northern welfare states will be diluted by immigration; little support for the claim that the livelihood of the developed world's unskilled workers will be swamped, or that the developing world's skilled labour force will drain away. Quite the opposite, this literature provides firm ground for questioning the economic, moral and political logic of today's control regimes.

It is these discoveries that motivate the book before you. My ambition is to draw from a wide body of literature to provoke a broader and more honest discussion about international migration. In doing so, I hope to present the disparate arguments in a way that is accessible to the general reader.

While the motivation for this argument can be found in the remarkable gap that separates public opinion and academic research on the subject of international migration, the argument's form was clearly moulded by three disparate pressures: the warning of sceptics, the passing of time, and the comments and criticisms of many helpful friends and colleagues.

Over the course of writing this book I have faced many formidable warnings about the pointlessness of arguing for a world with free mobility. These caveats have not been heeded. While I recognize that a world characterized by free mobility seems only a distant possibility today, I fear that we ignore it at great cost. It is surely not pointless to have the discussion. Even the most sceptical reader must accept the utility of considering counterfactual scenarios. The history of political thought is filled with examples of the motivational power of utopian visions. What harm can be done by considering the impossible, especially if such considerations can inspire us to more noble and just action?

More importantly, how can we be so certain of what is possible (or not)? Modern history should remind us of Machiavelli's caveat about the fickle nature of *fortuna*. The Cold War's abrupt end illustrates the remarkable pace of regime change, once a regime's legitimacy is called into question. Who could have imagined the fall of the Berlin Wall in the spring of 1988? How can we be so certain that a world free from passports and visas does not lie around the next bend of history?

Discussions about free mobility are not common or easy, but neither are they impossible. Stifling discussion or ignoring the potential of free migration will not help us bridge the gap that today separates opinion, interest, perception and policy. It is for this reason that proposals for open borders are not pointless, even if such discussions will not win votes in the developed world (at least not in the first round of what is necessarily an iterative game). Perceptions can be changed. Indeed, perceptions *should* be changed when they no longer correspond to interest, and are held at the expense of others (at great moral cost).

This random walk of history has already affected the argument that follows. It is almost ten years since I first began to wonder about the potential for free mobility. An initial draft of this book was nearing completion when two planes crashed into New York's World Trade Center. Immediately, I realized that the world's political climate was bound to change in ways that would make an argument for free mobility less attractive. Indeed, I felt a need to reconsider such an argument in light of these dastardly developments. As a consequence, I put the manuscript and the argument on ice.

In January of 2004, my family and I moved to Dhaka, Bangladesh, for an extended stay. Dhaka is an incredibly vibrant and exotic place – the sounds, smells and sights of which should have provided me with ample distraction. But Dhaka's effect on me was quite the opposite. For residents of the developed world living in Dhaka, every day is a reminder of the phenomenal and unjust differences that separate our life chances from those offered to the average Bangladeshi. The city's poverty, density and general sense of hopelessness forced me to consider the millions of people who live beyond the developed world's fortress walls, in dire need of justice and immediate help. Life in Dhaka made me realize again the necessity of considering radical solutions to an unbearable problem. It is my hope that this book can generate enough fruitful discussion so as to alleviate some of that injustice.

Given the length of time separating this book's conception and its eventual delivery to market, I have incurred numerous intellectual debts. Many students, over the years and from distant and faraway places, have helped me grapple with the potential for free mobility. Their curiosity, comments and criticisms have helped me sharpen my thinking on the subject. The same can be said of the countless fruitful exchanges with colleagues, friends and neighbours. Discussions of free mobility tend to generate strong visceral reactions. Discussions with friends and colleagues make it possible to breach delicate subjects and explore in more detail the grounds for difference.

I am also indebted to Robert Molteno of Zed Books for embracing this project and nursing it towards completion. Robert exemplifies a good book editor. His timely advice and stewardship have been central to the manuscript's development: he has helped me focus the argument, sharpen the language, and made me aware of the breadth of my potential readership.

I owe my greatest debt of gratitude to several people who have read the entire manuscript, in its many varied forms. Among these are Michael Alvarez, Maggi Brigham, Dag Harald Claes, O'mano Edigheji, Robert Gillespie, Chris Hassenstab, Håvard Mykeltun, Bjørn Myskja and Sabrina Ramet. These friends and readers have helped me temper my exuberance and polemical rhetoric, consider alternative viewpoints, and focus my presentation. It would be a mistake to assume that they subscribe to the argument that follows: most of them have challenged it on many disparate fronts. In spite of these differences, each of them has lent me an open ear. A writer can ask for little more. Their help and advice can explain what is worthwhile in the project that follows. I, alone, am to blame for any of its shortcomings.

I

Introduction

If they can get here, they have God's right to come.

Melville[1]

'Help us, we suffer too much in Africa, help us.' This simple plea was written in the summer of 1999. While most appeals of this sort go unnoticed, we remember this one for being found on the dead bodies of two young refugees boys, stowed away in the landing gear of an Airbus that had recently departed from Guinea–Conakry. In a world where ideas, capital, goods and services float almost effortlessly around the globe, it remains a crime for two boys to escape their suffering in Africa. Worse yet, it is a crime that hundreds – if not thousands – of people die trying to commit each year.

On the outskirts of the developed world lies a no man's land littered with the dead bodies of those – like these two boys from Africa – who scramble for a better life. In both Europe and the United States, the death toll that results from today's restrictive immigration policies is astonishingly high: over the past decade, thousands of people have died trying to make their own private dash for freedom. In a single month, May of 2004, sixteen confirmed deaths occurred along the border separating Mexico from the United States. One of these was a 32-year-old Mexican woman from the state of Veracruz, who was found dead north of Amado on 14 May. Apparently this woman was abandoned by her smuggler (*coyote*) when she was not able to keep up with a group of immigrants crossing the southern Arizona desert.[2]

We should not fool ourselves. These deaths are neither isolated events nor dreadful accidents. These deaths, and the many more that go unnoticed, are symptomatic of national policies that restrict immigration to the developed world. While these people deserve sympathy and support, the policies of the developed world encourage its residents to ignore the humanity and suffering of those who flee from the many faces of tragedy. Instead of acknowledging our moral obligation to assist people in dire need, the developed world brands them as a threat to its well-being, treats them as criminals, and forces them into desperate acts that too often result in death.

There is no greater global issue. On nearly every other front, the pace and scope of globalization have impressed all but the most enthusiastic supporters. Under the twin banners of freedom and efficiency, consumers and firms have broken out of their parochial, national contexts to mingle in increasingly global markets. This nexus has brought both opportunity and hardship – unequally distributed across the globe.

For a very fortunate few, the greatest political and economic hardships are softened by exclusive, democratic, welfare states. But the vast majority of the world's inhabitants are less lucky. Born into poor, unstable and/or authoritarian regimes, billions of people have little possibility of escaping the economic and political oppression into which they are born. For both rich and poor, our political and economic fortunes are determined mostly by fate.

Instead of recognizing the dilemma posed by such global inequalities, we build citadels to separate rich from poor, lucky from unlucky. Like gated communities, the developed world keeps the developing world at bay. But this myopic response cannot hold. As distance in the world recedes with technological, social, demographic and political advances, the demand for international migration will surely grow. In the future it is doubtful that walls can be built high enough to deter the desperate. Today's status quo is untenable: we need to find a better means for resolving the differences that separate our two worlds.

This book offers a simple solution to these dilemmas: free migration. Because of the radical and provocative nature of the proposed solution, it is developed cautiously along two fronts. On the one hand, it is necessary to show that most claims about the catastrophic political, economic and social consequences of free mobility are unfounded. On the other hand, this book aims to show how free migration can resolve many of the economic and political dilemmas that face individuals and states in an increasingly interconnected global context. In short, the economic, political and social consequences of free human mobility are not as frightening, as threatening or as unrealistic as most pundits suggest. Indeed, a world without borders can be a more just and efficient world – one that enjoys a better distribution of the world's political and economic bounty.

A timely argument...

Many would question the timing of this sort of argument. The world is enmeshed in a clash of civilizations, and the pace and scope of globalization have provoked an identity backlash in most of the world's disparate regions. The rise and influence of new religious groups, the spread of sundry secessionist movements, and the popularity of maverick and xenophobic political parties are all evidence of how people today are engaged in a desperate search for their unique identities and places in a shrinking world.

At the same time, there seems to be increased fear about (and hostility to) the subject of international migration in the developed world, especially after the attacks on 11 September 2001. For example, a recent YouGov poll conducted for *The Economist* found that 74 per cent of British respondents believed there were too many people coming into their country. Most of these respondents were concerned about immigrants putting too much pressure on public services, but there were also concerns about the effect on 'racial balance', crime and the domestic job market.[3] The concerns of the British public are not unique – each developed country entertains its own anti-immigrant sentiment. In light of these developments and concerns, it may appear as an odd time to forward an argument for free migration.

Actually, the time has never been more appropriate. A broader discussion about the benefits of freer human mobility can show how greater international migration need not threaten. After all, by moving to a world with freer migration we don't throw ourselves into a chaotic world without political authority, laws and/or community. A simple glance around us reveals that free migration *within* states doesn't jeopardize our cultural identity, individual security, or the authority of local political institutions, laws and markets. Any fresh emigrant from Seattle to Selma (or from Stockholm to Seville) can assure us that cultural difference can be maintained in a context of free migration. Indeed, globalization makes it easier to sustain the immigrant's cultural ties and affinities. Better yet, free migration has the potential to deliver the sort of economic, political and social gains that are necessary for establishing our personal and cultural security while deterring terrorism around the world.

The time is right for this discussion because new (global) economic conditions are diminishing the role of national borders and fundamentally altering the state's ability to pursue unilateral policies/actions. This constraint on state sovereignty is everywhere recognized but in the realm of immigration policy. How strange it is that states recognize the futility and cost of trying to stop the free flow of information, goods, services and investments, yet respond to immigration in the same old (and futile) way: by sealing off their borders. It does not take a Nostradamus to predict that the time is near when states will have to resolve this contradiction and address the changing roles of borders and governments in a world characterized by economic, political and social integration.

In addressing this issue, we can provide a reality check to an extensive globalization debate. While the globalization literature is bountiful, it focuses rather myopically on those areas of globalization that are most visible and fully developed. We now know a great deal about the economic and political consequences of international capital and trade flows. By focusing on these established global networks, however, we lose sight of how restrictive global exchange appears to the world's most desperate denizens. The world is hardly a free or unified place for people who are unable to escape from economic, political or social tyranny. For desperate souls like these, today's opportunity is too often restricted to something like the landing gear of a departing Airbus. Worse, a dearth of studies on labour globalization helps to feed the fear that lies beneath most migration control regimes. There is simply not enough discussion of the potential that free migration offers to the world's most desperate residents.

The time is also ripe to recognize that today's migrant control regimes simply don't work. While many policymakers and analysts claim that 'uncontrolled immigration is an impossibility',[4] the opposite appears closer to the truth: controlling immigration is an impossibility! More realistic is the recognition by Jean-Pierre Garson, the OECD's expert on international immigration, that 'Some politicians shy away from these issues for fear of losing votes, but the facts speak for themselves: zero immigration is just pure fancy.'[5] No matter what the political culture and/or particular migration control regime, illegal immigration has only grown in recent decades: all developed countries, and many developing countries, have been forced to deal with it. Consequently, an enormous gap has opened between the intent and the reality of the world's migration policies. This gap should encourage us to rethink our approach to migration and reconsider the effectiveness (measured in any number of ways) of continued regulatory enforcement.

Indeed, demographic pressures within the developed world will make it difficult (at least costly) to continue ignoring the political and economic potential of international migration. The developed world's population is both shrinking (in number) and ageing. Across most of Europe, national birth rates are below their replacement rates. Russia and Japan face the same dire situation, while America and Canada are hovering on the brink. Soon there will be too few workers in these countries to pay for their elaborate welfare and social security needs (which they otherwise fight so hard to protect). Without an injection of young immigrant workers, the welfare of the developed world risks being retired along with its population.

Even today, the developed world relies on foreign workers to satisfy its current demand for jobs – at both high and low ends of the skills continuum – and to compensate for its own inability to adjust to rapidly changing market conditions. Former German chancellor Gerhard Schröder was perhaps the most frank among the developed world's political elites, when he announced that 'German education with its focus on heavy philosophical concepts does not turn out the people we want.'[6] Over the past decade, Europe and the United States have been tripping over themselves in a race to attract highly skilled, information-technology workers from abroad.

Finally, states continue to lose sovereign authority over decisions regarding international migrants, and it is time to recognize as much. An emerging system of international human rights already limits the state's freedom of action.[7] In this new international context, the state is no longer the exclusive subject of international law: states find themselves caught in a web of rights and actors that effectively trap their capacity for sovereign action with respect to immigration decisions.

In particular, resident immigrants already enjoy an expanding set of rights, upheld by receiving countries (often at lower levels of political authority). In effect, we see the emergence of a de facto regime, centred in international agreements and conventions, which limits the state's role. This is especially obvious in the European Union, where courts have regularly supported, and governments have extended, the rights of resident immigrants. For example, governments in Sweden and the Netherlands fund immigration associations, facilitate home-language learning, promote equal opportunities in the labour market, and allow immigrants to vote in local elections. Similar pressures can be found in the United States, where the federal government finds itself considering amnesty programmes for illegal immigrants on an almost regular basis.

International migration trends, and the decisions that affect them, are already challenging traditional conceptions of national sovereignty. Global economic integration, the economic needs of both sending and receiving countries, a de facto transnationalization of immigration policymaking – all are evidence of the need to reassess the potential of freer human mobility. The time has come to move discussion about migration away from the narrow focus on limits and controls, to a broader political and intellectual terrain that links immigration to the globalization of other factors.

... a *good* argument...

Once this need is recognized, we will find that there are solid historical, moral, political and economic grounds for arguing that free migration can bring a drastic improvement to today's social, economic and political conditions. Indeed, these arguments constitute the main (positive) contribution of this book (Chapters 3 to 6).

The economic and political gains from freer labour mobility are similar in nature to the more familiar gains from globalizing capital and trade markets – but these gains can be extended to a much broader spectrum of the world's population. Of course, the beneficiaries of free human mobility can be found scattered unequally across countries, and around the globe. Residents of both the developing and the developed world stand to gain from free mobility, but these gains vary significantly across social groups and in terms of their size and effect. As a result, this book does not aim to prioritize the interests of developed-world or developing-world citizens – its objective is to show how the effects of international migration spread across the globe in uneven ways, and that the overall sum of these gains is clearly positive.

Having said this, however, it is important to recognize that the greatest resistance to free migration rests in the developed world. Most residents of the developed world assume that there are significant economic, political and social costs associated with liberalizing immigration controls. This resistance is grounded on hysterical arguments that exaggerate both the demand for, and the effect of, international migration. Rather than consider how migration might mitigate world tyranny, shrink world income gaps, resolve intergenerational pension deficits, and so on, the developed world cowers in fear of a pending catastrophe: where *tidal gates* are opened, allowing a *flood* of new immigrants that will *swamp* domestic economies and welfare policies in the richest states.

The truth is less ominous and more complicated: the pages that follow illustrate how free human mobility can benefit residents of the developed world, even when migration questions are framed in terms of narrow economic or political interests. More importantly, they will show that responses to migration can be motivated by a whole range of forces (including, for example, morality and prejudice) and that these forces may sometimes prevail over narrow economic and political interests. For that reason, the argument takes aim at a broad target: one that spans the moral, political, social and economic consequences of freer mobility.

While assessing these disparate arguments – as they play out in both the developed and developing worlds – you may find that one argument is more convincing than the others. This is not odd, as our disparate interests are affected in a variety of ways by international migration. Nevertheless, a reasonable argument can (and will) be made – on historical, moral, economic and political grounds – that a future world with free migration represents a significant improvement on the status quo for most people, in both the developed and the developing worlds.

While there are many political and economic motivations for abolishing border controls, perhaps the strongest argument for their dismantlement is moral in nature. Today's migration regime is terribly unjust: it distributes opportunity by fate, and has the effect of condemning people to life sentences in their country of birth. As such, the current regime tends to prioritize the rights of an imagined community (the nation), at the expense of sometimes desperate individuals.[8] This injustice is recognized by actors who span the political spectrum. For example, Soviet premier Nikita Khrushchev lamented the injustice of Soviet borders in his memoirs:

> Why should we build a good life for a people and then keep our border bolted with seven locks?… I think it's time to show the world that our people are free; they work willingly; and they are building Socialism because of their convictions, not because they have no choice…
>
> We've got to stop designing our border policy for the sake of keeping the dregs and scum inside our country. We must start thinking about the people who don't deserve to be called scum – people who might undergo a temporary vacillation in their

own convictions, or who might want to try out the capitalists' hell, some aspects of which might still appear attractive to our less stable elements. We can't keep fencing these people in. We've got to give them a chance to find out for themselves what the world is like.[9]

While Khrushchev wrote about the injustice of border controls that restrict emigration, American president George W. Bush has voiced concern about the injustice of controls that restrict immigration:

> Their search for a better life is one of the most basic desires of human beings. Many undocumented workers have walked mile after mile, through the heat of the day and the cold of the night. Some have risked their lives in dangerous desert border crossings, or entrusted their lives to the brutal rings of heartless human smugglers. Workers who seek only to earn a living end up in the shadows of American life – fearful, often abused and exploited. When they are victimized by crime, they are afraid to call the police, or seek recourse in the legal system. They are cut off from their families far away, fearing if they leave our country to visit relatives back home, they might never be able to return to their jobs.
>
> The situation I described is wrong. It is not the American way. Out of common sense and fairness, our laws should allow willing workers to enter our country and fill jobs that Americans have [*sic*] are not filling. We must make our immigration laws more rational, and more humane. And I believe we can do so without jeopardizing the livelihoods of American citizens.[10]

Giving people the opportunity for a better life is the right thing to do: it will empower individuals in the world and encourage a more just (and legitimate) system of international governance. For many of us, this moral argument trumps all the others as we grapple with the injustices that mark our globe. In short, an argument for free human mobility is not only a reasonable argument; it is a *good* and just argument as well.

An initial argument can be made by tracing the history of human mobility – a history that is often ignored in contemporary discussions about immigration control (and, for that matter, in broader globalization studies). It is common today to assume that national controls on human mobility are natural and long-standing. In doing so, we ignore or discount most of human history, where migration has been understood as a fundamental need and where welcoming foreigners has been seen as an act of civility. All human societies are products of migration, but our current perspective blinds us to this historical truth and has us imagine that our communities are hermetically sealed from the outside world.

While the history of human mobility is conveniently forgotten, we take for granted the political and economic gains that accompanied it. After all, it was during a previous era of globalization, when great 'waves' of migrants washed upon the shores of the New World, that America developed her economic and political prowess. America's strength and flexibility crossed the Atlantic in a fleet of migrant ships, beckoned by Emma Lazarus and the promise of a new life. It is these tired, poor and huddled masses, yearning to breathe freely, that populated and built the United States into the hyper-power of today. As the *New York Times* journalist and popular author Thomas Friedman never tires of noting: it is the USA's very adaptability – itself a product of its diverse immigrant stock – that lies at the core of its strength and staying power.

While this may seem obvious on reflection, it is less obvious to see (or understand) how these waves of emigrants affected their sending countries. A great exodus of surplus labour from Europe to the New World strengthened the political and economic power of the labour that remained. This strengthened class position led to the extension of democratic suffrage and the development of the modern welfare state in Europe.

During an earlier era of globalization, international interconnectivity was not a damper on progressive political action; it stoked its flames! Atlantic economies, linked by capital, goods and *labour* flows, were drawn together; the differences separating rich and poor were quickly eroded by powerful human incentives. As a consequence, the world was awash with progressive political movements; movements that established representative democracy, workers' rights and the foundations of the modern welfare state – in both sending and receiving countries.

By contrast, the bounty of today's globalization is accessible only to the lucky few. The world's richest individuals have exploited a global economy to amass unimaginably large fortunes (in 2002, Bill Gates was estimated to be worth $52.8 billion, while Warren Buffet managed a meagre $35 billion). At the same time, there are more than a billion people who somehow manage to live on less than one US dollar a day. It would seem that our shrinking globe is inhabited by people who live a world apart.

While the uneven economic benefits of globalization are already well documented (and will be discussed in the chapter that follows), the political consequences are poorly understood. Contrary to idyllic promises of the *End of History* and the universal triumph of liberal democracy, we live in a world scarred by tyranny and injustice.[11] These regimes exist, in large part, because people remain prisoners of territory. If given the chance to leave, who would remain in a country ruled by a tyrant? What tyrant could afford to pursue policies that emptied the state of its people (and with them its power)? Why else is it so difficult to imagine a tyrant ruling Texas?

If people were free to move, they could vote with their feet. In such a world, countries would need to coax foreign labour in the same way that they now entice foreign investors. The fear of losing workers would force states to pay closer attention to their needs and demands – encouraging the development of welfare states, education systems, training programmes, and so on. It has happened before and it can happen again.

While noting the potential of free migration, it is important not to exaggerate its scope and size. After all, there are significant social and personal constraints that limit a prospective emigrant's ability and willingness to consider international migration. Most people, given the opportunity, will not choose to move from their family, friends and home. Indeed, most immigrants yearn to return home, and many eventually do. It is only under the most hopeless conditions that potential emigrants consider the exit option, and only a fraction of these have the character, contacts and resources to carry it off. Nevertheless, and in spite of the fact that it is neither a common nor a costless option, migration can make all the difference in the world for a desperate family in search of a better life. While the costs of exit will remain too high for most people, the simple threat of exit can be an effective means of reminding governments, around the world, of the interests they have pledged to serve.

These are the sorts of argument that this book pursues in greater detail. Its conclusion, stated bluntly, is that we can expect the liberalization of national border controls to benefit the world's poorest inhabitants more than a truckload of World Bank analysts. It can also provide significant economic and political gains to residents of the developed world. In both political and economic terms, this is a win–win situation. Better yet, freeing people from the shackles of national citizenship will encourage states to compete with one another in maintaining a viable citizenry in a more just and peaceful world. In the most simple terms, we might say that there are few good reasons why people should remain prisoners of territory, and about three billion good reasons why they shouldn't.

...but a difficult argument

If the potential gains from free migration are so large, why are there so few advocates for free mobility, and why does the argument remain so controversial? What keeps us from considering the benefits of free migration?

Consider the mainstream globalization debates: most contributors completely ignore international migration. In effect, globalization's supporters and detractors find themselves unlikely accomplices in their neglect of migration issues. This silent conspiracy is all the more stunning when one considers that migration controls are the only area where states have actually tried to expand their sovereign control in the face of globalizing pressures! Neoliberal advocates of globalization embrace free trade and capital mobility, yet refuse to extend their liberalization argument to the movement of people across national borders. Critics of globalization wish to return to a world where the nation is sovereign, where one's life chances are determined mostly by fate, and where economic and political inequality in the globe will continue to grow. Both camps choose to ignore the potential that free migration offers to reverse and/or temper the inequalities and injustices that accompany globalization.

Perhaps the reason for this silence is the appearance of a monolithic body of conventional wisdom that regards free migration as too difficult, too costly, too dangerous, or too unrealistic to consider. To be sure, the conventional wisdom governing attitudes and approaches to migration is strongly critical of free human mobility. As a consequence, there are several popular arguments for maintaining national systems of border controls, in both the developed and the developing worlds, and each of these needs to be considered (and refuted) before the world is ready to embrace a discussion about the broader benefits of migration.

There are also a number of ominous political obstacles that stand in the way of any broader discussion concerning international migration. Public attitudes in the developed world are strongly anti-immigrationist, and most people – in both developed and developing worlds – continue to believe in the state's sovereign right of exclusion (i.e. to control passage across national borders). In addition, many particular interests are threatened by increased international migration, and we can expect these interests to oppose any liberalization of the world's migration regime. Like conventional wisdom, these interests and attitudes must be addressed and/or changed before it is possible to imagine (let alone reap) the benefits of freer human mobility.

Given the importance and influence of these potential sources of opposition to free mobility, the closing part of the book (in particular Chapters 7 and 8) is dedicated to describing, appraising and addressing each of them. In addition, however, there are two other obstacles that stand in the way of this argument, and these lend themselves to the book's introduction.

First of all, any advocate of freer human mobility finds himself or herself snuggled up to rather strange ideological bedfellows. As the earlier quotations from Khrushchev and Bush have attested, there are few political issues today that can animate such a wide swath of the political spectrum. On the one hand, we find support among small and disparate groups of radicals and anarchists who question the state's use of force in restraining human mobility. On the other hand, we find support in the editorial pages of the business world's leading newspaper, the *Wall Street Journal*, which has frequently implored its readers to support the right to migrate.[12] This sort of ideological diversity plays certain havoc with any attempt at political mobilization.

As you will soon discover, much of the following argument shadows a liberal position. Indeed, it is possible that many liberals (or even libertarians) will find themselves in remarkably familiar surroundings.[13] Thus the *Wall Street Journal* openly advocated free mobility in a Fourth of July editorial by proposing a US constitutional amendment: 'The yearning masses offer us their talents, ambitions and obviously unbreakable spirit. In return we acquire a renewed view of our own difficult past and, if we are true to that past, a reason for confidence in our future.'[14] In doing so, the *Journal* recognized that 'Perhaps this policy is overly ambitious in today's world, but the U.S. became the world's envy by trumpeting precisely this kind of heresy.'

In fact, many advocates of free mobility consider the *Wall Street Journal* a very uncomfortable ally. These people find themselves to the left of the political spectrum, but still somewhat removed from mainstream party positions. They trace their historical legacy back to a time when the left embraced internationalism: a legacy that has been forgotten and/or tarnished by the century-long attempt to construct 'socialism in one country'.

With this historical perspective, and contrary to popular perceptions, advocates of free human mobility embrace international markets, on the one hand, and a belief in active government, sovereign democracy, and a strong and vibrant welfare state, on the other. Indeed, by embracing free migration they hope to create greater wealth and opportunity, while encouraging states to become more responsive to resident demands. While this sort of argument has its roots in the history of the left, it is an argument that should appeal to readers from across the ideological spectrum.

Finally, this sort of argument is difficult because of its speculative nature: it asks you to consider a hypothetical thought-experiment about a future, unknown, state of affairs. How can we possibly know what a future world with free mobility will look like? On questions such as these, we should always be leery of those who speak with certainty. Unfortunately, most of today's political debates on immigration ignore this caveat and assume that there are simple answers to these difficult questions. Worse, today's political pundits use these simplistic responses to restrict a wider debate about international migration.

The simple fact is that we are unable to make accurate forecasts about the consequences of such radical changes. But neither this, nor the fact that they appear politically untenable, suggests that we should treat them as irrelevant or inevitably malignant. As the pages below will illustrate, careful consideration and discussion can answer many of the questions we pose. They can also help us examine and discard some of the more ridiculous assumptions that girder today's policy debates.

Two Paradoxes of Globalization

> Globalization, as defined by rich people like us, is a
> very nice thing ... you are talking about the Internet,
> you are talking about cell phones, you are talking about
> computers. This doesn't affect two-thirds of the people in
> the world.
>
> Jimmy Carter[1]

Globalization, in its contemporary form, generates enormous inequalities; it is these inequalities that motivate this book. In this chapter, these inequalities are mapped along two fronts, economic and political, and are described in terms of globalization's two paradoxes. Inequalities on both fronts are then juxtaposed against a third development associated with globalization: an enormous rise in the number of displaced peoples. In short, while globalization has expanded opportunity and prosperity for many in the developed world, this world has closed the gates of opportunity to millions of desperate refugees, displaced peoples and migrants. As globalization shrinks the world as we know it, its most desperate inhabitants are finding fewer and fewer places of refuge.

Economic Inequalities

Over the past few decades we have witnessed an incredible liberalization of world markets for a variety of goods and services. This liberalization has created vast new fortunes, but it has also ravaged the local economies of the world's poorest inhabitants.[2] The result has been a growing cleavage between rich and poor, both across countries and within them. This is the first paradox of globalization: *as the world draws closer together in the wake of remarkable technical, market and political developments, it is being pulled apart by growing inequalities.*

These inequalities were recently mapped in the World Bank's *World Development Report 2000/1*, where income figures were used to divide the globe into four groups: high, upper-middle, lower-middle and low income countries. This map is reproduced as Figure 2.1. With such a map of the world we can clearly see how the earth's surface is still covered with low and lower-middle income countries. Most of Africa and a large swath across South Asia are mired in poverty.

In stark contrast to these conditions, market liberalization has brought phenomenal wealth for relatively few. In 2001, with the world's economies hovering on the edge of recession after a year of market turmoil, the number of 'high net worth individuals' (i.e. those who are able to invest more than $1 million) increased by 6 per cent to 7.2 million – mostly in North America and in Europe.[3] They are not alone: the number of poor people is also increasing. These diverging trajectories reveal a cleavage that can be illustrated with two remarkable sets of descriptive statistics. First, the assets of the world's three richest billionaires are more than the combined GNP of all the least developing countries (and their 600 million people)![4] Second, nearly half of the world's population (2.8 billion people) live on less than $2 a day (about 1.2 billion live on less than $1 a day)![5]

Figure 2.1   Map of poverty

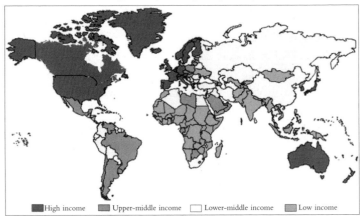

| High income | Upper-middle income | Lower-middle income | Low income |

Source: Simplified from World Bank, *World Development Report 2000/1*, p. 273.

This cleavage is also reflected in national comparisons, where the World Bank found that the richest countries' 1995 per capita GDP was 37 times higher than that of the poorest countries (an increase from 18 in 1960).[6] In other words, we live in a world where 80 per cent of the global population live off a mere 20 per cent of global GDP. Despite much rhetoric to the contrary, conditions have not improved for the world's poorest; over the past three decades, the number of Least Developed Countries (as classified by the UN) has grown from 25 to 50. These countries are home to 10 per cent of the world's population (some 614 million people), but their share of world imports (0.6 per cent) and world exports (0.4 per cent) is minuscule.[7]

Unfortunately, this trend has deep historical roots. A recent study by a senior economist at the World Bank shows that the ratio of GDP per capita of the richest to poorest countries has increased dramatically since the 1870s.[8] In 1870, the income ratio separating the world's richest and poorest countries was 8.7:1; in 1960 that ratio had increased to 38.5:1; and by 1990 it had climbed to a staggering 45.2:1 – a sixfold increase! Measured in another way, the average absolute gap in the per capita income of all countries (from the leading country) had grown from $1,286 to $12,662 between 1870 and 1990. These growing income differentials occurred during a time when international trade and investment flows were increasingly liberalized (but international migration flows were largely cut off).

Significant economic cleavages are also opening within countries – in both the developed and the less developed worlds. The Harvard economist Dani Rodrik argues that deeper economic integration 'is exposing a fault line between groups who have the skills and mobility to flourish in global markets and those who either don't have these advantages or perceive the expansion of unregulated markets as inimical to social stability'.[9] These disadvantages are reflected in the 18 per cent of the United States' 81 million full-time workers who earned below the official poverty level in the early 1990s (compared to just 12 per cent in 1980). A recent OECD report has documented the extent to which these cleavages can be found across the developed world, where the poorest decile's real income declined in the 1970s and 1980s. Others have extended the analysis to the developing world as well.[10]

Previous responses

Today's policy responses to these growing inequalities need to be understood in light of previous policy debates. Throughout the 1970s and 1980s, it was common to argue that the plight of the world's poor resulted from an international system of trade that was inherently biased against them. Poor countries that engaged in international trade suffered from crippling terms of trade; they became increasingly dependent on an international economy that worked to their disadvantage. At the time, there were three common responses to the perceived dilemma: some advocated a coordinated international attempt at righting the terms of trade, to the greater benefit of developing countries (i.e. the UNCTAD strategy[11]); others advocated economic autarky and endogenous development; while the most radical response advocated world revolution as the only means to free poor countries from the yoke of international dependency.

The dependency perspective proved increasingly unpopular in subsequent decades. Undoubtedly, there are several reasons for this. Among them is that most of the concerted efforts at UNCTAD proved to be ineffective at influencing international terms of trade. More significantly, perhaps, is the fact that a handful of Asian 'miracle' economies managed to break out of the dependency trap and engineer impressive records of economic growth (e.g. Taiwan, South Korea, Hong Kong and Singapore). In addition, national politics, worldwide, underwent a substantial ideological shift to the right in the wake of collapsing communist regimes in Russia and Eastern Europe. The new liberalism that resulted provided fertile ground for the growth of a new strain of development policy. For whatever reason, dependency theories were eclipsed by a more market-friendly development paradigm.

Throughout most of the 1980s and 1990s, poor economic performance was largely explained by too much political interference in naturally equilibrating market (and political) mechanisms. Active trade unions, central banks and (sometimes) well-intentioned governments were corrupting the 'correct prices' necessary to generate strong economic performances. Development became less baffling; it simply depended on 'getting the prices right'. (How these specific lessons were derived from the East Asian miracle economies, however, remains a mystery.) Once prices were right, private markets would allocate resources more efficiently, official state assistance could be reduced, and the market would be free to deliver robust economic growth.

In 1990, John Williams (at the Institute for International Economics in Washington DC) put together a list of the sort of policy initiatives that Washington was then urging on Latin America.[12] This 'Washington Consensus' of market-friendly reforms (fiscal discipline, tax reform, trade, finance, investment and exchange-rate liberalization, deregulation, privatization, etc.) became a template for economic success in the developing world. Over time, implementing these sorts of reforms became the necessary price paid by poor countries in return for international aid and financing.

After two decades of globalization and liberalization, support for these sorts of market-focused reforms is unravelling. International lending bodies have become more sensitive to public outrage over the human and social costs that are increasingly associated with these types of reforms. Both the IMF and the World Bank have embraced more comprehensive development strategies, where poverty reduction and debt relief are emphasized. While these changes acknowledge the role of public policy as a complement to economic liberalization and reform, they are hardly sufficient for dealing with the enormous problems facing the developing world.[13] We are still offering bandaids to economies on life-support.

Today's response falls under the rubric of the Millennium Development Goals (MDGs), a set of development targets agreed to by the international community, which centre on halving poverty and improving the welfare of the world's poorest by 2015. In particular, world leaders have agreed to eight specific and measurable development goals: the first seven focus on reducing poverty, hunger, illiteracy, gender inequality, child and maternal mortality, disease, and environmental degradation; the eighth goal calls for a global partnership for development, with targets for aid, trade and debt relief. With remarkable optimism, the world community declared in September 2000: 'We will spare no effort to free our fellow men, women, and children from the abject and dehumanizing conditions of extreme poverty, to which more than a billion of them are currently subjected.'

Not surprisingly, progress in meeting these goals has been less than inspiring. Apparently, some effort *is* being spared in freeing our fellow men, women and children from the abject and de-humanizing conditions of extreme poverty. Unfortunately, the first report on our progress in meeting these goals shows that most MDGs will not be met by most countries, given current trends. In order to achieve the MDGs on time, this *Global Monitoring Report* concluded that there is an urgent need for all parties to scale up action.[14]

What is common to each generation of reform proposals is that they provide little hope or opportunity to the poor, as individuals. In the parlance of contemporary policymakers, the poor remain 'disempowered'. In these approaches to development, economic success depends critically on the actions of governments or the international community; economic failure is blamed on an international system characterized by unequal exchange, harmful government interventions, and/or disingenuous attempts at liberal reform. Either way, as governments and international organizations fiddle around with getting the prices right, the world's poor become relatively poorer.

To summarize, the cleavage separating the world's richest and poorest inhabitants appears to be increasing, both internationally and within countries. Although the status quo is untenable, the solutions offered are both piecemeal and ineffective. While a handful of countries have managed to escape the dependency trap, it is unrealistic to expect that world poverty will be significantly reduced by following their example. A more radical treatment is required to cure these economic ills.

Political Inequalities

While global economic inequality may be the most obvious reason to consider a world with free migration, it is not the only one. As the above discussion implies, the key to economic success lies in the hands of national (political) officials. Whatever the proposed solution, states play a pivotal role in framing effective markets, coordinating responses, encouraging growth, and so on. But the world's political landscape is scarred by many of the same inequalities that we find on the economic terrain. Here, too, an individual's fortune is determined more by birth than by effort.

The situation is exacerbated by the fact that political and economic inequalities tend to draw on one another; persecution and poverty are inexplicitly linked. In short, political and social liberties are highly correlated with wealth; poor countries tend to be illiberal and/or autocratic. For example, only 9 of the world's 48 Least Developed Countries in 2000 (about 19 per cent) were free.[15] To the extent that poor countries are mostly unrepresentative, their governments may not be interested in significantly improving their citizenry's conditions. Indeed, as economic inequalities continue to rise in the world's richest democracies, it is perhaps naive to expect poor autocracies to pursue more populist policies aimed at decreasing economic inequalities.

Political inequalities, broadly defined, can be understood as the second motivation for considering an argument for free human mobility. Here, too, developments can be categorized as paradoxical: *at a time when the number of democratic states is expanding rapidly (concomitant with democracy's prominence as the only legitimate form of government), its sovereign scope and popularity among the established democracies is in retreat.* As with the first paradox of globalization, this requires further elaboration.

The rise of democracy

At first glance, developments on the political front are encouraging.[16] We passed through *The Democratic Century* at *The End of History*; political and academic pundits have delighted in the spread of democracy and exulted in the expected peace dividend they

Figure 2.2   Map of freedom

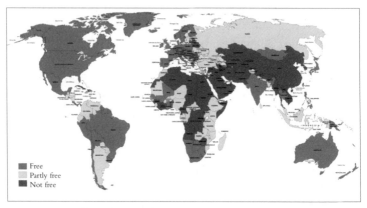

Free
Partly free
Not free

Source: www.freedomhouse.org/pdf_docs/research/freeworld/2003/map2003.pdf.

hope to reap. In this case, the rhetoric appears to have statistical support: today 3.4 billion people (about 58 per cent of the world's population) are said to reside in democratic states.[17] This represents a remarkable increase over the past century: in 1900 there was not a single state that could meet today's democratic criteria, and in 1950 only 14 per cent of states would be characterized as democratic, using today's criteria.[18]

While these examples are heartening, there are grounds for a more sober evaluation. After all, there are nearly 2.5 billion people (the remaining 42 per cent of the world's population) who continue to reside in non-democratic states. The vast majority of these (almost 80 per cent) live under authoritarian regimes. In celebrating the victory of democracy, we mustn't be complacent in accepting the plight of these 2.5 billion people. Much work remains.

Nor is life without hardship for denizens of the new democracies. Statistical indicators for democracy tend to focus on institutional components that are easy to measure and compare. As a result, they do not always capture the sort of phenomena that we usually associate with good and just government. In an influential 1997 article in *Foreign Affairs*, Fareed Zakaria suggested that as many as half of the democratizing countries in the world today are so-called 'illiberal democracies', where democratic elections are held without the constraints of limited government (in the form of a strong rule of law).[19] The resulting elections often produce populist leaders, and little formal protection for minority groups and their interests.

This distinction between liberal and illiberal democracies can be illustrated with reference to the 50 LDCs mentioned above. It has already been noted that only 19 per cent of these states are categorized as 'free' by Freedom House's indicators. But almost half of these states (i.e. 22 states, or 44 per cent) can also be categorized as democratic. Thus, in this small sample of the world's poorest states, we find 13 democratic but not 'free' states. The same pattern can be found in the full Freedom House sample: while most of the world's population lives under democratic rule, only about 39 per cent of us live in free states.

Exacerbating matters is the fact that many of these democracies are in new, unconsolidated and potentially unstable states. Across Europe, Asia and Africa the world has seen an explosion of new states. Thus, much of the increase in democratic (and free) states is a function of a few autocratic states dropping off the face of the earth, and being replaced by several new, more democratic states.

The expanse of 'unfree' states can be easily illustrated if we used the Freedom House 'Freedom Index' to map the global distribution of free states in 2003. Like the World Bank's 'Map of Poverty', Figure 2.2 provides a clear picture of the extent to which free states are a minority in the international system. The sorts of freedoms that the developed world holds dear do not extend much farther than their own doorsteps. As with wealth, freedom is largely confined to small pockets on the globe.

This development is significant for helping us understand the statistical rise in the number of democratic states, but it also makes it easier to understand the rising number of internal conflicts. Of the twenty-seven major armed conflicts that occurred in 1999, all but two took place within national borders.[20] In short, the spread of new, unconsolidated, states is creating appalling conditions with little security for millions of people. The threat of civil war, political conflict, human rights' violations, and so forth, has seldom been greater.

Declining confidence in the developed democracies

While conditions in new democratic states are grounds for concern, developments in the richest, established, democracies are also worrisome. If opinion research is any guide, the West's liberal democracies are experiencing something of a legitimacy crisis. Starting in the 1960s, support for – and confidence in – both politicians and democratic institutions has been in decline in nearly every developed state. In eleven of the fourteen countries recently surveyed by Susan Pharr and Robert Putnam, confidence in the national assembly (parliament) declined, with especially strong drops in Canada, Germany, Britain, Sweden and the United States.[21] On average, public confidence in the institutions of liberal democracy declined by 6 per cent over the 1980s. Consider some of their examples:

- fewer than 40 per cent of Americans trusted their government to do what was right;
- 67 per cent of Canadians asked felt that their 'government doesn't care what people like me think';
- only 24 per cent of Britons expressed quite a lot of confidence in the House of Commons;
- only 19 per cent of Swedes had confidence in their Riksdag (parliament);

- 84 per cent of the Italians surveyed said that politicians 'don't care what people like me think'.[22]

There are several additional indicators of declining faith in representative democracy. The party system of Western Europe – which for so long seemed frozen – now seems to be shattering under the strain of globalization. Electoral participation rates are falling across the developed world. The disintegration of Japan's Liberal Democrats; the obliteration of Canada's Progressive Conservatives, and the populist appeals of the 'new' right in many developed democracies are further indicators of electoral volatility. Finally, faith in the core institutions of representative democracy is being challenged, as states as different as Italy and New Zealand opted to change their electoral system (in almost opposite directions), or settle their electoral differences in court (witness the 2000 US presidential election).

Large public demonstrations against international organizations, such as the 1999 Battle of Seattle, are also indicative of this growing public frustration. The protesters in Seattle came from every corner of the globe, representing a broad swath of interests, united in their opposition to the expanding power of the World Trade Organization (WTO). Nearly 75,000 workers, students and activists filled the streets to protest the way in which powerful people, corporations and institutions were making important decisions behind closed doors. Ordinary citizens, frustrated by their inability to influence national policy on international decisions, demanded a say in decisions that affect important aspects of their everyday lives, such as food safety, labour rights and environmental protection.

Despite encouraging trends in the growth of new democratic states, significant political inequalities remain: both among countries and within them. Millions of people find themselves prisoners of political regimes over which they have little or no influence. Even citizens of liberal democratic states are increasingly aware of how their own opinions seem less and less relevant. Like economic inequality, political power in the world is distributed unequally between democratic and non-democratic states. Worse yet, the political power of the individual, as a democratic citizen, seems to be diminishing in the face of globalization.

Growing Demand for Migration

The previous sections have outlined how globalization has resulted in some alarming paradoxes; paradoxes that will likely remain if we confine our discussion to existing development paradigms. Political and economic inequalities continue to exist (and are arguably growing) in a world that is – to all intents and purposes – shrinking and becoming more integrated. One consequence of these growing inequalities is a world scarred by more and more civil wars. In 1993 and 1994 alone, internal conflicts worldwide forced an estimated 10,000 people *a day* to flee their homes, in the form of internally displaced people, refugees and/or illegal immigrants.[23] Thus, to escape poverty, repression and internal conflict, millions of people each year are forced to emigrate.[24]

The UN estimates that perhaps some 150 million people (or 2.5 per cent of the world's population) today live outside their country of birth.[25] This is a surprisingly high figure, given the degree and nature of restrictions placed by states on human migration. Today's potential emigrants must negotiate a number of hurdles. In some countries, exit restrictions still prohibit them from leaving. But even if a potential migrant lives in a country that allows free exit, there is not a single country that is willing to accept immigrants open-armed. Instead, any potential emigrant faces a myriad of restrictions and qualifications, as rich states effectively filter out all but the most oppressed, those with family ties, and/or the most diligent.

A pyramid of opportunity

To capture the range of prospects facing the world's poor and oppressed, we can imagine the situation in terms of a pyramid of opportunity. At the bottom of this pyramid is a large and growing mass of Internally Displaced Persons (IDPs). The international community has been slow to recognize their plight, and most end up as prisoners in dangerous territory – with little hope to escape their individual dilemmas. Increasingly, lower- and middle-income countries tend to occupy a zone of political turmoil. Many states in Africa, the Middle East, and across Asia demonstrate little or no capacity to govern. Forced from their homes by armed conflicts, internal strife, unimaginable human rights' violations and other atrocities, the internally displaced remain within the borders of their own countries – yet are dispossessed by their own governments. The headlines from Liberia, Nigeria, Sierra Leone, Sudan, Uganda and the Republic of Congo – to name just a few – tell of once unimaginable atrocities. This turmoil produces millions of internally displaced people, who effectively fall outside of the protection offered to international refugees.[26] The Special Representative of the UN Secretary-General for Internally Displaced Persons (IDPs) estimates there are between 20 and 25 million IDPs worldwide, while some estimates are as high as 30 million.[27] Most of these IDPs are in Africa (up to 16 million), but significant numbers can be found in Asia, Europe and the Americas. For these new 'domestic' refugees, hope and opportunity are in very short supply.

Modern states fiercely defend their traditional right to determine who may (or may not) enter their territory. The only sector of immigration over which governments have surrendered some discretion is the so-called humanitarian stream of international refugees. This constitutes the middle stratum of the pyramid of opportunity. Their predicament is preferable in that the international community has at least recognized their dilemma and promises some assistance.[28] But domestic pressure in potential host countries has generated a great deal of creative treaty reading, and the world's richest states have cut back on their intake of international refugees. As a result, the number of registered refugees is today around 11 million persons annually, down from 17–18 million in the early 1990s. Contrary to public perception in the developed world, most of these refugees end up in (neighbour-ing) developing countries: Armenia, Guinea, Yugoslavia, Djibouti, Liberia, Azerbaijan, Iran, Zambia and Tanzania all have higher percentages of refugee populations than does Sweden (the most generous of the OECD countries).[29]

At the top of the opportunity pyramid are those who manage to migrate, either legally or not, to the developed world. These are the luckiest of all – even though the threat of death shadows their journey, as illustrated in the introductory chapter. The numbers of these immigrants are relatively small, but they manage to dominate the developed world's headlines. The International Labour Organization (ILO) estimates that global labour migration may be on the order of 30–35 million economically active persons, with their 40–50 million dependents.[30] The UN figures that the United States is the world's largest net migration host, bringing in some 16.7 million people between 1970 and 1995 – an average of under 700,000 immigrants a year.[31] Across the OECD, the stock of the foreign population rose by over 13 million between 1988 and 1998 – or, on average, just about 1.3 million people a year.[32]

The most resourceful of the world's poor and oppressed enter the developed world illegally. Their numbers are notoriously dif-ficult to calculate, but are probably less than the legal migration levels. The most often cited statistics for the number of illegal immigrants comes from Britain's Home Office estimates that about 30 million people are smuggled across international borders every year in a trade worth between $12 and $30 billion annually.

This is a phenomenally large number, and probably overstates the problem.[33]

Along the US–Mexican border, the most famous crossing point, estimates hold that perhaps 200,000 to 300,000 people cross illegally each year;[34] but the actual number may be greater or smaller.[35] Another way of gauging the traffic is to note that at least 2,000 people have died trying to cross the US–Mexican border since 1998.[36] While it is difficult to estimate how many illegal migrants currently reside in the USA, a 1986 amnesty programme encouraged 3.1 million people to come forward and legalize their status. Current estimates suggest that some 5 to 6 million illegal immigrants now reside in the USA.[37]

Illegal immigration into Europe has risen along with the expansion of the European Union. Indeed, it is commonly held that immigration to the EU now exceeds that to the USA. Mafia rings based in Istanbul, Tirana, and other East European countries control a very lucrative business smuggling people into Europe, through Spain, Italy, Greece and Finland. Although these markets are difficult to trace, it is estimated that some 500,000 people are smuggled annually into the European Union.[38] As in the USA, hundred perish each year in the attempt: since 1993, UNITED for Intercultural Action estimates that more than 4,500 people have died trying to enter Europe illegally.[39] As a consequence, it is estimated there are about 3 million illegal immigrants living in Western Europe today.

To summarize, the number of immigrants to the developed world are minuscule when compared to the annual number of refugees and IDPs produced and settling in the developing world. To contrast these differences, consider the situation in two countries in 1999. In that year, perhaps 1 million people may have entered the USA, as either illegal or legal immigrants. In the same year, the UN estimated that some 2.6 million IDPs were distributed within the government-controlled areas of Sudan.[40]

If humanitarian reasons are not in themselves sufficient to provide a response to the inequalities of the existing system, the real threat of these inequalities (in the form of increased inflows of refugees and immigrants) should entice residents of the developed world to take these problems seriously. For whatever reason – humanitarian, moral or self-serving – something needs to be done.

3

Some Historical Perspective

I believe that, anthropologically speaking, migration is an irrepressible human urge. People have always wanted to move to places with more spiritual freedom, greater political liberty or higher standards of living (and the satisfaction of basic needs in their country of origin does not constitute a threshold at which the urge to migrate suddenly vanishes or loses its legitimacy). The more tolerant the receiving state, the more attractive its spiritual freedom and political liberty; the richer it is, the stronger its economic pull. When tolerance and wealth go hand in hand, man-made laws can attempt to regulate migration but they cannot suppress it.

W.R. Böhning[1]

It is not uncommon to assume that today's system of international border controls, and the passports and visas that accompany them, are permanent historical landmarks – natural and central parts of the international order and national sovereignty. The truth, as usual, is much more complicated, and quite different: the issuance of national passports constitutes but a blip on the historical radar, and international controls on migration are mostly a product of the twentieth century.

Before World War I, with the exception of just a few countries (e.g. Japan), states did not place constraints on the movement of people across borders. That war (and the fear of foreigners that it generated) led the UK to impose a compulsory passport system in 1914 and this legislation was continued after the war; the USA followed suit with an Act in 1918, as did many other states. To arrive where we are now, states began to ratchet up migration controls with each conflict in the twentieth century. As a result, international migration has become more and more narrowly defined in terms associated with the costs of war (in particular, refugee and asylum status) or (less legitimately) poverty.

This chapter outlines this peculiar turn of historical events. For most of recorded history, political authorities have found it too costly, too difficult, or simply unnecessary to control migration within and across territory. When controls were used, they were most often to protect the migrant himself or herself (not to restrict his/her mobility), and were most often the product and authority of local officials. Over time, such controls can be understood in terms of the larger political and economic ideologies of the period that produced them. Thus, controls were local and personal when sovereignty was divided and local, and grew to become an integral part of the state's sovereign powers during the mercantilist period.

There are two features that are unique to the current international migration regime. The first (and most obvious) feature is the extent of the modern state's control. Never have central political authorities had so much influence over the important life-choices of their resident populations. Throughout history, repressed people have exploited (if not always enjoyed) the option of exodus; since the First World War this option has effectively ceased to exist. Second, there is a curious inconsistency between the nature and extent of controls on human freedom and the dominant ideology of our time: liberalism. As we shall see, the free, rational individual – unbound by authority – is a principle tenet of liberalism. It is odd, then, that political and economic liberalism has come to blossom at a time when political authorities effectively shackle these rational individuals to a given territory.

Together, these two historical anomalies should make us question the durability of the current regime. Indeed, today's immigration regime can be understood as a peculiar response to the demands of the First World War. At the close of those hostilities, the world community faced an important regime crossroads: it needed to decide between returning to the more liberal migration regime from which it came, or to choose a course of greater and more permanent restrictions on international mobility. After a brief period of vacillation, the world community chose the latter path.

This chapter will *not* try to explain why this exceptional path was chosen – such an explanation would lead us too far astray from the task in hand. Rather, the aim is to contrast the contemporary regime with previous regimes in an effort to underscore its uniqueness. Once this historical distinctiveness is recognized, it makes little sense to assume – as today's migration debate does – that national barriers to international human mobility are natural, necessary or constant.

Migration in the Long Arc of History

Of course, the idea of controlling entry and exit to one's territory goes back much further than the twentieth century. There are even some willing to claim that this tendency is as old as humankind itself: that we have a deep socio-biological need to protect and return to our territory. In other words, people – like dogs – need to mark and defend their territory. But the history of migration argues against simplistic analogies to the animal kingdom.

For most of history, migration has been a part of life. Territory was not owned, but shared or borrowed, and people moved cyclically or periodically, following hunting, gathering and/or pastoral cycles. Conceivably, it is in this way that the world became populated as the original inhabitants of the world dispersed. In early human history, nomadism was central to life, identity and culture, as well as defining the world historical map (witness Attila and Genghis Khan). Both the Haan (in China) and the Vikings (in Northern Europe), to note two prominent examples, established large territorial domains build on migration. Similarly, the Roman Empire was a melting pot of different nationalities, harbouring a population that was at one time almost 90 per cent foreign-born.[2]

More recently, but before the Industrial Revolution, migration was essential to the settlement of early medieval Europe and an integral part of early modern life in Western Europe. In the countryside, regional migration routines were part of the agricultural cycle, central to family formation, and to the supply of the rural labour force. Throughout Europe, groups of nomadic traders, such as the Gypsies or tinkers, travelled freely to sell their wares. In short, for much (if not most) of Europe's early history, migration was a necessary part of economic survival. Though it is unlikely that these migrants avoided xenophobia and local repression, they usually didn't have to worry about the state actively restricting their movements.

In the Muslim world, as well, migrants were generally welcomed. The concept of *Dar-al-Islam* (the House of Islam) reinforced earlier traditions of free movement by stressing the essential unity of Islamic civilization and the artificiality of imposed territorial divisions within it. But migration in and out of the House of Islam was also facilitated by Islamic law. Visitors from non–Muslim states were allowed to enter the House of Islam under an *amān* (safe conduct), obtained beforehand from any Muslim. Such an *amān*, if granted, transformed the status of the visitor (*harbī*) from a state of war to one of temporary peace and security. Under Islamic law, the *harbī* becomes a *musta'min*, a person who is clothed with security as long as he remains in the Islamic world. This legal device facilitated exchanges across frontiers that separated Muslim and non-Muslim worlds.

Better known is the way in which migration has been used to escape political and religious persecution. World history is filled with examples of ethnic or religious exodus. The most significant of these lie at the centre of the West's historical tradition: Moses leading his people from Egypt across Sinai and into Canaan; the Jews' expulsion from Spain; the Protestant emigration from the Spanish Netherlands; the Huguenots' departure after the Revocation of the Edict of Nantes...

In a similar way, Alan Dowty considers the significance of earlier migration patterns by asking us to imagine the world's map only a thousand years ago:

> There were no Germans in Berlin, no Russians in Moscow, and few Turks in what is now Turkey. Spain was mostly Moslem, the southern Ukraine was inhabited by Turkish tribes, and most Bulgarians lived in Central Asia. There were no Thais in Bangkok or Malays in Singapore, and most of present-day Vietnam was occupied by the ancestors of today's Cambodia. In Africa, Bantu-speaking peoples, who now occupy most of Sub-Saharan Africa, were still confined to the center and the east coast of the continent. Most strikingly, of course, the New World was inhabited only by native American Indians.[3]

In short, for most of human history, migration was understood as a fundamental need; welcoming foreigners was understood as an act of civility. As the great Ancient Greek traveller and geographer Strabo noted in his *Geography* (XVII.i.19): 'To drive away strangers is to act like barbarians.'

Unfortunately, these acts of barbarianism became more common with the ascent of modern conceptions of nationhood and sovereignty. This is not to say that there weren't severe restrictions on international travel and residence before the modern period. Most infamously, under the Manchus (1644–1912), any Chinese found abroad was subject to beheading. But there has been a radical transformation in practices over the last century, and these changes have been driven by developments in Europe. Here, the creation of a modern passport system allowed states to monopolize and legitimize the authority to control human movement. These developments signalled a new era in human affairs, and it behoves us to examine them more closely.

The original notion of a 'passport' can be traced back to the English reign of William the Conqueror, at the turn of the first millennium. Apparently, William was afraid that other political entrepreneurs might wish to follow his example (and attempt to reconquer England). In response, William established a network of castles along the southern coast of England to repel a potential invasion. This network contained five key control points (the Cinque Ports): with castles at Hastings, Romney, Dover, Hythe and Sandwich. Formal entry to England at the time required official approval to pass through one of these five ports: hence the term 'passport'.

The practice of issuing travel documents to foreigners became customary in the late Norman period. But these documents were not used to control or stop migration and/or travel; rather, they were issued for the itinerant's benefit. Travelling documents were used to protect foreigners who had a legal right to free passage across a territory. In fact, clause 41 of the *Magna Carta* (1215) expressly guaranteed merchants (who had not previously been forbidden to enter England) unhindered travel in accordance with ancient and lawful customs.[4] While the sovereign retained the right to expel or exclude specific groups of aliens, any alien could freely enter England without the explicit permission of the sovereign.

Of course, there have always been private and local controls on movement, and it is important not to overlook or underestimate them. Under various forms of serfdom and slavery, lords and slaveholders held the power and right to determine their servants' right to move. Since as late as the sixteenth century, imperial ordinances in several European states limited the movement of Gypsies and vagabonds, and tied servants firmly to their masters. Even in England, a 1381 statute forbade all but the higher classes to leave the kingdom without a licence.[5] However, most of these controls were relatively ineffective and not understood as part of the state's sovereign power.

The fact that explicit legal controls were uncommon was not just a simple reflection of contemporary conceptions of international law and/or notions of sovereignty. Legal controls were cumbersome and expensive; after all, there were more ways to enter England than through the five ports on the southern coast (a lesson the Vikings had learnt with great success!). Territorial coastlines and boundaries were impossible to control, and people – in practice – were free to rove, as they liked. In other (more contemporary) words, limitations on travel were supply – not demand – driven. The potential emigrant had to overcome two significant constraints: personal allegiance and cost.

Before the modern state had become the dominant political actor, migration flows varied with the strength of personal allegiances and the size of the emigrant's wallet. Long-distance migration at the time was very costly, but not illegal (in most cases). Indeed the political ease of migration is reflected in the movements of the period's better-known subjects. The life of the squire, author or knight of the Middle Ages was a hectic one, as he moved from country to country, in search of employment, excitement or escape. As a result, Europe's cultural heritage is filled with the colourful exploits of marauding heroes and heroines.

The Mercantilist Period

It is commonplace to argue that the international system of states was created in 1648, with the Peace of Westphalia at the end of the Thirty Years' War. In Europe, the nation-state became the predominant political unit, and personal obligations were forced upward, from the local lord to the national sovereign. Throughout the Renaissance period, a new international system of conduct was being mapped by a number of contemporary theorists, who themselves moved from one country to another selling their genius (or escaping from tyrants). To take a prominent example, Francesco de Vitoria (1492–1546), heralded as the founder of international law, held that 'It was permissible from the beginning of the world, when everything was in common, for anyone to set forth and travel wheresoever he would.'[6] These sentiments were echoed in the works of Hugo Grotius (1583–1645), Samuel von Pufendorf (1634–1692) and Christian Wolff (1679–1754).[7] Indeed, in his *Law of Nations*, Emmerich de Vattel (1758) explicitly argued that no nation could, without good reason, refuse perpetual residence to a fugitive. All of these (now classic) scholars recognized the state's duty to permit transit of aliens, and (in certain cases) to permit their residence.

As political power rose from feudal lords to the sovereign, the distance between servant and master increased, straining personal bonds of obligation. Notions of personal obligation were no longer sufficient to keep people at home, and states found it necessary to impose controls on movements of peoples and goods, especially those that were most valuable to the sovereign. With the subsequent rise of mercantilist thought, the control of productive (or strategically important) labour became an issue of national strategic concern. People, as labour, came to be understood as a scarce resource. Given the era's relatively sluggish demographic growth rates, the increasing demands for labour (in both productive and military spheres), and the ambition to colonize new worlds, states found it necessary to increase their control over demographic resources.

Mercantilist states came to place a premium on their domestic populations, discouraging emigration (while enticing immigration from competing states). This common perception was captured by Jean Bodin, the great French theorist of sovereignty, who held that 'Il n'est force ni richesse que d'hommes.'[8] States maximized their sovereign power by acquiring a surplus of skilled labour.

During this period, migration itself was not shunned; only outward migration was restricted. The dominant states in Europe (e.g. England, Germany and France) imported reserves of labour from their immediate surroundings (e.g. Ireland, Poland, Italy and Belgium, respectively), and ambitious peripheral states followed suit. In Russia, the reigns of both Peter the Great and Catherine the Great capture this mercantilist spirit, as they imported Western craftsmen and ideas in their efforts to modernize the Russian Empire. Throughout mercantilist Europe, borders were open to foreign workers in principle, especially skilled craftsmen – even when they remained closed for the trade of goods. But outward migration was discouraged by a variety of means. The resulting pressure on wages (and its unequal distribution of incomes) was accepted in exchange for the possibility of maintaining international competitiveness.

Although emigration to competing states was discouraged, emigration to the colonies was promoted. Thus, for three centuries, Spain, Portugal, France and Britain exported legions of migrants to help settle North and South America, as well as large tracts in Africa and Asia.

When voluntary migrants proved to be too costly or too few for its needs, Europe encouraged forced labour migration from Africa, and (later) indentured workers from Asia. Incredibly, the volumes of forced migrant flows were of the same order of magnitude as those of voluntary Atlantic migrations. Thus, it is estimated that some 15 million slaves left Africa prior to 1850, while another 30 million indentured servants were forced to move in the century following the abolition of slavery.[9] European traders moved slaves from West Africa to ports up and down the Atlantic seaboard of both American continents. By the nineteenth century, indentured workers from South Asia were taken to East Africa, Malaya, Fiji, Guyana, Jamaica, Suriname and Trinidad, while Chinese workers were recruited to work in Southeast Asia (especially Indonesia, Thailand, Malaya and Indochina), and to build the US West.

The New World was populated and built with the sweat and effort of migrant labour. Imported labour, especially skilled labour, was highly attractive to these young and growing states. For example, the United States' economic policy in the early post-revolutionary period was decidedly mercantilist in nature (in stark contrast to its later, more liberal, attitude), and this neo-mercantilism extended to immigration policy. In particular, Alexander Hamilton, Secretary of the Treasury under President George Washington, proposed an actively mercantilist policy to Congress as a way to avoid the hegemonic dominance of Britain (and other European powers), and as a way to spark domestic economic growth. Following Hamilton's advice, the USA actively encouraged the immigration of skilled labourers, and capitalized farmers.[10]

These sorts of constraints are entirely consistent with the dominant (mercantilist) ideology of the time. Migration was seen to be part of the state's economic policy arsenal: it was encouraged if it was seen to strengthen the state's economic resources; it was discouraged if not. But this sort of state influence in economic affairs stands in stark contrast to the 'night-watchman' state that usually characterizes liberalism. In the centuries that followed, liberalism would become the reigning ideology – and the state would lose many of the economic powers it enjoyed under mercantilism.

The Liberal Period

With the advance of the Industrial Revolution – and the liberal ideology that accompanied it – free trade in goods, capital and services became more commonplace among the developed countries. Over time, this liberalism was allowed to extend to human movements as well. At the theoretical and philosophical level, liberalism was well suited to accommodate free human mobility. In practice, however, early liberal states introduced a number of measures to control and monitor domestic and international movements. In one of history's many ironies, restrictions on human liberty were spreading at the very time when democratic movements throughout Europe were beginning to impose their own will upon sovereignty. While the lowest orders of society were being liberated from the feudal shackles that had once bound them to their birthplaces, democratic states were increasingly imposing more restrictive controls on their mobility internationally.

Some of the first full-scale legal restrictions on migration appeared with the rise of liberal thought and its success in the political sphere; in Europe they were largely a response to the French Revolution. Because of the nature of controls that were associated with the old regime, freer mobility was an important call of the revolution – if a controversial one. Indeed, the revolution itself commenced with the destruction of passports; the French Constitution of 1791 guaranteed 'liberté, d'aller, de rester, de partir'.[11] But the revolutionary leadership quickly imposed new restrictions on both internal and international movement. In the following year (1792) a new – and strengthened – passport law came into effect in France.

Fears of a flood of Jacobian emissaries sparked strong doses of Francophobia and migration controls in Britain, America and even Switzerland (among other places). At first, the controls were narrowly defined, short-lived, and contained 'sunset' clauses. For example, the English Alien Bill of 1793 was explicitly designed to operate over a short and specific period of time. The impending Napoleonic wars encouraged France to adopt similar legislation: for example, its Passports Law (1797), which many interpret to be the starting point for modern aliens' legislation.[12] With the passing of each threat, laws like these were eventually rescinded. But new, more restrictive, legislation popped up with each new bout of political turmoil in the years that followed.

Between these periods of conflict, human migration spread rapidly. The price of travel decreased significantly during this period (mostly because of the rise of large shipping and railroad concerns), making it easier for the world's poor and displaced to move to new harbours of hope. At the same time, new and more global markets were developing in a way that both encouraged and facilitated long-distance migration, as well as migration across geographic regions (such as Europe, Asia and Africa).

In the late nineteenth and early twentieth centuries, African and Asian emigration was also substantial, if understudied. These areas experienced a number of demographic and economic trans-formations that encouraged migration flows that were broadly comparable in timing and size with those that we find in Europe and the New World. For example, rubber plantations in Southeast Asia and the rice fields of Manchuria enticed massive migration flows that often took place beyond the direct influence of Europe. Indeed, if we embrace a broader historical time-frame, we find that the long-distance migration flows to Southeast Asia and the Far East were almost as large as those that were crossing the Atlantic. Between 1846 and 1940, some 55–58 million people left Europe for the Americas. Over the same period of time, 48–52 million people left India and Southern China for Southeast Asia, the Indian Ocean Rim and the South Pacific. Concomitantly, another 46–51 million people left Northeast Asia and Russia for Manchuria, Siberia, Central Asia and Japan.[13]

Still, most of the literature on this period focuses on the Atlantic migration system. By the closing decades of the nineteenth century, in the wake of the first great depression and a series of catastrophic harvests, there were substantial migratory flows crossing the Atlantic. The Irish exodus to the United States is perhaps the best known, but several European states experienced massive out-migration during this time. Timothy Hatton and Jeffrey Williamson estimate that immigration may have augmented the New World's labour force by over 30 per cent; while depleting the native labour force in the Old World countries on the periphery of Europe (e.g. Denmark, Italy, Norway, Portugal, Spain and Sweden) by some 15 per cent.[14] In total, it is estimated that over 50 million people left Europe for the Americas in the century following 1820.[15]

Some 50 million people could flee to economic and/or political safety because there were few legal restrictions on human movement at the end of the nineteenth century. Indeed, international norms were committed to the notion of free human mobility, as evidenced in the communiqués of various meetings of the Institute of International Law, for example in Hamburg (1891), Geneva (1892) and Lausanne (1898).[16]

Characteristic of the era, an International Emigration Conference in 1889 could declare: 'We affirm the right of the individual to the fundamental liberty accorded to him by every civilized nation to come and go and dispose of his person and his destinies as he pleases.'[17] These international norms were also reflected in national law. For example, immigration to the United States was mostly unregulated before 1880: anyone who could afford the trip was let in. Indeed, foreigners were often welcomed, such as was done in an 1845 meeting in Philadelphia, where a group declared they would 'kindly receive [all] persons who came to America, and give them every privilege except office and suffrage'.[18]

Even in the 'old world', open immigration was becoming increasingly common. Thus, on the eve of World War I, a German observer surveyed the changing political landscape:

> Because in recent times the position of foreigners has grown much different from before ... most modern states have, with but a few exceptions, abolished their passport laws or at least neutralized them through non-enforcement.... [Foreigners] are no longer viewed by states with suspicion and mistrust but rather, in recognition of the tremendous value that can be derived from trade and exchange, welcomed with open arms and, for this reason, hindrances are removed from their path to the greatest extent possible.[19]

A more famous observation of the liberal nature of the prewar period (and the opportunities this period offered for residents of Britain) comes from John Maynard Keynes. This rather lengthy passage captures the spirit of the era marvellously, as viewed by the British bourgeoisie:

> What an extraordinary episode in the economic progress of man that age was which came to an end in August, 1914! The greater part of the population, it is true, worked hard and lived at a low standard of comfort, yet, were, to all appearances, reasonably contented with this lot. But escape was possible, for any man of capacity or character at all exceeding the average, into the middle and upper classes, for whom life offered, at a low cost and with the least trouble, conveniences, comforts, and amenities beyond the compass of the richest and most powerful monarchs of other ages. The inhabitant of London could order by telephone, sipping his morning tea in bed, the various products of the whole earth, in such quantity as he might see fit, and reasonably expect their early delivery upon his doorstep; he could at the same moment and by the same means adventure his wealth in the natural resources and new enterprises of any quarter of the world, and share, without exertion or even trouble, in their prospective fruits and advantages; or he could

decide to couple the security of his fortunes with the good faith of the townspeople of any substantial municipality in any continent that fancy or information might recommend. He could secure, forthwith, if he wished it, cheap and comfortable means of transit to any country or climate without passport or other formality, could dispatch his servant to the neighbouring office of a bank for such supply of the precious metals as might seem convenient, and could then proceed abroad to foreign quarters, without knowledge of their religion, language, or custom, bearing coined wealth upon his person, and would consider himself greatly aggrieved and much surprised at the least interference. But most important of all, he regarded this state of affairs as normal, certain, and permanent, except in the direction of further improvement, and any deviation from it as aberrant, scandalous, and avoidable. The projects and politics of militarism and imperialism, of racial and cultural rivalries, of monopolies, restrictions, and exclusion, which were to play the serpent to this paradise, were little more than the amusements of his daily newspaper, and appeared to exercise almost no influence at all on the ordinary course of social and economic life, the internationalization of which was nearly complete in practice.[20]

This normal, certain and permanent state of affairs proved anything but. With the outbreak of World War I, every state began to impose drastic restrictions on movements. This, in itself, was nothing new; but these controls were not lifted with the end of hostilities. After World War I, there would be no turning back to Keynes's liberal idyllic; even its memory is blurred in contemporary reflections.

The New Liberal Period

Increasingly, liberalism and migration controls proved to be rather comfortable, albeit unlikely, bedfellows. The political economy of the late nineteenth century was built on a rather curious contradiction, which continued to hamper economic study into the following century. Liberal trade theory rested on the assumption of international factor immobility (e.g. capital and labour); the rise in international trade in commodities was seen as a separate development from the international movement of capital and labour. In short, these models assumed that the movement of capital and labour were only free within one of the two countries in the model. In the mercantilist context, where labour and capital flows were usually directed among states of Empire, these assumptions were not too unreasonable.

However, as liberalism spread, and empires fell, these assumptions became more problematic. The empirical world came to mimic the models, rather than the other way around. With the rise of liberalism, flows in goods and capital were encouraged, while controls on migration were strengthened. As we shall see later, this development not only produced significant political and economic consequences, it allowed a severe contradiction to embed itself deep within liberal ideology. In the name of liberalism and of democracy, nation–states imposed increasingly stringent legislation to keep out unwanted émigré populations (e.g. on the basis of disease, occupation, skin colour, intellectual capacity, nationality, etc.). On the threshold of the twentieth century, the Western world experienced a radical regime shift within the liberal paradigm: gone was the era of liberal migration regimes and relatively free mobility; in its place rose a new liberalism built with the sweat and effort of subjects who were, in effect, prisoners of territory.

In the immediate aftermath of World War I, the limitations of a system that presumed mutually exclusive citizenries became very evident. The plight of 'stateless' citizens came to dominate the political landscape, and the need for a new international system for refugees became evident. In the early interwar period, some 10 million people took flight in an effort to return home, or to escape persecution. In the West, the plight of stateless citizens became a pressing political issue, as refugees fled from the new

Communist regime in Russia. Worsening matters, a Soviet decree of 15 December 1922 denationalized most of them – rendering them stateless and invalidating their travel documents.[21]

The international response to the refugee crisis was quick, if ineffective. For a brief moment in history it appeared as though the world would return to a more liberal migration regime – that the major powers would rescind their migration controls as they had after earlier conflicts. Thus, in 1920, the League of Nations convened an international conference in Paris to deal with the difficulties created by the new passport regime. This conference issued a number of recommendations aimed at reducing the unwonted peacetime restrictions on movements. The following year, a conference of the International Parliamentary Union met in Stockholm to condemn the passport system, and to call for more freedom of movement.

Yet a solution to the immediate postwar refugee crisis was not found in an international consensus to solve the plight of the stateless. States were unwilling (or afraid) to return to the prewar world of free migration and they fought to maintain their new powers. The immediate solution, limited as it was, can be understood as the result of a single individual's undying efforts: that of the Norwegian explorer, Fridjof Nansen.

Very early in the Russian refugee crisis, Nansen reluctantly agreed to become the League of Nations' High Commissioner for Refugees and to coordinate an international response to the problem of document-less refugees. As states were unwilling to dispose of their right to issue passports and control immigration, Nansen's inventive response was to create new, stateless, passports for the refugees. Introduced in 1922, these 'Nansen passports' were effective identification and travel document for stateless (at first mostly Russian) refugees. By September 1923, thirty-one governments had agreed to respect the documents, and their terms of arrangement.[22]

Although the Nansen passport system was an ingenious solution to the problems at hand, it suffered from a serious shortcoming (in light of an international system that allowed states to discriminate against immigrants). While these refugees finally had identification documents, recognized by many important states in the international system, these documents still did not guarantee a right of admission to the issuing country! Although this aspect made it easier to get governments to distribute the passports, Nansen was unable to persuade these states to assume any responsibility for the passport holders. Stateless refugees now had stateless passports, but their plight remained dismal.

In 1938, more concerted efforts were made to help the growing numbers of refugees from Germany and Austria. Again, the League of Nations convened a conference (this time in Evian, France), where delegates expressed their commitment to humanitarian assistance. While all the representatives bemoaned the degree to which they had already been saturated with refugees, only the Dominican Republic made a concrete offer of admission.[23] The eventual plight of these (mostly Jewish) refugees is already well documented.

By the outbreak of the Second World War, a great opportunity had been lost. As the threats and hostilities grew with Nazi expansion, states again ratcheted up their immigration controls. This pattern is consistent with state action in the face of war throughout the century. What was different this time was that the control regime from the First World War had not been dismantled before the new restrictions were introduced. Rather than returning to a system of war-based immigration restrictions, the international community came to see these restrictions as a normal and permanent instrument of sovereignty.

With the end of World War II, refugee numbers again exploded: it is estimated that there were some 30 million refugees, 11 million of whom were outside their countries of origin at the war's end. The League of Nations' successor, the United Nations, produced a number of subsequent organizations to deal with this flood of refugees in Europe: the United Nations' Relief and Rehabilitation Administration (UNRRA) in 1943, followed by the International Refugee Organization (IRO) in 1946 – which itself was succeeded by the creation of the UN High Commissioner's Office for Refugees (UNHCR) in 1949.

Unlike trade in goods, services and investment, there would come to be no postwar International Code of Conduct in regard to the nature and scope of migration restrictions; migration restrictions were considered to be solely matters of national sovereignty (while exchange rates, for example, were not). Worse, those international organizations that were concerned with human mobility suffered from divided and overlapping authorities. Thus the International Labour Organization (ILO) addressed issues concerning foreign workers; the United Nations' High Commissioner for Refugees (UNHCR) addressed refugee problems; and the United Nations' Economic and Social Council and its Conference on Trade and Development (UNCTAD) were mostly concerned with stopping emigration from developing countries.

By the end of the twentieth century, it was no longer possible to find any coordinated attempt to return to a regime with free migration; the world's focus remained trained on the need to accommodate the movement of refugees and asylum-takers – movements that were closely associated with the destructive wars that scarred that century. Suffering two major (world) wars, and countless smaller ones, war refugees and political asylum-seekers have become the new face of migration. In the fervour of war, and national responses to it, the age-old principle of free migration was buried under a growing pile of nationalist and xenophobic sentiments. During the brief periods when the developed world was not consumed by war, the immigration focus shifted to so-called economic refugees. But these immigrants remained illegitimate and mostly unrecognized by the international community at large.

Although international law allows for the right of exit from a given country, it does not recognize the corresponding right of entry into another. In particular, the 1948 Universal Declaration of Human Rights acknowledges the need for people to defend themselves against tyranny and oppression beyond the last resort of rebellion, and explicitly recognizes the dignity and equality of all members of the human family. In practice, however, this recognition is only window dressing. The Declaration's Articles 13–16 apply directly to migration: in particular, Article 13 declares that everybody has the right to move within the boundaries of a given state, to leave any country, and to return to one's own. (Article 14 protects asylum seekers from prosecution; Article 15 gives rights to a nationality; and Article 16 asserts that the family is the natural and basic unit.)

These 'basic human rights', as they are called, were established in the immediate aftermath of the Second World War. Since then, little has improved for the potential immigrant. The 1985 Declaration on the Human Rights of Individuals Who Are Not Nationals of the Country in Which They Live made this clear:

> Nothing in this declaration shall be interpreted as legitimizing any alien's illegal entry into and presence in a State, nor shall any provision be interpreted as restricting the right of any State to promulgate laws and regulations concerning the entry of aliens and the terms and conditions of their stay or to establish differences between nationals and aliens. However, such laws and regulations shall not be incompatible with the international legal obligations of that State, including those in the field of human rights.[24]

Today there is not a single state that allows free access to all immigrants. Of course, some states have been more liberal than others,[25] but a relatively small proportion of the world's population could and/or can enjoy these liberties. Until states are willing to accept new immigrants, the international right to leave a state is a shallow one.

Conclusion

The objective of this chapter has been to remind us of the unique historical conditions in which we reside: never have there been more formal restrictions on the right of individuals to move as they wish. Free mobility, and the political, social and economic liberty it encourages, has a long and distinguished history, while the contemporary powers of states to control that movement is surprisingly young.

This might be the first lesson we can draw to curb some of the most ridiculous assertions in today's migration debate. Contemporary restrictions on immigration should be seen as a unique response to the pressures generated by World War I and the nascent democratic movement. In that sense, our international regime is a historical anomaly, in at least two ways. First, there is a glaring contradiction between the dominant ideology of liberalism and the alleged needs of liberal states to restrict severely their citizens' freedom of mobility. Second, and more obviously, the nature and extent of these restrictions on human mobility are unparalleled in human history. As we begin to discuss potential solutions to some of today's most pressing international problems, we mustn't be complacent in thinking that national barriers to international human mobility are either necessary or permanent.

In addition, however, a second important lesson can be drawn from this brief historical overview. When we look back over the history of human migration, it is clear that this history cannot – and should not – be characterized in terms of large, uncontrollable floods. Even when there were few legal restrictions, migration flows tended to be limited and driven by their own internal logic. Its history suggests that migration is a highly selective process: only certain people leave and they tend to travel on highly structured routes to very specific destinations. As a result, migration flows tend to exhibit patterned or system-like natures that impose their own regulatory forces. Once a migration system reaches its point of saturation, there are inherent correction mechanisms that limit future migration: immigration levels automatically decline over time, and we begin to see considerable return migration. In short, the history of migration suggests that each migration system is limited in duration and geography: there is little historical basis for worrying about an unending flood of immigrants in a world without border controls.

sciences. If people some day will enjoy the same freedoms as those enjoyed by buyers and sellers of capital and/or goods and services, it is likely that a moral argument will hold strongest sway.

Consider a familiar example that illustrates the power of moral arguments in the face of strong opposing interests: the successful extension of the democratic suffrage. At the expense of real political power, enfranchised elites have consistently expanded suffrage to include workers, the propertyless, women, blacks, youths and others. Although it is often forgotten, initial democratic gains were made in the face of an ingrained antipathy to democratic ideas (before the First World War), and *all* the gains were made at the direct expense of entrenched interests. The motivation for this apparently irrational behaviour was mostly moral indignation, a changing economic and social context (that brought with it new ideas concerning sovereignty, legitimacy and citizenship), and a strong (if often implicit) threat of violent overthrow.[3]

There are four obvious parallels to contemporary conditions with respect to migration. First of all, birthplace remains a natural contingency that is morally arbitrary. Second, a small but wealthy elite control the globe's political and economic purse strings, at the expense of the vast majority. Third, the many facets of globalization are radically changing the way in which we experience and think about sovereignty, legitimacy and citizenship. Finally, a world of shrinking space and growing inequality is a potent recipe for social upheaval: Burke's fears of the 'swinish multitude' or Mill's of the 'uncultivated herd' are not unlike the fears that motivate those who wish to restrict international migration today.[4]

Moral arguments for free mobility can be developed along two fronts. The first front runs along universalistic and egalitarian lines (as an end in itself), where free mobility is seen as an intrinsic moral principle and recognized as a universal and basic human right. This is a strong argument with a long and distinguished pedigree, and it enjoys an elegance that is hard to dismiss. More significantly, this sort of argument has made much political headway in the postwar period.

The second argument is an instrumentalist argument for free mobility, where free migration is seen as a means to achieve greater moral ends (in particular, economic and political justice). The clear advantage of this line of argument is that it avoids many of the problems associated with recognizing and granting universal human rights. Instead, the focus of this argument is on recognizing the moral obligation to help people escape from grave economic and social injustices. As the second chapter illustrated, these inequalities and injustices are rife at the global level, and impute to the developed world a moral obligation to improve the conditions of the world's poorest denizens. In short, a moral argument for free mobility can be directly related to the global level of social, economic and political equality – the larger the differences, the stronger the moral argument for open borders.

In the end, moral arguments are the easiest arguments to make for free mobility. In fact, of all the arguments that are canvassed in this book, the moral arguments for free mobility are the most visible: many, if not most, of the political theorists who write on this subject question the morality of contemporary migration restrictions. For the lay reader, however, the moral arguments for free mobility are probably unfamiliar – and even fly in the face of conventional wisdom and political practice. Consequently, these arguments require some elaboration.

Mobility as a Universal Right

The purest moral argument for free mobility holds that migration should be recognized as a universal and basic human right.[5] The success of this argument depends on two related factors: (1) our willingness to accept universal human rights as a principle for ordering and evaluating human activity; and (2) a recognition of the shortcomings of the more common argument that compatriots enjoy a moral preference or priority. This latter (more common) argument usually assumes that states play an important – even necessary – role in providing security and fundamental civil, social and political rights, and that states can only do so behind closed borders.

At least since the end of the Second World War, human-rights-based arguments have made steady political headway. The 1945 Charter of the United Nations actually begins by reaffirming a 'faith in fundamental human rights, in the dignity and worth of the human person, in the equal rights of men and women and of nations large and small'. Although these fundamental human rights were (and are) often sacrificed on the altar of state sovereignty, they were frequently used to criticize states that did not subscribe to liberal democratic principles (read the constitutions of the USSR, China, and a handful of state-socialist satellite states). More recent attempts to hold formerly sovereign officials (e.g. Augusto Pinochet, Slobodan Milošević, and even Henry Kissinger) accountable for their alleged crimes against humanity provide evidence of the growing political relevance of these sorts of arguments. Popular demands for human rights – including both greater economic justice and political freedom – are on the rise, and increasingly legitimate.

If we accept the principle of universal human rights, then there are strong grounds for recognizing the right of free mobility as a core human right.[6] While many continue to argue over what constitutes core human rights, the general idea is that freedom, justice and equality belong to everyone (not only to privileged citizens of specific states). From this very broad definition, it is possible to defend the human right to migrate in all three terms (freedom, justice and equality).

Actually, there is a long and distinguished history of recognizing mobility as an essential freedom. In ancient Greece, the

Delphic priests regarded the right of unrestricted movement as one of the four freedoms distinguishing liberty from slavery.[7] This understanding can also be found in the work of Thomas Hobbes, who held that

> Liberty, that we may define it, is nothing else but an absence of the lets and hindrances of motion … every man hath more or less liberty, as he hath more or less space in which he employs himself … the more ways a man may move himself, the more liberty he hath.[8]

Indeed, a natural right to liberty figures prominently in the classical natural rights' doctrines. Within this concept of liberty lie a bundle of specific liberties, of which free movement was always one of the most fundamental (at least within the boundaries of a nation).

For these reasons, freedom of movement became central to the liberal philosophical project, and lies implicitly at the core of most contract theories.[9] After all, the central notion of 'government by consent' holds that citizenship is a voluntary act; the right to leave a country implicitly serves to ratify the contract between individuals and society. If a person who has a right to leave chooses to stay, that person signals a voluntary acceptance of the social contract. From this follows his/her obligations to society. But if an individual doesn't have the option of leaving, then society's hold on him/her is based on coercion. As Bruce Ackerman noted:

> The liberal state is not a private club: it is rather a public dialogue by which each person can gain social recognition of his standing as a free and rational being. I cannot justify my power to exclude you without destroying my own claim to membership in an ideal liberal state.[10]

This notion is clear and obvious in the foundational works of John Locke and others. Locke insisted that the very nature of the social contract implied the right to withdraw from it:

> Tis plain then ... by the Law of right Reason, that *a Child is born a Subject of no Country, or Government.* He is under his Fathers Tuition and Authority, till he come to the Age of Discretion; and then he is a Free-man, at liberty what Government he will put himself under; what Body Politick he will unite himself to.[11]

This is a classic statement of liberalism, and the right of personal self-determination. Such statements were repeated again in both the American and French Revolutions. Indeed, Thomas Jefferson was perhaps the most explicit on this point – asking Virginia's delegates to the 1774 Continental Congress to remind King George that

> our ancestors, before their emigration to America, were the free inhabitants of the British dominions in Europe and possessed a right which nature has given all men of departing from the country in which chance, not choice, has placed them, of going in quest of new habitations, and of there establishing new socie-ties under such laws and regulations as, to them, shall seem most likely to promote public happiness.[12]

In short, early liberal thinkers considered the freedom of movement to be a natural right, giving it precedence over all prerogatives asserted by the state. Although many modern liberals have subsequently devalued the right of free movement, it is still defended by some contemporary observers, and this prerogative lies at the core of most open-border arguments.[13] For example, Maurice Cranston holds that the freedom to move is 'the first and most fundamental of man's liberties'.[14] While Joseph Carens, more provocatively, argues: 'Citizenship in Western liberal democracies is the modern equivalent of feudal privilege – an inherited status that greatly enhances one's life chances. Like feudal birthright privileges, restrictive citizenship is hard to justify when one thinks about it closely.'[15] From here, the moral argument for open migration is straightforward.

For a number of rather obvious reasons, modern moral philosophy tends to prioritize universalism and impartiality. Indeed, it may even be argued that universality, egalitarianism and impartiality are the defining features of morality itself. If we apply these moral standards to citizenship/residency, it is necessary to question the 'right' to be born into (or reside in) any given country.

When our citizenship cannot be understood as a moral birthright, but is understood in terms of the luck of the draw, then all the advantages that are derived from that fateful event are also difficult to defend in moral terms. Thus we can question the moral legitimacy of an unequal distribution of national resources,[16] or the ability to inherit the advantages of a national economy and/or polity (e.g. advanced means of production, developed systems of communication, administration, education, etc.). As described in the second chapter, these 'chance events' are the most important variables in determining one's life chances globally. Despite their importance, individuals have little scope for influencing them.

From a universalistic moral perspective, it is necessary to ask why the rights of freedom, justice and equality are distributed by a relatively arbitrary rule (the luck of birth), rather than guaranteed to individuals.[17] From an egalitarian moral perspective, we should expect that the distribution of 'life chances' should be roughly equal. To the extent that none of the expectations generated by either of these perspectives is met, it is possible to question the morality of a system based on subjects who lack the freedom to migrate.

The morality of closed borders

Before we can accept a moral argument for free human mobility, we need to examine critically the more common assumption about the morality of national systems of governance. After all, isn't there a moral urgency to nearness? Don't we have a moral obligation to our nearest brethren? If so, can this 'nearness' be extended to fellow citizens of a nation-state?

William Godwin, the eighteenth-century utilitarian philosopher, offered a famous example that might help us to think about these questions. Godwin asked us to suppose that our house was on fire, with two people trapped inside: our mother and a great public benefactor who is visiting. He then tells us that there is only time to rescue one of the two before the roof collapses (killing the other). Godwin asks us: whom should we rescue? Remarkably, Godwin – on utilitarian grounds – encourages us to choose the benefactor. Today, most people would find this a ridiculous argument, and many might hazard to suggest that great moral comfort can be found in rescuing one's mother. The reason for this is that we often think about the strength of moral obligations in terms of nearness to home. Without arguing Godwin's point (allowing us to rescue our mothers, at the expense of the Archbishop Fenelon), we might challenge the common assumption that this sort of moral priority can be extended to citizens who are, in effect, strangers.

Morality starts nearest to home

We tend to presume that compatriots, or fellow nationals, take moral priority over foreigners. This presumption is often based on a sort of ripple (or concentric circle) conception of morality. From this view, we grant moral priority to those nearest us, and extend it with decreasing strength to those farther and farther away. As Alexander Hamilton argued in the debate over ratification of the US Constitution:

> The human affections, like solar heat, lose their intensity, as they depart from the center; and become languid, in proportion to the expansion of the circle, on which they act. [Thus] we love our families, more than our neighbours, more than our countrymen in general.[18]

In short, it is common to assume that individuals perform some sort of moral calculus that prioritizes family, friends, benefactors, neighbours, clients, co-workers, and so on. It is not difficult to extend this logic another step by offering compatriots moral priority over those further from the moral (individual) centre. While this sort of intellectual prioritization is common, is it right?

In a 1988 *Ethics* article, Robert Goodin lists a number of explicit cases in international law where foreigners are actually granted better protection than compatriots.[19] Among these are the right to take property for public purposes from our compatriots (but not from foreigners), and the right to conscript or tax fellow citizens (but not foreigners). Goodin suggests that the common intellectual prioritization of citizens over foreigners may not be so common in practice: 'in the present world system it is often – perhaps ordinarily – wrong to give priority to the claims of our compatriots.'[20]

Goodin explains the privileges of citizenship in terms of the need to match territorial boundaries to protectors. Citizenship is only a device for holding certain officials responsible to particular persons. Thus, for Goodin, the relevant moral boundaries are to be drawn around people, not territories. Obviously, these boundaries can be drawn at a variety of different levels and there is no reason, morally, to prioritize the nation-state.[21]

A related argument concerns the (moral) right of communities to live their own separate lives without undue influence from other people and communities based on different premises. If you believe that communities have a moral right to autarky and non-intervention, then the moral argument for closed borders comes rather easily.[22] From this position, it makes sense to limit moral concern to those who are nearest.

If we grant this argument its premisses (that there exist autonomous and autarkic communities, uninfluenced by the outside world), it is easy to follow. But such premisses are rather difficult to defend. Communities are not autarkic, and it is doubtful that they ever have been. Culture, ethnicity and community are all products of the centuries – where 'foreign' and 'local' have continually blended in unequal and complex ways. This argument will be developed more in Chapter 8. For now, it is enough to recognize that the identity of the individual or the community is much more fluid than these premises allow – making it difficult to demarcate clearly between us and them.

Neither are immigration controls the only (or even the most effective) means of maintaining a strong sense of community and/ or identity. Communitarian arguments against open borders often exaggerate the influence of immigrants on culture, while ignoring the potentially more threatening impact of trade, investment and television (to name just a few pernicious agents). Alternatively, these critics often ignore the more constructive tools available to communities for creating or actively producing a common sense of community in the absence of borders.

This distinction is all the more vacuous when we consider the fact that the modern state is so large that it consists mostly of strangers. In such a state, moral obligations are extended to some strangers (those with the right colour passport), and not to others. Once we begin to employ multilayered notions of moral obligations, we get stuck asking a series of very difficult questions concerning the balance of conflicting moral claims. By granting universal rights to individuals, regardless of citizenship, we can avoid these tricky issues by denying the priority of different levels of significance.

Indeed, communitarian arguments often assume that modern democratic states are built on shared communities of language, culture and ethnicity. In its boldest form, this argument assumes that there was once a pristine and autonomous cultural history to nations, and this pristine culture has been (and should continue to be) protected from foreign erosion. It is also common to assume that political stability requires a certain degree of cultural stability and cohesiveness. Each of these assumptions is questionable.

Like the general community argument, such arguments rest mostly on myths derived from nineteenth-century historical romanticism. If it were true that there were such things as distinct, unique and autonomous communities, then open borders might undermine that uniqueness, and rip the moral fabric of autarkic communities.[23] But it is not true, and modern states almost always incorporate more than one nation. As any introductory student of comparative politics is aware, nations and states are not coterminous. To the extent that there is a moral argument for isolating nations (as communities), the stronger moral argument may lie with eroding state power – and (concomitantly) allowing nationalities more autonomy.

Worse, attempts at trying to secure cultural and ethnic autonomy come recklessly close to racism, as is evidenced by the Heidelberg Manifesto, a recent statement from fifteen prominent German scholars and university professors:

> Biologically and cybernetically, nations are living streams of a higher order, with different systemic qualities that are transmitted genetically and by tradition. The integration of large masses of non-German foreigners and the preservation of our nation thus cannot be achieved simultaneously; it will lead to the well-known ethnic catastrophe of multi-cultural societies.[24]

States guarantee public security and civil rights

Historically, liberal principles and the development of civil rights have gone hand in hand with the state. This cannot and should not be denied. But history has also shown us that the sovereignty of the modern state is no guarantee of respect for individual rights. In short, the relationship between national sovereignty and individual rights is complex.

Perhaps the most legitimate argument for defending fixed borders is the need to maintain comprehensive systems of civil, democratic and social rights of citizenship. After all, many critics argue that liberal, democratic and social constitutions require some sort of closure in order to protect and guarantee the rule of law, and essential civil rights.[25] Open migration is said to threaten these rights on two fronts. First, the sheer migration inflow to an open state could have drastic consequences for employment, social security, public service, and so on. The second alleged threat comes from the import of alternative/competing principles or culture. Let us examine each threat in turn.

The first threat is directly addressed in the following chapters (in particular, Chapters 5 and 6). In these chapters it is suggested that there is no compelling reason to expect that increased migration flows will necessarily lead to an erosion of long-term political and economic gains. Even in a world characterized by open borders, states would continue to play an active role in offering and protecting civil, social and political rights. Indeed, it can (and will) be argued that states will actually need to compete with one another to offer more attractive citizenship bundles in a world with free human mobility. After all, many member states in federal unions (such as the United States) allow fairly simple 'citizenship' rules for citizens who move across state borders. For example, most states grant residency benefits to migrants who have stayed in a state over one year.[26]

Nor is there any reason to suggest that a world characterized by free mobility will be one that is without territorially bounded societies. To the extent that some amount of 'closure' is required for democratic decision-making to function stably, these requirements can be easily met at a variety of different levels of government (local, county, state, regional, whatever) – it does not require fixed and restricted state membership and/or closed borders. Indeed, citizenship can – for all intents and purposes

– remain exclusionary (though voluntary). By choosing to be a citizen of a country, migrants are actively choosing *not* to be members of other countries.

The second argument, about the cultural threat of immigration, builds on two assumptions: (1) that some cultures are naturally and permanently antagonistic or alien to democratic values; and (2) that a large inflow of people from these cultures can jeopardize existing democratic cultures. Subsequent chapters (7 and 8) will elaborate on how both of these assertions are without merit (and often condescending). For now it is enough to note that cultural values are learned, and exposure to these values (e.g. a lengthy residency requirement) will allow citizens to learn appropriate political and social behaviour. As a result, it is possible for democratic cultures to assimilate cultural and religious currents (for example, within Christianity and Islam) that were once profoundly hostile to democratic values.

Of course, most idealized notions of democracy are based on some sort of common history and practice, embedded in particular ethnic or national traditions; but these are simply that – idealized notions. The practice of democracy is about finding solutions to such differences. The only common value that is required for democracy to function is an assumption about the equal moral worth of individuals.[27] It is both dangerous and wrong to suggest that democracies depend on cultural homogeneity – especially when these arguments are used to legitimize exclusionary policies.

The real problem with this argument is that it prioritizes states' rights over those of individuals. As Joseph Carens reminds us,

> the state is a social institution, not a human individual, and an artificial creation, not a product of nature. The justification for dividing up responsibilities among states in the first place rests upon the claim that this arrangement is good for human beings, and so, judgment of legitimacy must focus in the first instance on the system as a whole. The legitimacy of any particular state

is thus initially derivative from the legitimacy of the system as a whole. The fact that a particular state fulfils its primary responsibilities will not make it legitimate if the system as a whole is illegitimate, and the system as a whole will be illegitimate if its way of allocating responsibilities fails to serve human beings as well as some feasible alternative.[28]

This is not to suggest that we must subscribe to the liberal view that the individual's needs are always prior to the community's. In fact, a communitarian argument for open borders is both possible and fruitful (if not yet proposed). At this juncture in the argument, however, the point is limited to recognizing the moral difficulty of justifying the rights of states when they come into conflict with the rights of individuals.

A related moral argument for restricting migration is the need to offer minimally adequate assimilation policies for both residents and immigrants. It is clearly inappropriate to offer different economic and civic guarantees to immigrants (from those that are offered to residents/citizens). Critics argue that the expense of an open borders policy may undermine the state's ability to offer equal guarantees to immigrants, or to lower the overall level of guarantees offered to both residents and immigrants. While the latter may be true, it provides little moral cover for an argument that would restrict international migration. It is both embarrassing and patronizing of the developed world to presume that it can decide what is best for the world's poorest and most exploited: we should let potential migrants decide for themselves whether they are willing to settle in a place that offers more or less opportunity, guarantees and/or obligations.

Finally, there is the issue of security. While this is an issue that is addressed in more detail in Chapter 8, it remains a constant companion to any discussion of open borders. After all, many would hold that a moral argument can be made for closed borders if it can be shown that a large inflow of migrants represents a threat to public order. The most common security argument parallels Garrett Hardin's famous lifeboat argument: it doesn't do anybody any good if a lifeboat is swamped with too many people.[29] By welcoming too many immigrants, a state may actually be threatening the very political and economic refuge sought by the migrant.

There are two reasons for questioning the applicability of the lifeboat analogy. First, the rich countries' lifeboats are far from full – and even the most pessimistic accounts of inflows do not represent the same sort of threat that is implicit in the analogy. The capacity of rich countries to absorb millions of people is very elastic; a long drive across the American West can easily confirm this. A significantly large inflow of immigrants may affect the standard of living of the world's richest populations (whether it is for the better or for the worse remains to be seen) but it is not a threat to their existence.

Second, if there actually was a security threat to immigration, the appropriate response would be to monitor, not to halt, the inflow. Another, more useful, analogy can be drawn from freeway traffic. In principle, freeways are open to everyone. However, during rush hour a sudden and large inflow of cars might inconvenience people. For this reason, political authorities do have a right to restrict access (e.g. lights, special lanes, etc.) in places where congestion is a problem and threatens the public's interest. But such a constraint is of a different order than outright restrictions. To conclude, the security argument for maintaining closed borders is either exaggerated or easily avoided by employing alternative (monitoring) approaches.

The examples above have been used to suggest that a strong moral argument can be made for thinking about human mobility in terms of a universal human right. At the very least, these examples and arguments should prompt us to be critical of the more common assumption about the moral priority of compatriots (near strangers at the expense of distant strangers). Not only is there a long tradition in political philosophy that recognizes the right of free mobility, but there are practical benefits as well. By recognizing the right to move as a universal right, we can avoid the difficulties and ambiguities of prioritizing between different levels of moral significance.

While many advocates of closed borders have legitimate concerns about the need for community closure, security and stability, it is questionable whether any of these needs will be challenged by a world with free mobility. Cultural cohesiveness and stability are important community assets, but they are more the product of common, lived, experience – than any sort of ethnic or national purity. If we discount recent tradition, there is little justification – moral or otherwise – for choosing nation-states as the appropriate level of closure. Nor is there any moral basis for providing nations, traditions and communities with rights, especially if these rights are seen to clash with individual (human) rights.

The Instrumentalist Argument

Despite the increasing popularity and influence of moral arguments framed in the form of a human, universal right, some may object.[30] Others may react to the strong liberal premises of such arguments – that the individual is assumed prior to the community.[31] Still others believe that enough moral goods are generated by the existing order and that there is no good reason to jeopardize these goods by moving to a new, unknown, state of affairs. It is possible to be sympathetic to all of these objections, and embrace yet another moral argument for free mobility. This argument is more practical in nature, and does not require that we accept the existence of human rights, or prioritize the individual at the expense of the community.

This instrumentalist moral argument holds that the current international system is immoral so long as it continues to produce significant global inequalities (social, political and economic). Because the current arrangement produces unjust and immoral results that benefit citizens of the developed world, these citizens have a moral obligation to right these wrongs. That obligation could be met by freer immigration, or by other means. Thus, this approach does not focus on free mobility as an end in itself, but sees free mobility as a means for achieving a greater moral end. In this way, the instrumentalist argument includes a sort of implicit moral threat: if rich states aren't willing to help poor states and reduce global inequalities, then inhabitants of poor states have a moral right to secure justice by voting with their feet.

In other words, if we accept the status quo – where states' rights are prioritized at the expense of the individual's – citizens of developed states have a moral obligation to minimize global economic and social inequalities. Rich states already have a number of instruments with which they can address these social inequalities, the most common of which is official development assistance. Most of these instruments will allow nations (or communities) a great deal of cultural autonomy. While this has long been recognized, rich states do not seem to take their moral obligations very seriously. The instrumentalist moral approach recognizes this, and seeks alternative means to meet these moral obligations.

In 1997, Thomas Pogge suggested that the economic commitment associated with this type of moral responsibility was shockingly low. His calculations suggested that a mere $75 billion (about 0.4 per cent of the GDP of the developed countries, or one-third of US military expenditures) could double the current income of the world's poorest 1,300 million inhabitants.[32] This sort of economic package could make a significant impact on the lives of the world's poorest inhabitants, with little noticeable impact on the (individual and/or national) economies of rich nations.

These economic gains, in turn, might encourage more positive political developments. Despite the relatively small costs involved, the developed world's moral obligations remain unfulfilled.

While some aspects of the current state system are morally defensible, the end product is surely not. The most appalling aspect may be the apparent lack of incentives for states to help the millions of poor and oppressed people of the world. By allowing individuals a chance to improve their own conditions, we provide an important incentive for correcting this moral imbalance. In doing so, we place pressure on rich states to take their moral obligations more seriously. (After all, one important way of staving off international immigration is to alleviate the economic and political injustices that incite it.) In short, this perspective sees free migration as a means for securing other moral goals; free mobility needn't be seen as a moral end in itself.

Criticisms of the instrumentalist argument

The most common rejoinder to the instrumentalist argument is that contemporary migration, especially legal migration, seldom includes the world's very poorest or most oppressed. After all, international migration requires some basic resources (e.g. language, information, money, contacts, etc.), making it unattainable for large segments of the world's oppressed population. Critics argue that opening borders will not eliminate all inequality, and that the right of free mobility cannot be extended to all because of significant resource constraints.

This sort of rejoinder is suspect on three grounds. First, there is no reason to confine ourselves to all-or-nothing arguments. If open migration can minimize some of the moral injustices that characterize today's global condition, it is a moral improvement on the status quo. Second, as is illustrated in the chapters that follow, those developing-world residents who don't emigrate may actually benefit from the increased voice and influence that accompany a real threat of exit. Finally, the second-order effects of outward migration may improve the conditions of those who remain. If outward migration helps the economic and political development of sending states, as the historical record suggests, then even the poorest can expect to benefit from an increase in global migration.

A second, less common, objection comes from the communitarian camp. While recognizing the injustices (and their accompanying moral dilemmas) of the current system, these critics worry that open borders may undermine the authority and power of states (the alleged protectors of community). In a sense, this objection mimics the concern about security and coherence, noted above. After all, as Michael Walzer (quoting Sidgwick) suggests: 'To tear down the walls of the state is not to create a world without walls, but rather to create a thousand petty fortresses.'[33]

To the extent that our concerns are with community (and not with states), there is no good reason to mourn the potential decline of large states. It is possible, and increasingly common, to disagree with Walzer's contention that contemporary politics requires the kind of largeness that states provide.[34] Rather, the benefits of size reflect an earlier time, when war and commerce depended on vast national resources. Indeed, it is quite possible that a world made of smaller, less powerful states, would be a more peaceful, egalitarian, world. Monopolistic and/or oligopolistic power is seldom celebrated in the economic sphere; it seems peculiar to wish them upon the consumers of political, social and moral goods.

In short, it is not unfair to suggest that both objections to an instrumentalist moral argument miss their mark. If we recognize states' rights, and the power they imply, we must also recognize the moral obligations associated with these rights. Few, if any, observers are willing to characterize the current distribution of world resources (economic, political, social) in moral or just terms. By advocating free mobility we don't need to argue that all inequalities will dissolve, only that there will be fewer than under existing conditions. Given today's distribution of power, resources and influence, this should not be too difficult to achieve.

Conclusion

In an attempt to understand contemporary arguments for restricting international migration, this chapter has engaged the moral argument for border closure. This argument holds that the state system is here and now, that such a system provides (fairly) strong bonds between citizen and ruler, and that the status quo produces a degree of justice and comfort for more people than any other feasible (alternative) system. The conservative nature of this argument makes it a difficult target to attack, as we really don't know what alternatives are feasible. This is the argument's strength. In moral terms, however, it remains a weak argument. In effect, this argument holds that the current system is good for those of us who are lucky enough to be born into affluent democratic states.

The higher moral ground lies with a universalistic conception of human rights and opportunities. This argument holds that individuals should enjoy a universal right to move in order to escape poverty and oppression. In the words of Angel, a Mexican peasant (and illegal immigrant to the USA): 'There are no frontiers for hunger. You have the right to look for opportunity wherever you can.'[35]

As we have seen, however, this argument is also open to criticism. Communitarians are concerned about the threat to the nation and community posed by free mobility, while realists are concerned about the effect on national sovereignty and states' rights. Both groups seem to be concerned about the impracticality of the proposal, preferring instead to stick with the status quo (even though many recognize the injustices associated with it). This chapter has endeavoured to show that these concerns (the threat to community and national sovereignty) are either exaggerated or morally inferior to the free mobility argument. The next chapter will address many of the political concerns in greater detail.

Finally, some may be leery of the larger attempt at trying to secure human rights as a basis for political exchange. For these people, the concept of human or universal rights is too diffuse and contingent upon diverse political and social contexts. These critics argue that it is the contexts themselves, not the 'rights' that they produce, which should attract our attention. For these critics, this chapter offers an instrumentalist argument for free mobility. Free mobility may be the most effective way of righting moral wrongs internationally. By empowering individuals to choose their own contexts, we can force states to react to the moral imbalance, and we can provide the poor and oppressed with real hope and opportunity.

5

A Political Argument

[I]t is nearly impossible to secure compliance with drastic state demands if people are able to vote with their feet.

Aristide Zolberg[1]

The political consequences of a world without borders are not understood and are hardly studied. In this terrain, the rhetoric runs high, while the analysis runs shallow. Most observers are unwilling even to consider the 'bogey' of free labour mobility, discarding the idea with simplistic references to the chaos that is expected in a free world.[2] This chapter aims to prune some of this rhetoric gone wild; it offers – in its stead – a new approach for understanding the relationship between migration and political development.

We can begin by jettisoning the most frightening depictions of a world without borders: most of these stories are generated by a simple fear of the unknown, or from short historical memories. Migration itself does not threaten political authority or community. Rather, interstate mobility encourages state and local officials to communicate and cooperate to solve common problems. While some of this new cooperation may undermine national instruments of sovereignty, the sovereignty itself does not disappear – it is simply reconstituted at new levels of political authority. The real bogey of globalization is the argument that the demise of national sovereignty is akin to the demise of all sovereignty.

Yet many of the fears generated by these pessimistic accounts are worth considering. For example, the respected economist Milton Friedman suggested that the welfare state was incommensurate with free immigration.[3] Citizens in the developed world might fear that a rush of new immigrants will undermine their hard-won civil liberties. Others rightfully question the security of states without borders, the protection of property rights, or the threat to democracy from immigrants with different political and cultural backgrounds. Political authorities fret about the difficulty of imposing unpopular policies when citizens can vote with their feet. These are, of course, legitimate questions that need to be addressed if advocates of free mobility are going to have any impact on public opinion in both the developed and the developing worlds.

The lack of any systematic analyses of the effects of migration on sovereignty may be one of the reasons that open borders are associated with chaos, political levelling and the demise of the developed world's welfare states. Pessimism and fear often ride posse with ignorance. What little work has been done in recent years is not directly related to evaluating the political consequences of international migration. Rather, the work in this area tends to focus on how host countries control migration flows, and evaluate their (in)effectiveness.

This literature sees national control regimes as part of larger nation-building projects, the result of domestic interest group pressures, the rights-based politics of liberal states, state interests – broadly defined – or changes in the international system.[4] At a more general level, there are studies that see migrants as a surplus pool of labour (an industrial reserve army) that is more politically exploitable (as it is unregulated, non-unionized and cheap).[5]

Although these studies are useful for understanding the policy responses of developed states, they leave a whole host of questions unanswered. How does migration affect sovereignty and/or democracy? Who wins by increasing migration? Who loses? What costs/benefits are associated with greater migration? Can international migration encourage a more just distribution of political capital? What will the political landscape look like in a world with free migration? To answer such questions we must go beyond the existing literature and start anew.

Such an approach will be hampered by a number of obstacles, common to any project considering future hypothetical scenarios. In particular, we can expect that any estimate of the political consequences of open borders will vary significantly according to the investigator's initial assumptions regarding three important parameters: the level of analysis, the size of the migrant stream, and the length of the temporal horizon. After all, the effects of migration might differ when analysed at the individual, national or international levels. For example, individuals might benefit from free migration, even if nations don't. Similarly, we might expect the political effects to vary with the size of the potential migrant stream: larger migrant flows might require greater political adjustments, while smaller flows might be accommodated without significant political fallout. Finally, free migration might distribute gains and losses unequally over time. It is conceivable that states, individuals and/or the international system might incur short-term losses but long-term political gains from freer human mobility. These sorts of caveats are important to keep in mind as the discussion develops. For now, however, the state of the existing literature remains so underdeveloped that we must set these concerns aside in order to trace out a larger (and less detailed) map of the political terrain.

We can begin with a provocative thought experiment. The first part of this chapter asks the reader to consider the injustice of a national regime that was routinely criticized in the international arena: the apartheid state in South Africa. In doing so, this part of the chapter has two immediate objectives. The first of these is to point to some uncomfortable similarities between apartheid and contemporary international law.[6] In addition, however, the South African example helps to emphasize the shortcomings of an international system that grants states carte blanche authority in matters of 'internal sovereignty'.[7]

The main body of this chapter develops a more constructive (positive) approach to understanding how increased mobility affects sovereignty. Here it is suggested that greater mobility will increase the bargaining power of individuals in their negotiations with the different faces of sovereign power. Freer mobility will not only make it easier to escape (and undermine) unjust regimes like the apartheid state in South Africa; it will also boost the individual's capacity to influence decisions in democratic states. In short, freer migration should strengthen the political hand of individuals as citizens – allowing them to create states that are more responsive to their political demands.

These conditions will also affect the nature of relations among states. If citizens become more mobile, and if states need to worry about alienating or scaring off a potentially mobile citizenry, we can expect states to compete with one another in attracting citizens (or exert effort to deter potential emigration). This sort of state responsiveness should encourage the development of stronger international regimes and cooperative institutions aimed at facilitating international exchanges. This is, after all, what we see happening between states in federal systems (such as the USA) and in the burgeoning European Union. Arguably, this new institutional context is better suited for dealing with the global nature of contemporary politics. After all, the biggest stumbling block to more effective international solutions has been the reluctance of powerful states.

The Problem with Closed Borders:
The Case of Apartheid

In a most glaring way, the apartheid state in South Africa reflected many of the injustices and shortcomings of the nation-based concept of sovereignty. With no real recourse to exit, the vast majority of South Africans were forced to live an impoverished economic and political life for half a century. This poverty was implicitly encouraged by an international system that turned a blind eye to matters of internal sovereignty. In this respect, the South African experience parallels that of many tyrannies: having no recourse to exit, and with little chance of influencing domestic policy, residents became prisoners of territory and circumstance.

The South African case provides a disturbing and familiar image of how our current international system encourages elite and unjust concentrations of power. For almost fifty years, from 1948 to 1994, this despicable state in South Africa survived in an international system that was mostly critical of its modus operandi, and where the vast majority of its residents were opposed to its rule. Yet even under these ideal conditions for regime change – with enormous resistance, both internationally and domestically – apartheid's governors were able to maintain their grasp on power.

Arguably, South Africa may not be the best case for studying how the contemporary system allows pariah states to exist and multiply. Indeed, the twentieth century was littered with states that were bloodier and more aggressive. But the South African example is useful in that most of its atrocities were committed under the robe of 'legitimate' politics. By and large, the apartheid state played by the rules of international politics. In return, the international community granted it sovereign control. In short, there was a legal basis to apartheid, with explicit references to democracy, sovereignty and national self-determination. In most respects, despite growing boycott pressures in the late 1980s, South Africa continued to be a legitimate member of the international community.

Indeed, there was a legalistic justification for every element of the apartheid regime, grounded in the needs of its total strategy.[8] This was not an absolutist state, unconcerned with the rule of law; this was a state that based its repression in legal terms, wrapped in the rhetoric of political democracy. In particular, apartheid was built on legal blocks with familiar, even comforting, sounding names such as the Internal Security Act, the Public Safety Act, the State of Emergency Act, the Maintenance of Law and Order Act, and so on.

The most common criticism of apartheid was that it denied the vote to a majority of its residents: those with black and coloured skins.[9] The importance of the vote is simple and obvious: in the absence of exit, the democratic vote is the best conduit of political influence. For this reason, representative democracy has come to be seen as the most just and legitimate form of rule. To over-throw repressive regimes, citizens in pariah states (such as South Africans under apartheid) are expected to organize an effective and democratic opposition. (It should be pointed out that this model is implicitly informed by the experiences of nineteenth-century Europe, where democratic opposition movements developed in an environment characterized by free international migration.)

Yet the lack of political voice was only one aspect of apartheid's injustice. Indeed, in the master plan for apartheid, the weight of repression rested on two other pillars: the use of 'migrant' labour and the state's 'homelands' policy. These two pillars were sup-ported by a number of different justifications and particular policy instruments over the decades, but the pillars themselves remained intact. These pillars, in turn, rested on an international system that – despite being vocally and highly critical of apartheid – employed many of the same repressive sorts of policy instruments. Apartheid was a political system of differentiation, grounded in the concept of nationhood, or autonomous self-development.

Relying on migrant labour

Ironically, one of the main criticisms of apartheid (both within and beyond South Africa) was the degree to which the movements of its coloured population were controlled and regulated. Since the 1920s, but especially after the 1948 National Party election victory, there were numerous restrictions placed on the movement of blacks in South Africa. Under the rubric of what were called Section 10 rights, black (and coloured) South Africans were only allowed to live and work in South African cities if they met certain conditions. In particular, Section 10(1) of the Native Law Amendment Bill passed by the House of Assembly in 1952, read:

> 10(1) No native shall remain for more than seventy-two hours in an urban area or in a proclaimed area ... unless
>
> (a) he was born and permanently resides in such area; or
> (b) he has worked continuously in such area for one employer for a period of not less than ten years or has lawfully resided in such area for a period of not less than fifteen years, and has thereafter continued to reside in such area and is not employed outside such area and has not during either period or thereafter been sentenced to a fine exceeding fifty pounds or imprisonment for a period exceeding six months; or
> (c) such native is the wife, unmarried daughter or son under the age which he would become liable for the payment of general tax under the Native Taxation and Development Act, 1925, or any native mentioned in paragraph (a) or (b) of this subsection, and ordinarily resides with that native.

Concurrent with the passing of the Native Amendment Bill, South African blacks came under the jurisdiction of the (misnamed) Abolition of Passes and Documents Act. This Act required all black South Africans, male or female, to carry a reference book that showed authorization to live and work in specific areas.

The point is that black South Africans needed official permission to travel and to work anywhere within the country. Specific permits were required to look for jobs, to take jobs, and then to change jobs. The requirement to register, and to produce the dreaded *dompas* (an internal passport), was both cumbersome and humiliating. To critics of apartheid, this represented a terrible injustice: it was understood as a major infringement on the sort of legitimate political liberties that should be granted to citizens of territorial states.

Now, gaze for a moment at the parallels to our own international system. With one eye, we see Europe and her offspring protecting their wealth from the invasion of poorer Southerners by imposing rigid controls on migration. With the other we see South Africa's European offspring protecting their wealth from the invasion of poorer surrounding Africans by imposing rigid controls on migration. Why is the Dane's advantage over the Somalian legitimate (and protected by international law), while the Afrikaner's advantage over the Xosi was not?

The homelands policy

The second pillar of grand apartheid was equally heavy and unbearable. Apartheid's critics fought against the state's development and implementation of a number of homeland, or Bantustan, authorities. Bantustans were areas reserved by the state's (white) authorities for black Africans. In the words of their creator, Hendrik Frensch Verwoerd, before the South African Parliament, in 1951:

> The fundamental idea throughout is Bantu control over Bantu areas as and when it becomes possible for them to exercise that control efficiently and properly for the benefit of their own people.

These Bantu areas were granted a degree of self-government and promised eventual independence. All black Africans were grouped according to a number of tribal antecedents, and each was forced to accept citizenship in his or her designated Bantustan.

With the Bantu Authorities Act of 1951 a system of local, regional and territorial 'tribal' authorities was established with limited executive functions. A special committee (the Tomlinson Committee) was created to evaluate the economic viability of these homelands, and found that they could not be sustained without massive state funding. Not surprisingly, the apartheid government was unwilling to make the necessary fiscal commitment; nevertheless, it proceeded to set up eight (later ten) distinct 'Bantu Homelands' in 1959 with its Promotion of Bantu Self-Government Act. Each of these Bantustans was given a degree of self-government, based on the principle of ethnicity.[10]

In the years that followed, some of the Bantustans developed autonomous political institutions. In 1963, the Transkei Constitution Act set up the first homeland legislative assembly; in 1970 homeland citizenship was imposed on all black Africans throughout South Africa; and in the following year (1971) self-government was given to the other homelands. In 1976, nominal independence was granted to Transkei, followed by Bophuthatswana, Venda and Ciskei in 1977, 1979 and 1981, respectively. In gaining independence, residents of these homelands lost their South African citizenship.

These homeland authorities were to become the foundation blocks for a new segregation policy based on the principle of separate development. Central to this new policy was the restriction of black mobility between rural and urban areas (as described above in the Section 10(1) legislation).

Arguably, the original intent of the Bantustans and their corresponding influx controls was to provide large reservoirs of black African labour for nearby white economic interests. Originally, the reserves were understood in terms of a political 'home' for all Africans, and a convenient way of excluding them from the polity of white South Africa. In the 1960s, however, the reserves were 'upgraded' with more autonomy, and showcased to the international community as an attempt to provide black Africans with the right to self-government.

Parallel to this new shift in emphasis on separate development and autonomous homeland policies, the government began to revise its strategy with respect to Section 10(1) rights. In particular, the Department of Bantu Administration and Development (BAD) began a sustained struggle to remove Section 10(1) from the statue books altogether. When they were unsuccessful in this, they tried to undermine Section 10(1) rights by employing a new forced-removal policy. Under this new policy, whole communities living in so-called 'black spots' were relocated from rural white areas to the homelands. By the mid- to late 1960s, urban removals were also becoming increasingly frequent.

In short, autonomous homelands were redefined in an attempt to help them withstand the new ideological winds that were blowing across the African continent. In the aftermath of colonialism, new nations were beginning to spring up across the continent, united under the banner of nationalism and ethnic self-determination. In the same way that nationalism in Europe was clearly exclusionary (you can't be Norwegian if you are Swedish; or Czech if you are Slovak), apartheid's officials used nationalism to justify continued segregation in South Africa.

Parallels to today's international system

Thus, nationalism and self-determination – two of the most significant political forces of the late twentieth century – were melded together to justify the new nature of apartheid: whites and blacks were to have their own separate spheres of influence, where they could exercise and enjoy the full privileges of a free society.

Obviously, this description is not meant to condone the apartheid regime or its policies by equating them with the concepts of nationalism and self-determination. Neither is it intended to suggest that these Bantustans ever won the degree of autonomy that is enjoyed by European states (for example). Rather, the intent is to focus on the similarities between the apparently legitimate notions of nationalism and self-autonomy, and their illegitimate application to Bantustans in South Africa. Why are these concepts acceptable at one level and not at the other?

In fact, the new homelands can be understood as a logical extension of the concept of national sovereignty, a concept that continues to dominate international relations. The apartheid regime was simply suggesting that Africans should gain control of their own (relatively worthless) piece of territory, over which they would have full political autonomy. Like the conditions that characterize contemporary notions of national (territorial) sovereignty, people from one homeland were not allowed to travel freely to another without the appropriate travel and residency documents.

The South African case is particularly noteworthy in that its apartheid regime reveals one of the main contradictions of our own international system. Although the apartheid state was consistently attacked for the unjust nature of its policies, very similar policies are commonly employed among nations, at the international level. Although the moral shortcomings of South Africa were obvious, most contemporary observers are unable (or unwilling) to see the parallels to our own international system.

Worse, given a nation-based or territorial conception of sovereignty, the 'fault' of apartheid lay implicitly at the feet of an ineffective democratic opposition in South Africa. In this view, legitimate regime change comes from within, when the dissatisfied masses unite to overthrow an unjust or unpopular regime. While individual states may provide illicit support for indigenous democratic movements, in public they expect citizens to overcome the enormous collective action, financial and military superiority of powerfully entrenched interests. This is both wishful thinking and unjust: as territorial subjects (with no recourse to exit), the cards are heavily stacked against individual residents or citizens.

In the aftermath of apartheid, additional shortcomings of this contemporary approach to development have become increasingly visible. Despite the ANC's impressive electoral victory, economic conditions for the vast majority of South Africans have not improved; nor has the ANC government managed to fulfil many, perhaps most, of its campaign promises. For many observers it appears as though the new democratic government has been hamstrung by its commitment to satisfy the demands of the international lending community. An aggressive liberalization of domestic markets for capital, goods and services markets has made popular economic reforms difficult, if not impossible. In short, policy in South Africa is aimed largely at attracting international support; the new constituents of democratic South Africa are not the poor rural black (and voting) population, but the class of mobile asset-holders who vote with their feet.

In the ashes of apartheid governance lie the seeds to real empowerment, but we need to dig to find them. Black citizens are now free to move about their country in search of better economic and political opportunities. This is a real victory, but it is limited to the territorial boundaries of the state. By contrast, South Africa is full of other asset-holders – white and black, foreign and domestic – who are not limited in the same way. Investors and producers, of whatever nationality, can move relatively freely in and out of South African territory in search of better conditions and larger returns. The resulting imbalance in opportunity of exit means that mobile asset-holders end up wielding greater influence over political outcomes.

While the battle for political democracy in South Africa has been won, the victory has proven pyrrhic. The new democratic government responds effectively to the influence of its loudest constituents – but the voice of influence is not being transmitted with the vote. Rather, the real voice of influence in contemporary politics comes with the threat of exit. As a consequence, the voice of most South Africans remains muted and ignored.

A Market-based Approach

It is one thing to point to the disturbing similarities between apartheid in South Africa and contemporary conditions in the international community. It is quite another thing to suggest that liberalizing border controls will empower individuals, threaten totalitarian regimes, and balance the growing asymmetry between governed and governors (or labour and capital). How can free mobility reap such significant political rewards?

To understand how freer migration affects political sovereignty, consider the following hypothetical example from the supermarket. As consumers, we choose daily among competing products on the supermarket shelf. These products offer a sundry mix of qualities and quantities, at varying costs, so that we can choose the product/price mix that is best, given our preferences and income.

Now, imagine that you are a long-time consumer of a given product, say Soapy Soap, produced by a large, responsible, firm called Cleaner Products Inc. For whatever reason, and with great surprise, you discover one day that Soapy Soap is not the same wonderful product that it used to be. As a concerned consumer, you face three options: (1) you might try an alternative brand; (2) you might contact Cleaner Products Inc. and tell them how disappointed you are with the deterioration in product quality (while threatening to defect to an alternative product if something isn't done); and/or (3) you might do nothing but sulk.

This simple example is derived from an influential work by the economist Albert Hirschman.[11] Hirschman describes these three different feedback mechanisms in terms of what he calls 'exit', 'voice' and 'loyalty'. To the extent that there are alternative brands on the shelf next to Soapy Soap, it is relatively easy (and cheap) for us – the dissatisfied consumer – to 'exit' to another brand. For this reason, Hirschman expects consumers to rely most heavily on exit as a strategy to signal our dissatisfaction with a product. After all, writing a letter to the management of Cleaner Products Inc. requires quite a bit of energy (and the frustration needed to generate it)! Similarly, Hirschman recognizes that there are real costs to changing brands if we are loyal to a particular brand of detergent. These costs allow firms like Cleaner Products Inc. a cushion of time, within which they can address the problem to our (the consumer's) satisfaction.

It is possible to adapt Hirschman's argument in a way that can help us think about the effects of migration on political sovereignty.[12] In a context with free labour mobility (which reduces the cost of exit), the adaptation is fairly straightforward if we simply imagine states acting like firms, and citizens acting like consumers. If people are free to move from state to state, and can choose freely among states (or their requisite 'citizenship bundles'), states should begin to compete with one another – like firms competing for consumers. In short, with freer international mobility, citizens will be able to act more and more like consumers – choosing among citizenship baskets that best meet their preferences.[13]

Of course, it is not entirely unproblematic to assume that voters will act like consumers, or that states act like firms. There are, after all, very important differences that separate both sets of analogies. Neither is it appropriate to assume that a potential migrant has the same cold/calculating attitude to social uprooting as he/she does when changing his/her brand of detergent. Still, these types of assumptions – if problematic – are common in the social sciences, and they can help us to see things that aren't always immediately obvious.

It might also be noted that it is possible to generate other, less market-oriented, models for analysing political outcomes under conditions of greater human mobility. The advantage of this market-based approach is its ability to provide clear intuitive lessons and predictions on the basis of fairly realistic assumptions. To its detriment, the model conceives of community in terms of an aggregation of egoistic consumers – hardly a very appealing vision of community. To correct for this shortcoming, future research might consider the effects of free mobility on a Rousseau-inspired republican community model. For now, however, the discussion will be confined to an extension of Hirschman's market-based model.

By adapting Hirschman's model to examine how states might respond to citizen dissatisfaction in a context with free human mobility, it is possible to generate three explicit expectations about the effects of migration on political sovereignty. First of all, citizens will enjoy increased influence on issues of internal/domestic sovereignty. This is because voice is not only amplified by the threat of citizen exit, but the exit option itself provides another (new and important) means of articulating dissatisfaction. Second, states themselves will need to become more responsive to citizen demands or risk losing legitimacy, people and resources. Finally, and as a consequence of the first two expectations, we might expect to see states competing with one another in order to attract mobile citizen resources. A state without citizens would be as successful as a firm without customers.

As the last two expectations are derived from the first, it may be worthwhile to elaborate on why citizens can expect increased political influence in the context of freer international migration. In a world without borders, citizens will not have to rely solely on voice in signalling their dissatisfaction with government. As we saw in Chapter 2, the world is filled with examples where political voice is either muted or ignored. The potential for freer exit will provide citizens with another venue for signalling dissatisfaction; in doing so, exit can improve the quality and volume of voice *and* undermine those regimes where voice (thus far) has been muted. As the opening citation by Aristide Zolberg attests, it is difficult to imagine tyrannical regimes in a context with free human mobility.

In a world with free human mobility, voice and exit could become real alternatives – if unequal in cost. In the face of unwanted political changes, citizens will have two, complementary, means of influencing future outcomes. If traditional voice (the vote) proves ineffective at influencing the outcome, the citizen can threaten to (or actually) emigrate. This is, after all, what capital owners do today: they threaten exit if the political authorities don't deliver what they wish. Obviously, the cost of an individual's exit – even in an environment with free mobility – will remain very high (for personal, social and cultural reasons). Consequently, we can only expect it to be wielded under extreme conditions, or in response to policy decisions that are particularly important for the mobile citizen. Most of the time, voice will remain the most important avenue for signalling dissatisfaction, but the threat of exit will strengthen that voice substantially.

Hypothetical scenarios

To clarify these options, and the influence they wield, consider two hypothetical scenarios. On the one hand, we can imagine a citizen in today's world who finds him/herself living in a democratic regime that promises to curtail or limit future civil liberties (for example, as a necessary measure to fight terrorism). We might further assume that this citizen puts a premium on civil liberties, and wishes to protect them (even in the face of a rising terrorist threat). Under these conditions, this citizen is expected to use his/her voice (and, obviously, contribute in all the supporting activities of representative democracy – for example, support and assist sympathetic political campaigns, write letters to the local newspaper and political representatives, etc.) and hope that the larger political community ultimately shares the same political values. If this citizen finds him/herself in the minority, he/she must accept the democratic outcome, and hope for a better outcome in the next election.

Now consider the same situation in a context with free human mobility. In this context, the concerned citizen has an additional instrument with which to signal dissatisfaction: the vote *and* the threat of emigration. If voice proves to be ineffective in signalling his/her dissatisfaction with the new state of affairs, this citizen can threaten exit to a country that offers a better civil liberties' package, or – if things are really bad – he/she can actually emigrate to that country.

In this context, the political dynamics change for both states and citizens. Policymakers will be forced to consider more seriously the political fallout from unpopular decisions. Not only will they need to consider the exit-effect of their proposed changes, but they will need to consider these changes in light of the rights regimes of competing states. States with more attractive civil liberties regimes can expect to attract citizens that desire those rights. Individuals that prefer to live in a state with a more restricted set of civil liberties will be free to choose these.

Indeed, the most attractive consequence of the free mobility context is the freedom and power it offers individuals. Disgruntled citizens are provided with an opportunity to leave the political community and find one that better suits their own values.[14]

Those loyal and patriotic citizens who are committed to living in the state will be able to wield their voice more effectively, because it is accompanied by the threat of exit. Finally, the voice of ordinary citizens will be amplified to the level that other (more mobile) actors already enjoy. Today's threat of elite exit can then be matched by the threat of exit for the citizenry at large. As a consequence, we can expect states to be more responsive to broader citizen dissatisfaction.

In a world with free human mobility, the quality of the citizen's voice, because of the implicit threat to exit, is significantly improved. Better yet, voice is improved in both democratic and non-democratic regimes. With a real threat to exit (even when it remains an expensive alternative), states would be forced to respond to lapses in citizenship quality or risk losing power (read people and the revenues associated with them). States would rule over a citizenry that is both alert and inert (to borrow Hirschman's terms): alert citizens, through voice, could provide information to state officials about policy failures; inert citizens could provide the state with a cushion of time and resources within which they can respond. This is an ideal environment for encouraging effective state responses to dissatisfied citizens.

Recent evidence

While this argument may appear far-fetched, it is possible to provide examples of the way in which the threat of exit strengthens citizen voice. Of course, as few of today's citizens enjoy real freedom of exit, contemporary examples are relatively few and difficult to find. Still, these exceptional examples provide strong support for arguments about the potential power of exit.

The collapse of East Germany and the Berlin Wall represents just such a case, where the threat of mass exodus clearly affected significant policy changes in the home state. In August of 1989, a flood of would-be émigrés from East Germany tried to escape to the West via Hungary (and on to Austria, then West Germany). When the Hungarian authorities stopped trying to stave off this flight, some 30,000 East Germans had escaped to the West by the end of September. Concomitant with this human flight were a number of large demonstrations in Leipzig, Dresden, Berlin and other East German cities. These protestors were explicit in their intent *not* to leave. In stark contrast to their fellow citizens who chose exit, East German demonstrators rallied under the slogan 'We stay here': demanding greater input in policy at home.

This combined threat of voice and exit reaped significant political rewards. On 1 November, the East German cabinet reopened the country's border with Czechoslovakia. Two days later the ministers in charge of security and police resigned. After a reported 1 million demonstrators jammed the streets of East Berlin, the rest of the cabinet resigned. And still people continued to leave East Germany. In the following week, some 50,000 people were said to have left before the East German government eventually threw in the towel and announced that all of its border points were to be opened. On 9 November the Berlin Wall fell.

The Berlin Wall proved to be the Achilles heel of state socialist regimes in East Germany and across Eastern Europe. A week after the borders were open, the East German secret police force, the dreaded Stasi, was disbanded, and the leading role of the Communist Socialist Unity Party was renounced. Within the next few months, most of Eastern Europe fell victim to similar revolutions.

While there are many explanations for the fall of East Germany, the immediate threat of exit by large numbers of East German citizens was surely a significant factor. Because East Germans had an effective exit threat (they were welcomed in West Germany), the Communist authorities were forced to concede power or risk ruling over a state without citizens.

A similar, if more confined, situation can be found in Southern Africa today. In both Zimbabwe and South Africa, important land reform programmes have been hamstrung by the real threat of exit by white farmers (and the effective voice of those that have remained). In Zimbabwe, for example, 4,500 white commercial farmers (or about 1.4 per cent of the population) occupy 48 per cent of the best arable land – while millions of blacks are crammed into unproductive regions. President Mugabe's reforms aimed to acquire 5 million hectares of land from those white commercial farmers, and give it to poor black families.

The conditions in South Africa are not all that different, and the pressure for reform has been equally strong. The new democratic government in South Africa promised an extensive land reform package, aimed at three specific goals: (1) strengthening tenure rights for the rural poor; (2) land restitution for those who could prove that their family's land had been taken under apartheid; and (3) redistributing 30 per cent of all agricultural land to the rural poor.

While there is significant political support for the reforms among the black majorities, reforms in both Zimbabwe and South Africa have been very difficult to implement. In Zimbabwe, reform promises have been repeatedly broken, and the government's ambitions radically scaled back. In South Africa, the government had promised that all three of its goals would be met before the year 2000. By that date, however, the country was nowhere near achieving any of them. In both countries, the voice of a very small minority has been amplified by their very real threat of exit: white farmers in both countries enjoy exit options to Britain (and elsewhere). In the face of deteriorating (for them) levels of citizenship (e.g. land reform), some white farmers leave, but many stay and voice effective demands. The effectiveness of these demands rests critically on their implicit threat of exit, and the loyalty that is conveyed by their willingness to stay.

In these two, very different, examples we see the way in which a *real* threat of exit, combined with effective voice at home, can significantly influence policy outcomes. The examples are relatively unique in that both white farmers in Southern Africa and East German émigrés enjoy/enjoyed the possibility of settling elsewhere. This makes their threat of exit real and effective.

More common today are conditions in which people enjoy a restricted freedom of exit (i.e. the right to leave a country, but no corresponding right of entry elsewhere). It is for this reason that the political effects of migration are often misunderstood or corrupted. Under these conditions, the possibility of exit can, and sometimes does, coexist with (and may even encourage) tyrannical regimes.

For example, it might be argued that the flight from Serbia by thousands of younger and more educated Serbs (and non-Serbs) sapped the opposition of some of its more articulate and vibrant members and actually facilitated Milošević's increasingly harsh rule.[15] On the surface, an example like this might suggest that the threat of exit can also be used to create tyrannical regimes, as the opposition to tyranny flees to greener pastures. But we should be careful about drawing this conclusion. Such an example tells us little about whether Milošević's regime could have survived in a world without borders. After all, without the possibility of legal entry into other states, Milošević's rule was never truly threatened by an exodus (as the threat of exit was not credible for the vast majority of residents).

Historical evidence

At earlier periods in history, when international migration was a real possibility, both exit and the threat of exit were used to affect important political changes. For example, it is conceivable that exit played an important role in encouraging the democratic revolutions that shook nineteenth-century Europe. In a 1978 *World Politics* article, for example, Hirschman speculated that pre-World War I emigration might have sparked democratization and liberalization movements in several European countries. In a similar vein, Stein Kuhnle has suggested that pioneering welfare-state measures of the late nineteenth and early twentieth centuries (in Bismarck's Germany, Scandinavia and Great Britain) were all taken in light of high rates of overseas migration.[16]

Indeed, contemporary observers of the first democratic revolutions were acutely aware of the effect that emigration had on the politics of states that were losing their citizenry. In a prescient account of the importance of the American Revolution, the French economist Turgot wrote:

> The asylum which [the American people] opens to the oppressed of all nations must console the earth. The ease with which it will now be possible to take advantage of this situation, and thus to escape from the consequences of a bad government, will oblige the European Governments to be just and enlightened.[17]

The Political Benefits of Free Migration

While these examples are aimed to show how increased mobility strengthens the political hand of citizens, they also show how states will be forced to become more responsive to the citizen as voter/migrant. Holders of today's mobile assets (in particular finance capital) have already learnt this lesson, and it is one of the most important lessons of the burgeoning globalization literature.

After all, some factors of production are more mobile than others (by their nature and/or by political design); owners of these factors enjoy more influence – given their real threat of exit. Thus far, owners of financial capital have benefited the most from the liberalization of global markets – their political influence has grown in proportion to their real threat to exit. While there is some debate about how much labour benefits in this new context, it is not controversial to suggest that capital has benefited relatively more.[18]

Nor should these results surprise anyone. After all, this was one of the most important lessons learned by reformist socialists at the beginning of the last century. Despite the radical rhetoric of nearly every social-democratic party in Europe during the interwar period, none of them nationalized the means of production when they eventually formed or entered government. The threat of a capital strike has always hung heavily over the ambitions of socialists in government.[19]

Consequently, if there is a challenge to the welfare state, it does not come from increased labour mobility. In the simplest political terms, we might argue that the welfare state benefits domestic labour, at the expense of domestic capital.[20] If this is true, the future of the welfare state depends on the continued political influence of labour, relative to capital. Thus far, globalization has occurred faster in some venues than it has in others – this has introduced an imbalance of power between holders of mobile and immobile assets. To the extent that many forms of capital are already mobile, the domestic influence of its owners has increased with globalization (relative to that of immobile labour). In this light, an argument for increased mobility is an argument for balancing the political scale between holders of mobile and immobile assets.

In a world with free human mobility, states would need to protect and advocate workers' rights in a global environment. In the face of potential citizen out-migration, states may find it difficult *not* to offer more developed welfare states – for fear of losing their workforce. Thus, in the same way that states today compete by offering attractive investment havens for mobile capital, we can expect future states to compete with one another to attract increasingly mobile citizens/labour. While it is too early to say whether this competition will lead to increased policy convergence, we can expect citizen voice to be amplified, allowing it to be heard more easily (over the already significant voice of mobile capital) by national policymakers.

Here, too, anecdotal evidence suggests that the relationship between immigration and welfare state development is far from obvious. There is quite a bit of variation among US states (and, for that matter, European states) in the welfare options that they offer. After all, California is a huge magnet state for immigrants, yet it offers one of America's most developed welfare states. Indeed, many states today are already actively competing with one another to try and attract mobile workers both from within and beyond the United States – offering glossy PR campaigns and the promise of a bright future in their state. Clearly, and with apologies to Milton Friedman, inter-state human mobility in the United States and the European Union has not undermined the welfare state.[21]

In an international context characterized by free human mobility, states will find it increasingly difficult to pursue extremist policies. Frankly, it is difficult to imagine an apartheid state, or a Khmer Rouge, in a world that embraces free human mobility, and where the possibility of exit is real and threatening (to any rogue regime). This lesson should be drawn cautiously. There is some question as to whether or not states might act to exploit specific demographic niches. In a context of free human mobility, states might use hidden mechanisms to support self-selection and/or discourage the migration of certain subsets of labour (as can be seen in some 'exclusive' neighbourhoods today). There is also a distinct possibility that states might try to attract citizens based on specific criteria like race, sexual preference, skills levels, religion, and so on. Although this approach does not allow us to elaborate on these possibilities (or their likelihood), there is no reason to ignore them.[22]

Another (more hopeful) lesson concerns government accountability and efficiency. If citizens have an effective instrument to influence hesitant or unresponsive governors, it may be possible to jettison many of the inefficiencies associated with today's democratic regimes. A number of highly unproductive checks and balances were originally placed on governments in order to protect citizens from overzealous governors. The US Constitution is, perhaps, the best example of this. With a viable exit option, these sorts of checks and controls may not be necessary, as citizens have other means with which to respond to declining citizenship quality. In short, we might expect governance efficiency to increase in the new, more competitive, context. When states are forced to compete for mobile citizens, these sorts of institutional reforms are even more likely.

Also, the exit option offers a direct remedy for the growing citizen dissatisfaction with voice in most established democratic states, as described in Chapter 2. It would seem that many democratic states are becoming increasingly callous to voice; they are unable to respond effectively to dissatisfaction that is expressed solely by voice. One reason for this may be that society's most privileged groups have captured voice or already enjoy an effective threat of exit, alienating the larger citizenry. If this is the case, freer human mobility and the threat of exit offer a way to settle the political score.

All of these examples point to the important ways in which policymakers need to be sensitive to the potential threat of exit posed by mobile factor holders. Governments today, as they did in the interwar period, find it necessary to offer competitive tax and investment policies in order to avoid capital flight, and/or alienate potentially international investors. But governments today can discount the voice of workers and citizens because their threats are relatively impotent without the possibility of exit.

Finally, we might expect intergovernmental cooperation to improve in an environment where increased mobility continually challenges the authority of national officials. As suggested above, the demise of national sovereignty encourages the development of authority at new levels – both locally and globally. In the same way that European states are now developing intricate supranational and local bodies to investigate, develop and implement policies that affect citizens of all member states, a world of freer human migration will spark the need to develop stronger local and supranational solutions to global challenges.

Because of the inherent costs of migration, the level of labour mobility can never be expected to approach that of capital owners and investors. After all, the numbers of workers that threaten real exit are relatively small compared to their counterparts in the finance market (for example). Still, social science research suggests that we can expect competitive pressures among states, even with relatively low levels of mobility.[23] Either way, the dynamics of the arguments should be the same: the example of capital's increased voice (given the threat of exit) is illustrative of the gains we might expect for labour in a world with free labour mobility.

This handful of illustrative examples, plucked from history and around the globe, suggests that freer migration needn't threaten democracy or political voice. To the contrary, there are strong reasons to expect that increased mobility will actually strengthen democracy and the political voice of individuals – allowing them access to another channel of influence. This extension of influence is especially welcome in a context where policymakers are increasingly unresponsive to political voices that are limited to the ballot box.

This approach is admittedly simple, and based on rather crude assumptions about the relationship between citizens and states. In

6

An Economic Argument

> If we consider both the sending and the receiving countries
> as part of the same world, then – and on this every
> economist agrees – the overall effect of the migration on the
> average standard of living of the world's people is positive.
> The reason for this is that the migrant goes from a place
> where he or she is less productive to a place where he or
> she is more productive. This increased production benefits the
> standard of living of the community as a whole, as well as
> that of the migrating individual.
>
> Julian Simon[1]

This chapter describes some of the most important costs associated with an international regime that limits human mobility. In contrast to the scant literature that examines the political effects of international migration, economists have shown great and sustained interest in the issue. Indeed, it is not unreasonable to say that a majority of economists recognize that migration reaps economic gains, often very significant ones, as hinted by Julian Simon in the quotation above. These gains can be found at all levels: for immigrants themselves, for sending and receiving countries, and for the international system as a whole.

This is not to suggest that all economists agree that migration is only (or always) beneficial. There are many economic studies that show how immigration can have negative effects on the different aspects of the host country economy: on the wages of workers with specific skills levels; on the expenditures of local (as opposed to national) government; on different aspects of the welfare system, and so on. However, if the effects of migration are taken as a whole, over the long run, contemporary levels of migration seem to make good economic sense for most, if not all, receiving countries.

There may be two reasons why economists are more optimistic about the benefits of migration, relative to the public at large. The first is that economists tend to have a built-in normative preference for liberal freedoms and 'free trade'. Even advocates of restricted immigration allow that:

> The principles of free trade first enunciated by David Ricardo almost two centuries ago suggest that the world would be much richer if there were no national borders to interfere with free movement of goods and people. By prohibiting the immigration of many persons, the United States inevitably shrinks the size of the world economic pie, reducing the economic opportunities that could be available to many persons in the source countries.[2]

After all, in the study of economics, labour can be seen as just another factor of production (like land or capital), and any attempt to hinder this (or any other) factor from its most productive location is seen as inefficient or costly.

More significantly, economists have been introduced to a barrage of empirical tests in the past few decades that point to the economic benefits of immigration from across the developed world. As George Borjas, the indefatigable economist at Harvard's Kennedy School of Government, noted in a 1993 OECD report: '[T]he methodological arsenal of modern econometrics cannot find a single shred of evidence that immigrants have a major adverse impact on the earnings and job opportunities of natives of the United States.'[3]

This developing consensus among economists was probably not anticipated. In the late 1980s, voters in the developed world were increasingly concerned about what was seen then as a threatening rise in the number of immigrants. This concern provoked a plethora of diverse economic and policy analyses, in an honest attempt to evaluate the costs of this new 'wave' of immigration (with an eye towards reflecting it). The results surprised many of the authors, encouraging some to pursue 'revisionist interpretations' of the available evidence.[4]

Typical of the experience of many developed countries is the case of a small Norwegian town's reaction to increased immigration levels. In late 1999, the anti-immigrant Progress Party (Fremskrittsparti) managed to win a majority in the city council of Os, a small town just outside of Bergen. In the face of much national resistance, the new mayor, Terje Søviknes, announced that the town would begin to estimate the costs associated with refugees and immigrants in Os. The stated intent of these 'immigrant accounts' (as they were called) was to put a price on the cost of immigration, with an eye towards decreasing it. To the Progress Party's great surprise and political embarrassment, the immigrant accounts showed that the municipality was actually making money from its immigrants/refugees. Over the five previous years it appears that Os made 2.4 million kroner (around US$300,000) on its relatively small immigrant stream.[5] The political wind in Os now blows for increasing immigration – and away from local Progress Party support.

This sort of economic analysis has been undertaken in cities and states across the developed world. While this, in itself, is encouraging (as the results from Os suggest), these analyses have done little to improve our understanding of immigration issues beyond any particular community and circumstance. The reason is partly associated with the problem of competing definitions and assumptions in the existing analyses. However, the larger problem is symptomatic of the more general immigration debate: these analyses rely on a number of implicit and restrictive assumptions that compromise any attempt to generalize beyond them. In particular, as hinted at in the previous chapter, these studies assume that a number of model parameters are fixed. The most important of these include the expected volume of immigration, the relevant time horizons, and the appropriate level of analysis.

The first parameter concerns the expected consequences at varying levels of migration. Most empirical studies focus on contemporary levels of migration, and there is very little speculation about the economic benefits/costs of a free mobility regime. It is quite possible that low-volume migration brings economic benefit; while high-volume migration is costly to developed (receiving) countries. On the other hand, many sending countries may actually benefit from higher levels of emigration. For this reason, the anticipated size of the migration flows becomes a central – and highly uncertain – parameter in any attempt to evaluate the costs/benefits of free migration. The variance in these estimates can have significant consequences for any interest-based argument for (or against) free mobility.

The second important parameter is common to social-scientific studies: the problem of time horizons. Imagine a context where there is suddenly free human mobility. In the immediate aftermath of this change (whatever its impetus), it is possible that a very large number of migrants will flow out of poor countries and into rich ones. In this scenario, the short-term economic effects in host and sending countries could be detrimental, even devastating. Over time, migrants can be expected to flee from the worse conditions, and settle in more attractive places – like water in search of the lowest point. During this 'transition' phase, the economic consequences might be fairly mixed. Over the long term, however, we might expect significant economic rewards as people settle in ways that provide the most individual satisfaction, and where productivity, skills and wage levels are best matched internationally. In short, high-volume migration may have costly short-term consequences, insignificant medium-term consequences, and beneficial long-term consequences.[6]

The third parameter is also a common variable in social-scientific studies: the levels-of-analysis problem. This parameter varies with the proposed audience or beneficiaries of the (economic) gains from migration. After all, it is quite possible that migrants can expect significant personal gains, at the expense of the host country; or that the host country can expect significant economic gains, while the sending country suffers; or even that the host country experiences an economic burden, while the international community benefits. While most migration studies tend to focus on the economic effects on the host country, these effects may be different from those on the sending country, or for the international system at large.

As host countries tend to be richer, it is not difficult to understand why we find more studies that measure the impact of immigration in the developed world. For the same reason, there are fewer empirical studies on the economic effect of emigration (on sending countries) and even fewer studies on the costs and benefits from migration to the international economy. In theory, these costs/benefits could vary significantly from level to level. As a result, it is important to be aware of the varying costs and benefits at different levels of aggregation: individual and national costs and benefits are important – but so too are the aggregate effects.

Luckily, the last problem is not difficult to solve. To do so, this chapter presents the literature on economic migration in three sections: one that examines the effect on host countries, one that examines the effect on sending countries, and one that considers the aggregate (international) effects. As it is not controversial to assume that international migration will improve the living standards of those who migrate, this survey largely ignores the individual (economic) effects of migration. While the quality and quantity of data and analyses vary significantly across levels, this form of presentation allows us to look beyond myopic national studies and to consider the larger economic impact of freer migration.

In the end, there can be little certainty about the size of the economic benefits associated with free human mobility – too much depends on the particulars of these important parameters. Any specific analysis would require firm estimates of the volume of migration, a commitment to specific time horizons, and an explicit level of analysis for evaluating these costs/benefits. At this point of scholarship and history, these sorts of constraints would be fairly arbitrary and mostly meaningless.

On the other hand, we can be fairly certain that there will be significant economic gains from increased international migration – especially over the long run. This is a simple result of the fact that we can expect poor workers to migrate to places where their input will be used more productively. These gains can be expected in both sending and receiving countries, and to benefit the international community at large. The remaining pages of this chapter elaborate on this summary of the economics literature.

Before moving to this review of the literature, however, we should consider three important caveats. First, for fear of scaring away the general reader, this chapter has limited the discussion to a fairly general level. For those readers who would like to pursue the academic literature in greater detail, the accompanying notes provide some guidance. The primary objective of this chapter is to provide a broad, non-technical survey of a vast literature on the economic benefits of migration.

Second, much of the description below assumes that host countries tend to be developed countries, while sending countries tend to be developing countries. As a general rule of thumb, this is an accurate depiction of empirical circumstances. Still, it is important to keep in mind that there are developing countries that benefit significantly from international immigration (for example, those that rely on the immigration of professional and high-skilled workers) and developed countries that struggle with emigration issues (for example, Canada has its own brain-drain dilemma).

A third and final caveat concerns the significance of economic arguments. As you will discover, there are strong economic arguments for opening up international migration. In the end, these arguments are probably less important than the political and moral arguments already advanced. Sufficient economic gain, alone, will not be enough to convince the developed world to drop its border guard. Nevertheless, the economic argument for free human mobility remains important for three reasons. First, the economic literature on migration is quite developed, if not always directly relevant for our current purposes. Second, the technical nature of economic arguments tends to have a disproportionate effect on the decisions made by today's policymakers. Third, as mentioned briefly above, public perceptions tend to differ widely from those that are common among economists.

Host-country Benefits

Most of the economic work on migration has aimed to measure the economic impact of immigration flows into the developed world. Because of the United States' history as an important immigration magnet, there is a strong American component to this literature. However, parallel studies in a number of other countries tend to confirm the American results.

One of the most influential works in this field is Julian Simon's *The Economic Consequences of Immigration* (1989). Perhaps no other recent book has managed to spur economists and policymakers to reconsider the economic benefits of immigration.[7] At the time of the book's first publication, it was not uncommon to assume that US immigration rates were hovering at historic levels, and that these immigrants represented a massive draw on the national economy. Although it is possible to disagree with many of the author's political and philosophical positions, Simon's book offers an excellent and exhaustive introduction to understanding the economic consequences of immigration.

There is no easy or single measure of the economic benefits accrued to immigrant host countries. Some confusion is derived from the fact that conclusions often vary from measure to measure. The most common measures include the potential impact of migrant labour on local wages, public finances, as a replacement for an ageing workforce, and so on. These are the traditional venues of economic studies of immigrant effects, and we will turn to them first. In addition there are also more direct costs associated with maintaining the existing, closed-border regime. The end of this section will survey these (often ignored) costs.

Impact on wages

Contrary to public perceptions, most economists believe that immigration has had a significant and positive effect on American economic growth in the twentieth century. The historical record appears just as positive – the world's greatest economy was built mostly with the sweat of immigrant labour. Nevertheless, for a number of reasons, popular perception continues to hold that immigrants are a drain on the local economy. Most commonly, immigrant labour is assumed to be poor, unskilled and willing to underbid native wages.

This popular perception is misguided, on several fronts. First of all, immigrant labour, on average, may not be less skilled or workers, the wage effects on native low-skilled workers may be negative – as attested to by several recent studies. For example, the National Academy of Sciences Research Council estimated that immigration was responsible for 44 per cent of the decline in real wages experienced by high-school drop-outs between 1980 and 1994. In a similar vein (and in contrast to Simon's earlier analysis), George Borjas's *Heaven's Door* suggests that many of the USA's most recent immigrants are poorly skilled and educated, and compete directly with America's low-skilled workers.

On the other hand, there is a distinct possibility that low-skilled immigrants may not undermine the wages in those sectors where they find work. Of course, when low-skilled immigrants enter the developed world's labour market, the immediate effect on (low-skilled) wages can be negative. As a result of this initial reduction in potential wages, we can expect domestic workers to move to other sectors, or refuse to move into that (lower wage) sector. At the same time, domestic employers become more willing to move jobs into those sectors that are now characterized by lower wages. As a consequence of these diverse developments, it is possible that the local demand for labour can increase while its supply is shrinking. Under these conditions, wages in low-skilled sectors might actually rise along with low-skilled immigration!

Finally, it is possible that immigration decreases low-skilled workers' wages, but that overall wages in the developed world are not affected (or are even positively affected). After all, if low-skilled wage-earners lower the price of important consumption goods for the rest of the workforce, then real wages for the aggregate workforce will rise. It may be for this reason that the vast majority of studies on the subject find little or no impact on the *overall* wage or employment levels of native workers. For example, in the United States, a number of otherwise disparate studies have not found any harmful effects from immigration on native unemployment.[10] A recent OECD report concurs; relying on evidence from across the developed world, the report argues that immigration confers small net gains in terms of per capita output to the host country, with no obvious impact on native unemployment.[11] Though they vary in their use of datasets and methodologies, most studies find that the impact of immigrants on earning and employment opportunities of natives is usually rather small.[12] For example, a 1995 study in the *Journal of Economic Perspectives* found that a (phenomenally large) 10 per cent increase in the number of immigrants might reduce wages by (at most) 1 per cent.[13]

Nevertheless, some caution is required in employing these results for the argument at hand. Most studies concern themselves with current immigration levels – and are not directly relevant for estimating the benefits of free mobility. Few authors have addressed this possibility (or its consequences) explicitly, and when they do they become more sceptical. For example, Julian Simon explicitly shies away from endorsing an open-border policy because of the possibility of congestion and what he calls 'negative educational externalities'. The problems of congestion are fairly straightforward, and potentially serious. The second problem concerns how worker productivity is affected by surrounding skills levels. As immigrants may have skills that do not match the needs of the local labour market (e.g. handling modern computer and communications equipment), they may represent a different type of human capital with which the native workforce can cooperate. This could reduce the productivity of both native and immigrant workers over the short term (say five to ten years). However, if we balance these costs against the positive externalities produced by mixing different cultural experiences, it is not certain that the overall effects will be negative. Either way, it is regrettable that Simon dismisses a discussion of the free mobility context because it is politically implausible, 'and hence not deserving of much attention'.[14]

Indeed, a series of counterfactual studies have revealed that the developed world actually has most to gain from increased international migration. These studies will be described in more detail below, but we might note that one particular study found that today's level of international migration benefits the developed world to the tune of some US$38 billion. Better yet, this study estimates that if migration flows were allowed to increase, the developed world's gains would increase substantially: from a 1 per cent (global) increase in migration, the developed world could expect to gain US$155 billion – an increase of 10 per cent could reap US$1,537 billion![15]

Impact on public finances

The next economic issue concerns the potential effect of migration on public finances. It is common to assume that immigrants are a burden to public finances, as it is expected that they draw heavily on public services, while contributing little to public revenues. As a 1986 CBS/*New York Times* poll revealed, 47 per cent of Americans felt that *most* immigrants wind up on welfare.[16] Once again, public perceptions are challenged by the economic analyses: most economists conclude that immigrants actually make a positive contribution to public finances. Although there may be significant variations at different levels of government, when all levels of government are considered together, immigrants generate significantly more in taxes paid than they cost in services received. When we consider the demographic component of the immigrant workforce, this finding is not very surprising: most immigrants arrive in the prime of their working lives, with fewer children than native workers. Even those immigrants with children tend to draw less from the public coffers than the (demographically similar) native population.[17] For rather obvious reasons, illegal immigrants draw even less from the public coffers – while all groups, legal or not, continue to pay income and local taxes.

As with the question of wage effects, immigrants do not

make a significant negative economic impact on public finances – indeed, their overall contribution is probably positive. While these estimates might change with larger numbers, at different levels of government, and/or over various time horizons, the potential costs of free immigration appear to be small or non-existent.

Supplementing ageing workforces

Residents of the world's richest countries are getting older. Current demographic trends suggest that the populations in Europe and Japan are expected to fall around 15 per cent (in total, some 65 million people fewer) between the year 2000 and 2050.[18] In the United States, the overall population is expected to increase, but so too is its proportion of elderly people, as is the trend towards early retirement. These demographic trends represent a real threat to the developed world's living standards, and politicians on both sides of the Atlantic have begun a frantic search for ways to keep national welfare and social security plans solvent.

The overall economic impact of declining (and ageing) populations can be serious. The OECD estimates that the cumulative effects by mid-century could reduce the USA's living standards by 10 per cent, the European Union's by 18 per cent, and Japan's by 23 per cent (measured by GNP per capita, adjusted for terms of trade effects).[19] If accurate, these figures represent formidable political and economic challenges to the developed world. The most obvious solution to these changing demographic patterns is to complement the West's declining and ageing populations with younger immigrants. Indeed, America's past reliance on immigration is one important reason why the conditions there are relatively better than in Europe or Japan. There is an enormous potential supply of young immigrants who would be willing to work in the developed world, contributing to declining social security and pension plans. To the extent that immigration can replace these shrinking workforces, the national savings are potentially enormous.

Indeed, political authorities from across the OECD seem to be quite serious about raising immigration levels to help complement their ageing native populations. While political proposals of this nature are often difficult, the potential costs of not addressing the problem are massive. If it continues to restrict immigration, the developed world can expect to lose as much as a quarter of its standard of living by mid-century. This represents a formidable cost for countries that choose to continue their closed-border policies.

The direct costs of controlling borders

So far we have only examined the indirect costs of restricting immigration. Because these costs are an indirect measure of im-migrant influence, they are susceptible to a number of assumptions, many of which are difficult to establish. For example, the results of these studies often depend critically on the demographic and social make-up of the immigrant and native workforce, the size of the immigration flow, its locality, and so on. But states incur more direct costs to migration control as well – though these costs are seldom addressed. To maintain control over their borders, and to monitor immigration flows, states are burdened with a number of specific costs, both externally and internally.

External controls are perhaps the most visible, and include the need to maintain a military and/or police presence along national borders and to punish international carriers that have permitted travellers to enter without proper travel documentation. To get an idea of the amount of resources that this requires, imagine what it would cost for individual states in the USA to implement border controls. Then try to imagine the economic consequences of stopping and monitoring all interstate traffic. The line of cars waiting to enter California would probably stretch halfway up the Oregon coast! As ridiculous as it seems, this is what nation-states actually do.

In addition, governments need to pursue strong internal controls on immigration. For example, states need to monitor all employees to ensure that they are citizens or have permission to work; they must patrol the underground economy; enforce employer sanctions; issue national counterfeit-proof identity documents; expel illegal aliens; and so forth. These internal controls require a vast bureaucratic network that can interview, detain, register and monitor all legal immigrants (as well as asylum-seekers and refugees) in the form of a comprehensive national registration system.

Such activities bear significant control costs – costs that are often spread across several government ministries and levels. For that reason, it is not easy to obtain good hard figures for what it costs states to maintain their border controls. Worse, even with the money that is spent, it is generally recognized that the existing control systems are very ineffective, as hundreds of thousands, possibly millions, of illegal immigrants enter the developed world each year.

So what does it cost a state to try and keep immigrants out? The most obvious place to start is in the United States. After all, the responsibility for border control in Europe is still largely divided among European Union member states, making it difficult to track the overall costs. Also, the US example might make a good starting point, as its commitment to border control has been rather small (traditionally), especially before 9/11. This suggests that generalizations based on the American case might be conservative. Finally, great attention has recently been focused on American attempts at controlling cross-border activity, especially in the wake of the 2001 attacks on the World Trade Center and the Pentagon. What, then, does it cost for the United States to maintain its (relatively ineffective) border control system?

Throughout most of American history, the US Border Patrol (USBP) has been a fairly weak, and poorly organized, federal agency. When it was established in 1924, the USBP had only 425 officers and targeted mostly European and Asian immigrants. (At the time the United States had a guest-worker programme with Mexico, the Bracero Program, and was actually encouraging Mexican migration!) Actually, before the 1970s, the annual budget of the USBP remained smaller than many city police departments in the United States.[20]

Ironically, the neglected state of the USBP and the Immigration and Naturalization Service (INS) began to change at the very time that President Clinton was pushing hard for a North American Free Trade Agreement (NAFTA). While breaking down the barriers separating most goods and services markets in the United States and Mexico, the Clinton administration began an unprecedented effort to barricade the US labour market from Mexican immigrants. Between 1993 and 1999, the budget for the INS ballooned from $1.5 billion to $4.2 billion, making it one of the fastest growing federal agencies. To give an idea of how much money this is, $4.2 billion is equal to the amount that was allocated to the Federal Government's Commerce Department in 1998, and it is only slightly less than the total amount of money allocated for the federal government's foreign affairs in the year 2000 ($4.8 billion)![21]

Most of this expansion was focused on erecting a police barrier along the US–Mexican border. Here, the number of agents more than doubled during the mid-1990s, as several high-profile operations (such as 'Hold-the-Line', 'Gatekeeper' and 'Safeguard') increased border patrols in the most trafficked areas along the border. The increase in manpower and money allowed border guards to inspect around 500 million people a year (apprehending about 1.5 million people!) at various US ports of entry. Physical barriers were built to stop the inflow of illegal migrants: army reservists built a 10-foot-high/14-mile-long steel wall south of San Diego; in Nogales, another fence (15 foot tall and nearly 5 miles long) was erected by army engineers.

As if this was not enough, in 1996 the US government committed itself to developing an automated system to track the entry and exit of all non-citizens. The objective was to try and identify immigrants who stay longer than their visas allow – the main means of entry for illegal immigrants to the United States. This law was postponed for several years, because of concerns about the cost and difficulties associated with its implementation. Indeed, according to the *New York Times,* the Immigration and Naturalization Service explained that the technological costs alone were phenomenal and would require the authorities 'to process information estimated to be so vast that in one year it would exceed all the data in the Library of Congress'.[22]

In short, effective controls are not possible, and ineffective control systems are terribly expensive. In an attempt to gauge the cost of border monitoring and control under more 'normal' circumstances, the empirical examples in this chapter come from before 9/11. Since that time, the pressure to increase the state's presence on national borders has increased significantly across the developed world. In the US example, the overall costs of border control are actually much larger than the INS's annual budget suggests, as many of these control costs are spread out across a number of other federal, state and local agencies. When compared to the costs of monitoring international financial flows (which was jettisoned some time ago, because of their crippling size!), the physical control of a nation's border is an extremely costly endeavour.

Overall benefits to host countries

It is not possible to provide any exact or concrete figures on the benefits that the developed world might expect to generate by opening its borders. With the mark of a pen, a country such as the United States can expect immediate savings of at least US$4 billion a year by simply downsizing the enormous (and growing) police presence along its borders. Indeed, a recent IOM report estimated that the twenty-five richest countries spend US$25–30 billion a year on the enforcement of immigration laws.[23]

Even for those who believe that the costs of maintaining the current regime are manageable, these costs should be compared to those associated with maintaining parallel regimes in other sectors (e.g. capital and goods markets). The efficiency losses that were linked to maintaining national capital markets are probably similar to those associated with labour markets, and the cost of control were surely lower. Then again, twenty years ago these costs were seen to be too high for individual states to bear, and financial markets across the world were deregulated under pressure from free-floating finance.

Allowing immigrants to supplement the shrinking and ageing populations in the developed world might generate even greater national savings. Without the influx of younger immigrant labour, the developed world may find its standard of living falling rather substantially over the next fifty years. Here the economic argument for liberalizing human mobility is clear-cut and powerful.

Finally, although the indirect costs of migration are those that are most studied by economists, they are probably the least significant. Most studies find that states actually generate some economic benefit from immigration, but these gains tend to be relatively small. For example, a recent study by the National Academy of Sciences estimated that migrants made a net contribution to the US economy of US$10 billion.[24] The size of these gains should not distract us from their most important characteristic: the aggregate contribution to the country is *positive*!

Sending-country Benefits

If the developed world can expect to benefit from freer labour mobility, can we expect the developing world to suffer? This is, at any rate, the perception of many elites, in both the developed and developing worlds: there is a broad consensus that emigration from the developing world hurts poor countries. As in the developed world, the real costs to emigration from the developing world are difficult to establish, but there are many reasons to think that these costs are not as large as some would have us believe.

Unfortunately, there are few constituents willing or able to fund studies for measuring the effects of emigration on sending countries, or for the international economy as a whole. The lack of good data is another important constraint in this regard. Finally, the apparent lack of interest in the subject may be the result of a common perception that these countries will suffer a 'brain drain' if people are given an opportunity to emigrate. Although we can be certain that freer migration represents a significant improvement to the lives of millions of potential migrants, are the costs to the developing countries so large as to negate these gains?

At the most general level, we might say that the economic consequences of emigration parallel the sort of costs we have already considered in the previous chapter (about the political consequences of emigration). In the same way that the threat of exit should encourage political officials to respond to unattractive political conditions, the threat of labour emigration should encourage economic officials (e.g. employers) to reform or become obsolete. After all, why should we condemn people to live in a country that cannot utilize the potential of its own citizens?

Brain drain

When we focus on more particular costs, the calculus becomes more difficult. As already mentioned, the main cost of emigration to the developed world is usually ascribed to brain drain. Because brain drain is such a persistent concern, we shall address it again, in Chapter 8. For now it is enough to say there is a strong perception that doctors and computer scientists are streaming out of poor countries in search of lucrative careers in the developed world. It is easy to imagine how this sort of exodus might leave the developing world with few of the sort of experts needed to enrich and improve the lives of their fellow citizens. Indeed, recent history is filled with frightening examples that suggest emigration can produce significant loss of human capital (and smaller returns on educational investment) in developing countries. But, as we shall see later, there are a number of reasons to question whether these costs are as large as generally assumed.

Indeed, it is not certain that the effects of brain drain are as clear-cut as elite perceptions would have it. It is more likely that any brain-drain effects are complicated by many intervening factors – as brain drain is but one of several consequences of emigration. As the individual gains from emigration can be enormous, and as academics continue to debate whether migration increases the returns to education in the developing world, it is not unreasonable to assume that the costs of brain drain may be offset by other, more beneficial gains, generated by outward migration.

Emigration and development

In particular, emigration can influence economic development in four interrelated ways. First, international migration allows for a more efficient matching of international supplies and demand for labour. This generates enormous efficiency gains internationally, as described below in the closing section of this chapter. Second, emigration tightens the conditions that characterize sending-country labour markets (albeit often at the regional, not national, level), strengthening the bargaining position of the labour that remains. Third, migrant labour provides a large and dependable source of development capital in the form of remittances. We shall return to this issue shortly. Finally, returning migrants bring capital, skills and access to markets that benefit the sending economy. To understand these broader gains to the developing world, we might anchor this discussion in a more historical perspective.

Historical evidence

For classical economists, immigration and demographic factors played a central role in explaining economic growth. For example, the eminent Swedish economist Knut Wiksell openly advocated outward migration from Sweden in order to help the local (poor) peasantry.[25] As Harry Johnson had already suggested in 1967, the immigration policies of the developed world lie at the heart of the development problem.[26] For whatever reason, however, international migration seldom plays an influential role in contemporary discussions about development. Indeed, some of the most important textbook accounts of the European Industrial Revolution and economic development delegate little or no role to migration.[27]

Historically, however, the links between migration and development are both positive and well defined. There can be little question that the European economies benefited greatly from open migration to the New World at the turn of the previous century. Some of the fastest economic growth performances in the late nineteenth century (e.g. Ireland and Sweden) were major ports of emigration to the New World.[28]

In their impressive study of the *Age of Mass Migration*, Hatton and Williamson suggest that mass migration accounted for 208 per cent of the real wage convergence observed between the New and Old Worlds between 1870 and 1910.[29] While much of this convergence depends on corollary factors (e.g. capital accumulation forces, trade, technological catch-up, etc.), there is little doubt that most of this convergence can be explained by the mass migrations from Europe to the New World, or that emigration contributed to European economic growth and industrialization.

Several historians have shown how immigration can be used to explain the remarkable economic trajectories of both the New and the Old Worlds. For example, Brinley Thomas's impressive 1954 study documents how the early years of emigration to America were directly related to economic developments in Europe.[30] Thomas documents the way in which migrant labour from Europe made a niche in the American economy; from there it exercised a direct formative influence on the technical conditions of production and American habits of consumption. This, in turn, attracted more immigrants. For Thomas, the long-run consequences in America were clear: native-born and second-generation Americans ascended to the managerial, professional, skilled and clerical posts. This created a growing demand for common, unskilled labour – which was easily filled by the new immigrants. In this way, fresh immigrants didn't represent a threat to the American labour force, but bestowed prosperity on them. Although the scope for direct social mobility was restricted, there was still ample possibility for advancement from one generation to the next.

There is considerable evidence that emigration played a central role in the economic transformation of Europe during the late nineteenth and early twentieth centuries. International migration from the continent was then widespread, and the initiation of emigration was strongly correlated with the spread of industrialism. The now classic works of Harry Jerome, *Migration and Business Cycles*, and Dorothy Thomas, *Social and Economic Aspects of Swedish Population Movements*, suggest that European transatlantic emigration was closely connected to transatlantic business cycles.[31] In Europe, the transformation of agriculture and a growing peasant population created a surplus of relatively unskilled labour in search of livelihoods. This pressure for rural out-migration was diffused by emigration to the New World. In effect, emigration served as a buffer against the periodic upswings and downswings in the course of European economic development.

Even in postwar Europe, an abundant supply of labour was essential for maintaining its impressive growth record. Charles Kindleberger has shown how a large supply of available labour was a major factor in shaping Europe's remarkable economic growth in the 1950s.[32] Although this labour supply was not driven by immigration in all countries (e.g. it occurred naturally in the Netherlands and was transferred from the agricultural sectors in France, Germany and Italy), Kindleberger shows how it was an essential part of the economic growth recipe: countries that did not experience a substantial increase in the labour supply (the UK, Belgium and Scandinavia) grew slower; and when Europe's excess supplies of labour dried up in the early 1960s, so did its growth rate. Indeed, Kindleberger confirms the historical pattern from a century earlier by showing how the developing economies of the Mediterranean rim also grew when their excess labour emigrated northward.

In short, the historical evidence seems to suggest that migration is an important explanatory factor for economic growth in both the New and the Old Worlds. In allowing excess labour to leave areas where it is not prized (and to flow to economies where it is) international migration can generate prosperity in both sending and receiving countries. The skills, capital and technology that accompany these labour flows also have a significant impact on economic growth rates in both types of country.[33] In today's context, the most important of these may be the role that worker remittances play in the economies of the developing world.

Remittances

When today's migrants come to the developed world in search of economic riches, much of this new wealth is sent back home in the form of remittances to families and friends.[34] Although it is difficult to get a picture of what proportion of wages are sent home, it has been estimated that migrants, on average, send home about a $1,000 a year.[35] This is not an insignificant amount of money for an average family in the developing world, and can be seen as a direct economic benefit of emigration. When this money is spent in the sending country it can function as a domestic demand stimulus (with multiplier effects) in the local economy.

This may seem like small change, but the aggregate effects of remittances can be substantial. Even in today's world of regulated migration, remittances from migrants have enormous economic significance, and governments in the developing world often encourage migration as a way to attract much-needed foreign exchange. Not only is this important source of foreign exchange very large, it is relatively stable and mostly unaffected by the whims of political favour. It is for this reason that many of the poorest countries rely on migration as a means of maintaining economic solvency, and as a primary source of hope for the future. It is perhaps for this reason that the (then) Bangladeshi prime minister, Sheikh Hasina, held that the solution to her country's problems of poverty lay in migration:

> We'll send them to America.… Globalization will take
> that problem away, as you free up all factors of production,
> also labour. There'll be free movement, country to country.
> Globalization in its purest form should not have any boundaries,
> so small countries with big populations should be able to send
> population to countries with big boundaries and small popu-
> lations. Already, we have nearly two million working abroad.[36]

Migrant remittances aggregate to a substantial source of income for states in the developing world. For example, in 2003 world remittances totalled US$80 billion, up from $17.7 billion in 1980 and $30.6 billion in 1990! Although the real number is probably much higher – as this figure draws only from formal remittance channels – these remittance figures were double the amount of foreign aid, and ten times higher than net private capital transfers in 2001.[37] In some countries, such as Albania, the size of remittances dwarfs export revenues (153.5 per cent); but even in more developed countries such as India, Morocco and Greece remittances represent about 20 per cent of export revenues.[38]

In another example, a recent World Bank report, *Global Development Finance 2003*, noted that home remittances are a hugely important source of development capital and foreign reserves across South Asia: in Sri Lanka, remittances account for over 10 per cent of GDP; in Nepal, it would be appear, the economy would be in dire straits but for remittances; India was the world's second-largest recipient of remittances worldwide (in 2001, Indian workers abroad sent home a remarkable US$10 billion); in Pakistan, remittances tripled between 2001 and 2003; and in Bangladesh, remittance flows increased by nearly 50 per cent during the same time period.

Indeed, many countries actually encourage international labour migration: Turkey, the Philippines, South Korea, India, Pakistan, Bangladesh, Sri Lanka, Jamaica, Cuba, Barbados, Mexico, El Salvador and Nicaragua are all countries that are known to support emigration, either implicitly or explicitly. In a world with shrinking international aid budgets, and growing income differentials, remittances represent an important and dependable short-term economic lifeline for many families in the developing world.

In fact, a 1992 *Human Development Report* conducted an analysis of the cost to the developing world of immigration restrictions. The report began with an estimate of the number of workers who might emigrate given the chance (about 2 per cent of the developing world's labour force); then the report assumed that these workers would only earn a poverty-line salary in the developed world (some $5,000 a year or about $220 billion a year in total). Finally, the report assumed that between $40 to $50 billion would be sent home in the form of remittances each year. After calculating the multiplier effect of these remittances on the domestic economy, the UNDP estimated that 'immigration controls deny developing countries income (direct and indirect) of at least $250 billion a year'.[39]

Effect on wages

At the same time, emigration can have a significant effect on the wages of those workers who remain behind in the sending countries. With fewer workers remaining (after emigration), their relative bargaining power (vis-à-vis employers) increases – empowering them to demand higher wages. Computer-generated counterfactual studies of the economic impact of increased international immigration suggest that wages in the developing world could increase substantially, even at relatively low levels of immigration. For example, one study found that a 10 per cent increase in international migration might lead to an 11 per cent increase in the wage rates of non-migrating labour in the world's poorest countries.[40]

Overall benefits to sending countries

To summarize, the effects of migration on development are not well understood. In the short run, it seems fair to note that the economic costs of emigration can be important (though these costs are disputed). Not only do sending countries lose important skills, but they lose another person capable of paying taxes to help support the country.

At the same time, however, there are many positive externalities associated with emigration, and these probably outweigh the more negative (and disputed) effects associated with the brain drain. We can close this section by mentioning three of them. To the extent that international migration drains the rural labour surplus in the developing world, it can contribute to a convergence of wages between traditional and modern sectors of the economy (and, of course, between sending and receiving countries). The resulting rise in rural wages will force farmers and rural employers to pay a better wage (which, in turn, encourages multiplier effects) and/or adapt new (more productive) technologies. Second, these new conditions strengthen the relative bargaining power of labour vis-à-vis capital. This new bargaining power is partly the result of labour's increased (relative) scarcity, and partly a result of its threat to exit. Finally, emigrants introduce new capital and skills to the domestic (sending) economy. As we have already seen, international emigrants send a significant proportion of their wages home in the form of remittances – providing a new source of capital for small farmers and entrepreneurs in the home country. In addition, returning émigrés bring home skills and norms (along with their savings) that can rejuvenate the sending economy.

International Benefits

It should be fairly obvious by this point that the international effects from free migration must be positive. If both sending countries and receiving countries (not to mention the individual migrants and migrant families themselves) appear to benefit from increased freedom of movement, then the world as a whole must surely benefit. In addition, there are significant economic and social gains to be reaped from legalizing and regulating today's ugly human-smuggling industry. Despite these anticipated international savings, there are relatively few firm estimates of the worldwide economic benefits of free migration.

We can begin this discussion by returning to Hatton and Williamson's important book on the *Age of Mass Migration*. This book illustrates the important role that international migration played – at an earlier time – in levelling international income and wage differentials. Perhaps the lack of international migration may explain why income differences today between the world's richest and poorest countries (and within each) are on the rise.

Indeed, the overall economic gains from free migration may be so great that the world can no longer afford to ignore them. Such gains were found in a study conducted at the Indira Gandhi Institute of Development Research in India. This study estimated that by the year 2000, immigration restrictions would have resulted in a $1,000 billion loss in global economic growth![41] If true, this represents a phenomenal economic cost to the international system, and yet there have been relatively few attempts to try and elaborate on the potential gains of liberalizing migration regimes.

One way to come to grips with these potential gains is to employ computer-generated equilibrium models of counterfactual conditions. Without getting into the messy details behind these approaches, we can say that political economists have developed rather simple models of how the world economy works. These models can be used to predict the potential effects of an increase in different types of economic activity, including an increase in migration.[42] One of the most recent attempts at this sort of modelling calculates phenomenally large efficiency gains generated by a world with free international migration.[43] In the most reasonable (but unadjusted) scenario in this model, the world can expect an efficiency gain from the removal of immigration controls in the order of US$34.08 trillion! To provide some comparative context of the size of these gains, you need only know that the world's official funding for development totalled just US$65.5 *billion* in the year 2000. The potential impact from the private sector is also minuscule in comparison, as total foreign direct investment (FDI) to the developing world in the year 2000 was only US$ 1.9 trillion! When these figures are adjusted to compensate for workforce and efficiency differences, the estimated gains remain substantial – the lowest estimate being US$1.97 trillion. Indeed, even at lower levels of international migration, the gains remained substantial (actually, the marginal efficiency gains are larger for the first waves of migrants). In particular, the study estimated that a 10 per cent increase in international migration corresponded to an efficiency gain of about US$774 billion. In short, the international community can expect to reap incredibly large gains by simply allowing people the freedom to move.

Given the implicit parameters of these sorts of approaches, it is perhaps not surprising to find that freer mobility can generate worldwide efficiency gains and some improvement in the distribution of world incomes among nation-states. What *is* surprising, however, is the expected size of the gains generated by these models. These remarkable findings have been substantiated by several independent studies, and generally correspond with the historical evidence, as surveyed above.[44] In short, these findings do not appear to be spurious.

While it is important to recognize the limitations of these sorts of counterfactual analyses (and the underlying data and parameters/assumptions on which they rest), the findings remain important. The estimated efficiency gains of free migration dwarf any sort of gains that we can expect from other – more traditional – policy proposals (e.g. commodity price stabilization, debt cancellation, trade liberalization, foreign aid, etc.). Indeed, no other policy proposal being discussed today can deliver anything remotely similar to the scale of these projected gains. Clearly, free migration has the best chance of addressing the problems of world poverty.

Conclusion

In a recent *World Development Report*, the World Bank recognized that 'Well-functioning markets create opportunities for poor people to escape poverty.'[45] To this sentiment it might be added that the most effective solution to global economic and political inequality is escape, yet there is no free 'market' to accommodate these pent-up demands. The most liberating market of all remains off-limits to most of the world's residents, reserved for a small elite of economic and political professionals. In today's world, CEOs and high-skilled workers (such as professors and footballers) find it both possible and profitable to migrate; the world's most desperate people do not.

This chapter has aimed to paint a simple picture of what sort of economic sacrifice the international community is making by promoting a regime that effectively makes people prisoners of territory. The costs of this injustice are surely highest for the world's poorest inhabitants, who – by poor luck or fate – are born into poverty, with little avenue of economic recourse.

In the final analysis, economic arguments (in themselves) are probably not sufficient to encourage individuals or states to open their borders. On the one hand, the results of these arguments often depend on so many conflicting assumptions and model parameters that it is difficult to generate any confidence in them. On the other hand, the great fault of economic models is that they often presuppose that economic calculations dominate the rational individual's optimization basket. In practice, we can expect individuals to react to migration policy at a variety of levels – rational and irrational, economic and not. In addition, as argued in the previous chapter, citizens may reap significant political gains from freer human mobility. It is conceivable that individuals in the developed world would be willing to exchange these political gains for what little economic cost, or benefit, they might expect from increased international migration.

Even when the economic benefits are truly significant, they do not appear to be distributed in a way that will generate support among the population and the policymakers of wealthy and influential countries. To convince sceptics in these countries, we need to remind them of the historical uniqueness of our current international condition, as well as the moral and political costs associated with maintaining these restrictions. Last, but not least, we need to engage popular perceptions, public opinion and conventional wisdom about the costs, difficulty and danger of increased international migration. It is to these important perceptual realms that we now turn our attention.

7

Who Opposes Free Migration?

> The simple truth is that we've lost control of our borders;
> no nation can do that and survive.
>
> Ronald Reagan[1]

The proposal to liberalize international barriers to human mobility
is a radical one – it challenges both general conventions and
specific interests. It is evident that people are concerned about
the threats posed by migration, but much of this concern seems
to be provoked by unfounded scenarios that exploit public fear
and uncertainty. In this charged political context it is difficult
to distinguish between perceptions and interests, and a country's
immigration policies can be driven more by xenophobia than
by reason. Indeed, the anxiety surrounding migration is often
greater than the circle of people whose interests are directly
affected by it.

While much of the public anxiety with respect to migration
can be dampened with education, argument and dialogue, it is
important to recognize that real interests are indeed exposed to
the effects of migration. Like international trade, investment and
information flows, international migration challenges the status

quo, providing threats and opportunities unequally distributed within countries and around the globe.

On the path to free mobility stand a number of substantial obstacles. This chapter examines two of them. The first obstacle is perhaps the most daunting: public opinion in the developed world. People in the developed world are afraid of immigrants: they fear that immigration challenges their wealth, security and sense of community, and they have been willing to exert the political and military force needed to keep immigrants at bay.

The second barrier to free mobility results from public perceptions about the role and nature of the nation-state. Denizens of both the developed and the developing worlds cling to an anachronistic conception of sovereignty – one that implies a level of autonomy, isolation and self-sufficiency that no longer exists. In addition, these national containers of sovereignty collect political preferences in a way that provides little incentive to consider the opinions or interests of people that happen to find themselves on the wrong side of the container walls. As long as the nation-state continues to be perceived as a paramount, legitimate and useful vessel for aggregating political preferences, the struggle for free mobility will be an uphill one.

Finally, a third obstacle to freer mobility is the conventional wisdom that rules in both developing and developed worlds alike. In its many sundry forms, today's conventional wisdom is dead set on opposing free migration. People simply assume that an open migration regime will unleash a flood of poor migrants, swamping and overturning local cultural, political and security arrangements. While most of this book is directed at challenging this conventional wisdom, the following chapter addresses some of its most pernicious forms head-on.

For now, however, we will concentrate our attention on the first two, more perceptual, barriers to free migration. While these two barriers are intimidating, they are not insurmountable: with time they can become more like hurdles and less like roadblocks. Indeed, we shall discover that public opinion about immigration is much more pliable and nuanced than would first appear to be the case, and this opinion is remarkably detached from respondent interests. The dominance of the nation-state, the anachronistic notion of its sacrosanct boundaries, and simplistic conceptions of national interest are all being challenged by global developments that include migration (especially illegal immigration) as well as other types of international exchange. In short, both of these hurdles can be overcome with a more open and honest discussion about the role of states and the interests of individuals in an increasingly global context.

Suggesting that public opinion and traditional conceptions of the nation-state are important deterrents to any attempt at liberalizing border controls does not imply that real interests aren't threatened by increased migration, in both the developed and the developing worlds. It is important that these interests are not ignored; but it is equally important that the size or influence of these disparate interests is not exaggerated. After all, the impact of migration is not fundamentally different from the sort of impact we have already come to accept in return for freer trade and investment flows. For this reason, the later part of this chapter will examine which particular interests are most likely to be affected by freer human mobility.

Public Opinion

The biggest single deterrent to free international migration is the perceptions and attitudes of citizens in the developed world. The world's richest countries have shown a willingness to employ force along national borders to protect what they have from those who don't have it. Like a wealthy gated community, the developed world hopes to isolate itself from the injustice, poverty and misery that surround it.

In democratic states, public policy should reflect public opinion, and public opinion in the developed world is clearly opposed to immigration. For example, the 1995 National Identity module of the International Social Survey Programme (ISSP–NI)[2] revealed that only a very small percentage of respondents wanted their national immigration polices to be expanded (whether it was 'a little', 'a lot', or both combined). The most immigrant-friendly country in the sample was Canada, where almost 20 per cent of the respondents felt that immigration should be increased (yet only 5.9 per cent thought that immigration should be increased a lot – the highest national response in the sample). For most European countries, however, support for greater immigration was much lower (between 2.8 per cent of the respondents in West Germany to 8.4 per cent in Spain). Ireland was the only exception to this rule, with a positive response rate of 19.1 per cent – but Ireland (in contrast to the other European countries in the sample) is an outlier in the sense that it can be characterized as a 'sending', not a 'receiving', country. In the United States, only 8 per cent of the respondents favoured an increase in immigration rates – a response that was fairly indicative of the whole sample of twenty-three countries.[3]

Instead, there were very substantial majorities in support of more restrictive immigration polices. Some 54 per cent of all respondents thought that immigration rates should be reduced. As evidenced in Figure 7.1, the strongest support for reducing immigration levels was found in the Philippines, Eastern Europe and New Zealand (all about 59 per cent). In the United States and Western Europe, the responses were similar to the sample mean (54.9 and 55 per cent respectively). Indeed, each of the West European countries scored above 55 per cent, except Ireland (already noted) and Spain, where only 40 per cent of the respondents

Figure 7.1 Public opinion on levels of immigration

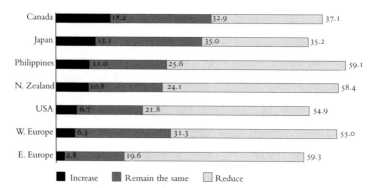

Note: Respondents were asked: 'Do you think the number of immigrants to [your country] nowadays should be...reduced a lot (1), reduced a little (2), remain the same as it is (3), increased a little (4), increased a lot (5).' On this graph 'Increase' represents the combined response scores for 'increased a little' and 'increased a lot'. Similarly, the 'Reduce' indicator combines 'reduced a little' and 'reduced a lot' responses. The graph shows those who expressed an opinion as a percentage. The difference (totalling to 100) are the respondents who couldn't or didn't choose between the different response categories. 'W. Europe' includes West Germany, Great Britain, Austria, Italy, Ireland, the Netherlands, Norway, Sweden and Spain. 'E. Europe' includes East Germany, Hungary, the Czech Republic, Slovenia, Poland, Bulgaria, Russia, Latvia and the Slovak Republic.

Source: Anna Maria Mayda, 'Who is Against Immigration? A Cross-country Investigation of Individual Attitudes toward Immigrants', IZA Discussion Paper No. 1115 (April 2004): Data Appendix 1A.

thought that immigration needed to be reduced. The nationalities in the sample that were most likely to express opinions about reducing immigration 'a lot' were Hungarians (56 per cent), East Germans (52 per cent) and Latvians (50 per cent).[4]

While these numbers suggest that there was significant opposition to immigration in 1995, the situation has probably worsened since then. In the absence of any good comparative indicators over time, we might suspect that public opposition to immigration has risen substantially in the aftermath of the terrorist attacks on 11 September 2001. Public debates and voting behaviour suggest that residents of the developed world are increasingly concerned about lax border controls and the threat of terrorists sneaking surreptitiously across unprotected national borders.

While public opinion about immigration is daunting, it is not monolithic. There is substantial and consistent variation across different political, social and demographic categories in support of immigration. For example, one of the strongest predictors of an individual's attitude towards immigration is his/her level of education and relationship to the labour market. Thus, highly educated people in the richest parts of the world tend to have more favorable impressions of immigrants, and about immigration.[5]

These patterns correspond to other individual features with respect to immigration attitudes. Older people in the developed world tend to favour immigration restrictions, as do individuals living in rural areas and smaller towns. Respondent attitudes regarding the impact of immigration on crime rates and the cultural effect of foreigners are also correlated with immigration attitudes. Not surprisingly, individuals who prefer multiculturalism are more likely to embrace immigration than those who prefer a more homogenous society (in terms of customs and traditions), while patriotic, nationalist and racist respondents are less likely to favour immigration. Finally, gender, individual (real) income, social class and trade-union membership do not appear to have a significant impact on immigration attitudes across states.[6]

In a more recent poll, conducted by Ipsos–Public Affairs and Associated Press in early May of 2004,[7] people were specifically asked about the influence of immigrants on the host country ('What influence do you think that immigrants have on the way things are going in your country?'). Responses to this question suggest that public attitudes about immigration are more subtle than the 'more or less immigration' surveys might lead us to believe: not a single country had a majority of respondents who felt immigrants were a very bad influence.

Figure 7.2   Immigrant influence

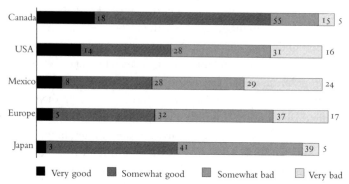

Note: Respondents were asked: 'Overall, would you say immigrants are having a good or bad influence on the way things are going in [your country]? Would you say very (good/bad) or somewhat (good/bad)?' 'Europe' includes the UK, Spain, Italy, Germany and France. The graph shows those who expressed an opinion as a percentage. The difference (totalling to 100) are the respondents who were 'not sure'.

Source: IPSOS–Public Affairs and Associated Press 2004.

In this poll, once again, the most favourable impressions about immigrants were found in Canada, where 73 per cent of the respondents found the influence of immigrants to be good or somewhat good (while only 20 per cent felt that immigrant influence was bad or somewhat bad). It would seem that Canadians have a remarkably positive impression of immigrants. In contrast, the Mexican respondents were the most critical: 36 per cent of them found the immigrant influence to be a positive one, while 53 per cent found it to be negative. In Japan, positive and negative impressions were equally balanced (44 per cent each), while the European sample (which included France, Germany, Italy, Spain and the UK) was the least favourable with respect to attitudes about immigrant influence. In Europe as a whole, 37 per cent of the respondents had a positive impression (combined good and somewhat good responses), while 54 per cent were negative. Finally, in the United States, 42 per cent of the respondents believed that immigrant influence was good or somewhat good, while 47 per cent thought the influence was bad or somewhat bad.

More revealing, perhaps, are respondent attitudes about whether immigrants took jobs that were desirable to, or held by, domestic workers (or whether they competed for the same jobs). Some 66 per cent of the respondents in the USA (and Canada) said that immigrants took unwanted jobs, while only 27 (and 18) per cent responded that immigrants took jobs away from host-country citizens. In Europe and Japan, the threat of immigrants stealing jobs was perceived to be even smaller: in Japan, as many as 75 per cent of the respondents said that immigrants took unwanted jobs; in Europe, the corresponding share was 74 per cent.

This glimpse of the polling data suggests that public attitudes are surprisingly open and nuanced. While opinions seem to be split over whether immigrants do more harm than good (broadly defined) to the host nation, there is substantial variation across states. Indeed, Canada's experience with immigration seems positively inspiring. More significantly, majorities in each country recognize that immigrants are not competing with domestic workers for jobs. These respondents seem to realize that immigrants are taking jobs that are not attractive to their fellow citizens – implying that the countries in question enjoy a net economic gain from migration. In short, public opinion is not as monolithic or as critical of immigration as we often assume.

The Undying State

The second obstacle to free mobility is less obvious and more deep-seated. This barrier rests on people's perceptions about the role and nature of the modern nation-state. As evidenced by the quotation from Ronald Reagan at the start of this chapter, there seems to be widespread consensus that the national interest, even the survival of the nation itself, depends upon control of the territory's borders. Reagan's ideological bedfellow, Margaret Thatcher, also noted Britain's fear of being 'swamped by people of a different culture', and the need to 'hold out the clear prospect of an end to immigration'.[8] While both of these giants of modern conservativism slashed away at government regulations and controls in the name of smaller (and presumably more efficient) states, they remained adamant defenders of the rights of states to use force to repel strangers.

The perception that national sovereignty is paramount (and associated with territorial boundaries that are firm, hermetic and exclusionary) is a historical creation – and a faulty one at that. Nevertheless, this perception remains as a second major obstacle on the path to freer human mobility. People continue to believe that national borders are sacrosanct, and that 'no geographic area can legitimately claim nationhood if it cannot control its borders and who may enter its territory'.[9]

Of course, the right to exclude was traditionally considered an essential, even defining, aspect of national sovereignty. This right was granted to the exclusion of goods, capital, services, foreign armies, even workers. There have been other defining aspects of sovereignty as well: the right to coin money, a monopoly on the use of force, national representation abroad, and so on. Over time, these traditional symbols and instruments of sovereignty have been eroded by international exchange: foreign goods, capital, services and production techniques are allowed – even encouraged – to penetrate national borders and to puncture static conceptions of national identity (as well as the regulatory regimes that had been constructed for their defence). In short, much of the damage to these traditional conceptions of sovereignty and national interest has already been done in the name of free trade and investment. Limiting international migration flows will not protect national icons in a world where business, capital, goods and services are already footloose and fancy-free.

Although borders and border guards are often the first visible consequence of successful national liberation movements, they are not necessary for the maintenance of political sovereignty. Denmark remains a sovereign country, yet it is possible to enter her sovereign realm from neighbouring states without confronting a border patrol. In the past, nation-based states have relied on exclusion and force as a means to contrive political communities. But in the wake of the twentieth century – that bloody century of nationalist struggles – we might question whether this practice is worth repeating. Thankfully, there are few states willing to follow Pyongyang's lead on this front.

Contemporary sovereignty is much more fluid than these traditional conceptions would allow. After all, nobody questions the sovereignty of European states, though many of them have jettisoned their right to exclude foreign nationals or to coin their own money. In a similar vein, we still recognize Canada as a sovereign country, despite her sharing a remarkably long and porous border with the world's only superpower (and economic powerhouse). Actually, recognition of the porous and amorphous nature of modern sovereignty is everywhere recognized and accepted, except in the realm of immigration policy. When it comes to international migrants, states and citizens still cling to the sovereign power of exclusion.

Worse, we embrace this outdated conception of sovereignty without reflecting on how today's regulatory regimes are themselves remnants of a time when a state's immigration policies were racist and explicitly eugenic. While we no longer subscribe to the beliefs that human qualities are determined by race, that some ethnic groups are superior to others, and/or that immigration controls can (and should) be used to protect a nation's racial or ethnic superiority, we embrace immigration policies that resulted from this type of racist mindset.

Finally, the international system that results from nation-based conceptions of sovereignty provides its own deterrent to any attempt at liberalizing human mobility. In today's international system it is difficult to imagine a context in which any one state would agree to liberalize immigration flows unilaterally. Any leading state can risk becoming a target of international immigration, if it – alone – opens its borders to the world's tired, poor and huddled masses, yearning to breathe free. The chances of immigrant flooding are much smaller if several countries adopt more liberal immigration policies concomitantly.

Unfortunately, today's international system lacks the institutional framework to facilitate this sort of cooperation and policy co-ordination. As we have already seen, international labour mobility lacks the sort of international institutional support that guarantees and advocates an international mobility of finance and payments (the International Monetary Fund) or the international flow of goods and services (the General Agreement on Tariffs and Trade, subsequently the World Trade Organization). Nation-states have shown little interest in monitoring the transnational flow of people, as compared to goods and money. As an illustration of the lack of interest in the subject, the United States has not bothered to collect emigration data since 1957.

Nevertheless, hope may be found in the sort of multilateral agreements that have been traditionally used to expand the realm of free trade. For example, it is not impossible to imagine a Most Favoured Nation clause applied to migration. Indeed, even the absence of a dedicated international body for managing inter-national migration can be overcome by piggy-backing on existing, if tangential, international frameworks. Recent discussions about Mode-4 trade in the World Trade Organization are encouraging in this respect, if somewhat myopic in practice.[10]

In short, the international system of nation-based states is not constructed in a way that will facilitate free migration, but there are no inherent obstacles that can't be overcome with sufficient will and ingenuity. Common perceptions of sovereignty based on exclusion and territorial control are hopelessly outdated and applied inconsistently to labour, goods and capital markets. These anachronistic perceptions lend themselves to ridiculously simple notions of national interest, as examined below.

National interest

It is with historical amnesia and contemporary blindness that we form our opinions about sovereignty and national interest and the effect on them of international migration. In this context, it is hypocritical and ludicrous to place the burden of defending an anachronistic notion of sovereignty on the backs of working men and women. Despite many warnings to the contrary, some of them by respected academics and policymakers, the legitimacy of today's nations does not depend on a state's ability to control its borders. Indeed, if this were the case, there would be few legitimate nations left standing, as the level of illegal immigration (not to mention trade, investment, cultural flows, etc.) has risen precipitously. Simply put: states cannot cordon off their territories from foreign influences. It has always been an exaggeration to suggest this was the case, but to argue it today is the height of nonsense.

Once we recognize the fluid nature of modern sovereignty, it is more difficult to embrace the concept of a unique national interest. Indeed, calculations of the national interest have always been complicated by the fact that each nation's interest is a series of aggregations that don't always add up. Despite this, many conventional arguments, reviewed in the next chapter, assume some sort of national interest with respect to the effect of immigration on culture, security, economic integrity, and so forth.

In the most extreme cases it may make sense to talk about a national interest. For example, in a country such as Bangladesh

– which suffers from tragic overpopulation – there can be little question that the country as a whole benefits from emigration. There are simply too many people, and too few resources, to sustain so many lives. Alternatively, it is possible to imagine a small rich country that must rely on immigration to satisfy its insatiable demand for labour. Thus, at the extremes of national experiences, it is possible to talk about clear national interests.

Yet for the vast majority of countries it is difficult to argue that a nation's interest is served (or not) by closed-border policies. When trying to consider a nation's interest with regard to international migration, we need to balance a phenomenally complex constellation of interests. Among the interests being tallied are an aggregation of individual winners and losers and an aggregation of different types of interests (e.g. moral, political, economic, etc.). These individual interests, spread across different dimensions, intersect in a plethora of ways that make it difficult, if not impossible, to speak of a single national interest. Different analyses will emphasize different aggregations and different priorities for aggregation.

Consider what would appear to be a straightforward example. As described in the previous chapter, recent academic research has begun to estimate the economic gains that the world can expect to reap by embracing greater human mobility.[11] In these economic analyses, very simple models are employed on existing conditions to estimate the economic gains from current levels of international migration. On the basis of such studies, we know that the developed world could be US$32 billion poorer should it close its doors to all immigration. In another scenario, it was estimated that the developed world can expect an enormous economic windfall (to the tune of US$1,537 billion) should it allow a relatively small (10 per cent) increase in international immigration. Of course, these studies could be conducted at the national level to get a firm (empirical) measure of national interest.

Either way, in either scenario, we find that the developed world can reap significant economic gains by *doing the right thing*!

While these sorts of estimates provide strong support for liberalizing national border controls on human mobility, it is important to note that they are generated by models that rest on a number of rather shaky assumptions. They are, in effect, the academic equivalents of elaborate castles made of sand. Other academics, less sympathetic to the plight of the international migrant, could generate other estimates, based on different assumptions. Realizing this makes it difficult to argue categorically about a region's (or a nation's) economic interest – whether in the developed world or in the developing world. To complicate matters all the more, we might recognize that there are no good reasons to prioritize economic interests over moral, cultural or political interests (for example). Individual interests – economic, political, social or moral – will always aggregate in complicated ways.

Diffuse and Particular Interests

Thus far we have seen how public opinion in the developed world is mostly opposed to increased immigration. Against this observation it has been suggested that opinions deviate significantly from aggregated individual interests, making it difficult to generalize about national interests on such a complex, multifaceted issue. It is time now to examine these sundry and particular interests more carefully, in both the developing and the developed worlds. What we will find, especially in the developed world, is a remarkable mismatch between particular interests and general perceptions.

Developed world interests

We can start with the developed world. Economists, in particular, tend to frame the discussion in the form of winners and losers (within the state). Thus, as George Borjas repeatedly points out in his recent book:

> This perspective on the economic consequences of immigration clarifies what is at the core of the immigration debate. The debate is not over whether the country as a whole is better off – the net gains seem to be much too small to justify such a grand social experiment. The debate is really over the fact that some people gain substantially, while others lose. In short, the immigration debate is a tug-of-war between the winners and losers.[12]

This sort of calculation begins by drawing up a list of classes, sectors and/or communities that benefit (either directly or indirectly) from closed borders. Calculated in this way, control regimes might be legitimized if they are shown to benefit a majority of interests within a given (host) state. The most common argument takes the following form: by assuming that immigrants complement capital, easily substitute for unskilled native workers, and are less substitutable for skilled workers,[13] we can expect businessmen to favour immigration, trade unions (especially industrial trade unions) to oppose immigration, and professional and skilled labour to be largely unaffected by (and thus uninterested in) immigration. In short, employers can be seen to gain from cheap access to unorganized labour; domestic workers can be seen to have their wages undercut by desperate immigrants.[14]

From this simple calculation of interest, you might infer that contemporary barriers to international migration reflect the political power of labour in developed states. Although this is a very common argument, it is problematic in at least two ways. First, it ascribes to labour a degree of political power and consciousness that is seldom evidenced in other policy spheres. If labour has been able effectively to protect its interests with respect to immigration, why has it proved so ineffective in blocking the detrimental effects from the globalization of other factors (e.g.

trade and capital market liberalization)? Why hasn't this politically potent labour movement managed to secure broader political victories (e.g. shortening the working week, extending vacation time, raising the minimum wage, etc.)? There is something here that just doesn't add up, as labour's interests are not being met consistently across policy areas. If nothing else, greater attention needs to be drawn to this question.

The second problem with this argument is that it does not mesh with the sort of variation we see in migration control regimes, across states. If this argument were correct, we should expect to find stronger control regimes in states that host strong labour movements (or 'left government strength'), and weaker control regimes where the political strength of capital is seen to dominate. But the relationship, if any, is quite frail: there is only a weak negative relationship between left party strength and the size of a country's foreign-born population.[15] In other words, states that have relatively weak labour movements (e.g. Japan, France, the USA and Canada) can vary significantly in the type of migration control systems they employ.

Perhaps this aggregation of interests (capital versus labour) is too narrow. After all, it is possible to imagine a much larger coalition of beneficiaries from international migration. Obviously, employers benefit from access to cheaper and deeper pools of labour, which they can easily tap and pipe into their profit shares. (Presumably, this is one reason that the editorial pages of the *Wall Street Journal* openly advocate free mobility.) In addition, however, central bankers can be seen to benefit by being spared the necessity of making difficult decisions; they would rather see the workforce expand with immigrant labour than be forced to make frequent and unpopular decisions to raise interest rates, with an eye to stifling growth and the threat of inflation. Alan Greenspan, the long-time chairman of the US Federal Reserve, has made this argument explicitly on several occasions.

The largest, yet most diffuse, group of potential winners from free migration may be consumers and residents in the developed world. If low-wage immigrants are allowed to produce local goods at lower wages, and if we assume that there is real competition in the local economy, then these lower wages should translate into lower prices for consumers (and higher real wages for the general workforce). Consumers in the developed world should benefit significantly from increased immigration from the developed world. These consumers should be familiar with this argument, as it has been used with great success to undermine national barriers to trade and investment.

Consumers, as residents and neighbours, might also benefit from the new incentives for firms to stay in the local community, rather than relocate abroad in the face of global competition. In today's globally competitive production climate, many firms from the developed world choose to relocate in low-wage regions. Low-wage immigrant labour could be used to deter a firm's decision to move abroad. If these jobs remain in the community, even if they are filled by immigrant labour, the community can expect significant multiplier effects from the fact that these (lower) wages will be spent in the local economy (on food, shelter, clothing, local sales taxes, etc.), rather than evaporating abroad.

In short, the greatest beneficiaries from international migration are widespread and include some of the most powerful interest groups in modern capitalist democracies: employers, central bankers and consumers. In opposition to these powerful interests stands a diffuse and varied group whose interests will be threatened by increased immigration. Although these groups tend to benefit from the existing control regime, they are a remarkably diffuse and otherwise ineffective alliance of interests.

As suggested above, the most common perception is that immigrants to the developed world compete with low-paid, unskilled workers. These workers are not usually known for the effectiveness of their lobbying campaigns, or for their influence on national policymakers. As these groups tend to be poorly organized, union support for them is often erratic, and varies from country to country.

Allied with these workers may be the clients of national welfare states.[16] These clients worry that their welfare states might be undermined by immigrants in at least two ways. First, there is a concern that new immigrant values might not correspond to those of the domestic population, and this – over time – might lead to a different type of welfare state. For example, it is conceivable that immigrant populations might prefer family-based assistance programmes rather than the government-supplied and more universalistic policies implemented in many of today's developed states. Second, welfare-state beneficiaries worry that a flood of immigrants will drain the pool of resources available to them. While both of these threats are real, their source is not limited to immigrants. International capital and trade flows, as well as a widening net of international obligations, are imposing significant constraints on the size and nature of national welfare states. Still, residents of the developed world find it easier to blame foreign immigrants than faceless foreign firms and/or international organizations.

Finally, people worry that their (national) cultural identity is threatened by immigrants – an issue addressed in greater detail in the following chapter. These concerns have only sharpened after policymakers in many parts of the developed world have come to embrace the 'Clash of Civilizations' perspective on world affairs. For example, women in Northern Europe – who have struggled to secure important rights and protections in their own national contexts – worry that these rights might be trampled by immigrants from more traditional or gender-conservative cultures. Similarly, residents of countries that enjoy religious freedom fear an inflow of immigrants who are less tolerant of religious pluralism.

These sorts of concerns are easy to detect in the opinion data, as well as in national debates over immigration.

These interests don't add up

When we line up and compare the particular (developed world) interests that we might expect to benefit or lose from increased human mobility, we find a striking disparity. While it may be useful for mapping out the effect of immigration on diverse interests in the developed world, this simple equation of interest just doesn't add up. On the one side of the equation one finds some very focused and influential interests, such as employers and central bankers, with broad public backing in the form of consumers and local residents. On the other side of the equation one finds a broad group of citizens, many of whom are not known for their capacity to influence policy. Most modern political analysts assume that smaller, more focused, and better-funded interests should prevail over diffuse, large and poorly endowed interests. How can it be that an alliance of low-paid, unskilled workers and the beneficiaries of the modern welfare state have managed to trump the most powerful interests in modern democratic states?

This apparent mismatch between interest and opinions is also evident in the lobbying landscape of developed states. Despite assumptions of broad and deep-seated opposition to greater immigration in developed states, there are phenomenally few formal lobbying organizations that are committed to restricting immigration. In the United States, where political lobbying is a highly developed and public art form, it is difficult to find many established interest groups opposed to more open immigration. Indeed, the most influential immigration lobby group in the USA is probably the American Immigration Lawyers' Association (AILA), which lobbied *against* the passage of legislation that would restrict legal and employment-based immigration in 1996. By contrast, the leading anti-immigration lobbying force is the Federation of

American Immigration Reform (FAIR), a group that is mostly anathema to mainstream politicians because of its extreme views on the environment and population-control policies.

More significant is the fact that today's immigrants are making their own voices heard, as their rising numbers command the attention of political elites in democratic states. Across the developed world, politicians are increasingly eager to attract the votes of immigrant populations that are becoming more politically active. In the United States, hardline Republican Party opposition to immigration has melted in response to the growing political muscle of Hispanic voters in key states such as California, New York and Florida. The position of the Democratic Party has also softened, as it no longer faces a trade-union movement that is strongly opposed to further immigration (see below). In Europe, demographic concerns have weakened opposition to immigration, as nations begin to engage in frank and open discussions about how to pay for future social security and pension schemes with a shrinking domestic workforce.

Given today's embrace of liberal economic theory and pluralist politics, and the lopsided equation of domestic interests, open immigration policies should be a slam dunk. Public opinion and perceptions of national sovereignty are clearly lagging behind developments on the ground – they reflect interests and opportunities that are no longer viable and that are increasingly challenged by the many facets of globalization. As the world and these interests continue to change, perceptions will surely follow.

Organized labour

The experience of organized labour provides the best example of how an evolving global context can affect changes in both interests and attitudes. While most people assume that the interests of organized labour stand in stark opposition to increased immigration, trade unions themselves see their relationship to immigration and immigrants changing radically in response to new economic, social and political realities.

On the one hand, unions are clearly aware that a substantial inflow of immigrant labour will bring downward pressure on their members' wages. Traditionally, this concern has been reserved for the effects on unskilled wages, but it is spreading rapidly to other areas and skill levels. Worse, unions worry that desperate and job-hungry immigrants might be used as strike-breakers to undermine labour's influence during industrial disputes.

On the other hand, unions realize that immigrants constitute a large pool from which they must draw future members. Unions in the service, office and hospital trades, for example, are being forced to re-examine their traditional hostility to immigration. Similarly, public-sector unions see low-wage immigrants as potential new 'clients' for the services rendered by their members. While it once seemed reasonable for unions to oppose immigration, this is no longer the case. More importantly, unions realize that they cannot oppose the immigrants themselves: once immigrant workers enter a country and join the local labour market, unions must organize them or risk a growing cleavage in the ranks of the working class.

The unions' precarious relationship to immigration is aggravated by the nationalist contexts in which industrial relationships have developed over time. Modern labour movements are as much a product of nineteenth-century nation-building as they are of industrialization.[17] After World War I, the power and influence of organized labour was increasingly intertwined with that of employers and the state; its authority was largely limited to an imagined community confined to a specific (national) territory. This nationalist foundation was fortified during the Cold War, as trade unions with internationalist ambitions and connections were quickly marginalized as Communist sympathizers, while unions that committed themselves to nationalist solutions became some of the most influential and powerful institutions in the postwar period. Although their level of power and influence varied significantly from country to country, the interests of labour organizations became firmly linked to the fate of the nation-state, and its ability to regulate and control the domestic economy. As the state's regulatory capacity and power grew, the presence of foreign workers within nation-states became an anomaly, and immigrants were increasingly regarded as both alien and temporary.

Against this historical backdrop, it is little wonder that today's trade unions are concerned about the effect of immigration on existing national bargaining and power structures. Their dominant frame of reference remains that of the nation-state and the national economic arena, where the structures for consensus development, decision-making and policy implementation were established. These structures, in themselves, depended critically on the national solidarity of workers, employers and the state – all of which were (once) allied in their opposition to foreign competition.

As the power and influence of the nation-state have been eroded by the sundry forces of globalization, and employers have explored and exploited new international production and investment sites, organized labour has been left to fight a battle long lost. The old tripartite relationships, upon which most of labour's legitimacy and influence rested, are already being undermined by globalization. In this new global context, the state has less authority and power to bring to the negotiating table, employers are less interested and committed to nation-based solutions, and labour finds itself wielding influence in a realm that is increasingly irrelevant.

Under these new global conditions, labour is forced to reconsider its relationship to international production and organization. This sort of re-examination is clearly evident in the developed country where organized labour has been least effective in securing its political objectives: the United States. Before 1980, the US union movement consistently supported every legislative initiative enacted by Congress to restrict immigration and to enforce its policy provisions.[18] In recent years, however, organized labour in the United States has changed its position radically, and its largest groups have come to embrace greater immigration. For example, the Executive Council of the American Federation of Labor–Congress of Industrial Organizations (AFL–CIO) announced in February of 2000 that it would support expanded immigration, lenient enforcement of immigration laws, and the legislative agenda of immigrants.[19]

In short, organized labour – the largest and most powerful organized interest that we might expect actively to resist immigration to the developed world – is being forced to rethink its traditional opposition to immigration. Some of its component skill-groups will undoubtedly be threatened by immigrant labour, but unions are looking for new ways to address these concerns, as they work to establish more international forms and strategies in response to the spread of globalization and the retreat of the state.

Developing world interests

As in the developed world, it is difficult to generalize about the nature of opposition to migration in the developing world. On the one hand, the developing world is filled with states that use emigration as an economic lifeline: actively encouraging emigration as a way to secure a dependable source of foreign income and to jettison some of the political pressures associated with economic underdevelopment. On the other hand, many developing states are concerned about their inability to retain skilled labour, especially the doctors and engineers whose skills are badly needed at home.

Using the same rough framework as above, we can map the potential winners and losers generated by emigration from the developing world, based on perceived economic interests. In particular, we can expect to find resistance among certain groups in the developing world – and this resistance will vary according to the nature of the domestic labour force and the type of emigration that is encouraged from the country in question. But interests in the developing world are not simple reflections or inversions of those found in the developed world: conditions on the ground can vary substantially. For example, we cannot blindly expect capital owners in the developing world to oppose emigration, as some developing countries are awash in an almost limitless supply of cheap and unskilled labour.

For this reason, it is fruitful to begin by distinguishing between two types of developing state: those with a relatively small, but poorly paid, workforce; and those, such as Bangladesh and India, that seem to have a limitless supply of cheap unskilled labour. In the latter group, we can expect to find few sources of opposition to greater emigration, unless it is the emigration of a highly specialized and demanded skill type. Indeed, we can expect that emigrants from this type of country might be encouraged to leave with government incentives and targeted government institutions to facilitate migration, remittances and repatriation. In countries that have an enormous supply of untapped labour, emigration (and the remittance flows that result) is crucial for economic survival, and we can expect few sources of opposition.

Alternatively, in those developing countries that are not swimming in bottomless pools of surplus labour we might expect to see an inversion of the sort of cleavages we saw in the developed world. In this context, employers should fear the effect of emigration on domestic wages and the workers' capacity to organize and capture a greater share of the political and economic pie. In these countries, emigration can draw down the nation's limited supply of labour; this increased scarcity brings with it greater influence and a better price. Thus, we can expect employers in these contexts to oppose greater emigration as it threatens their relative bargaining position in the local economy (and polity).[20]

Compared to the developed world, however, these pockets of opposition are relatively small and isolated. Even so, economic elites have always enjoyed inordinate political influence, and we should not be surprised to see that these groups can influence policy outcomes with respect to domestic labour market conditions. But historical experience suggests that employers find it more useful to improve the local conditions that influence emigration decisions (e.g. better wages, working conditions, and political contexts), than try to limit mobility itself. Either way, there are relatively few grounds on which to organize opposition to increased emigration from the developing world.

International interests

Having mapped the bunkers of opposition we can expect to find in both the developed and the developing worlds, it is time to consider three sorts of international interest that might oppose increased migration. After all, international migration reinforces traditional political cleavages and encourages new ones along mobility lines, as owners of more mobile assets benefit relative to owners of immobile assets.

First, and most generally, the liberalization of national border controls on human mobility will undermine the artificial barriers that now segregate life-opportunities by skill level. For example, under existing conditions, some forms of labour wield more influence than others, as they enjoy greater opportunities for exit. By liberalizing international migration we can help to shrink these inequalities in opportunity.

The cynics among us see an implicit international alliance of political and economic elites who employ traditional, even tribalist, fears to restrict the mobility of the masses, while they themselves move effortlessly across international borders. While it is almost impossible for a bricklayer to get permission to work in a foreign country, the upper management ranks of large multinational corporations – not to mention leading artists, athletes, professors, and other labour elites – have much less difficulty in accessing and exploiting international markets for their labour. Although these skill-based barriers to mobility are artificial (i.e. political constructs), they generate real and important differences in opportunity.

Second, and more obviously, the advantage of international mobility today benefits capital at the expense of labour, globally. To the extent that labour, as a class, is comparatively less mobile than capital, its political influence is limited by its inability to threaten exit. This is one of the lessons derived from Chapter 5. In other words, capital benefits more than labour from the new international conditions of investment and production.[21] Liberalizing restrictions on international mobility will level the international playing field.

The problem, as we have seen, is that modern labour movements are trapped in their nationalist legacies. Yet the internationalization of economic processes, across Europe and beyond, has radically changed the nature of contemporary industrial relations. At the same time, transnational collective action and the international organization of labour have proven difficult and evasive. For example, the European Trade Union Confederation (ETUC) was established as early as 1973, and represents 30 per cent of all workers in twenty-two European countries. Despite its age and scope of membership, the ETUC has proven remarkably ineffective at influencing European industrial relations and the policies that affect European labour. By contrast, the European Roundtable of Industrialists is widely recognized as a political and economic force in Europe. An even stronger imbalance can be found at the global level, where capital thinks and works on an international plane, while labour is confined (mostly) to national struggles and strategies.

This international ineffectiveness is the result of labour's traditional reliance on national frameworks. European labour, in particular, is accustomed to dealing in a tripartite setting, where it negotiates with an organized employers' organization and a strong state. The state, in these contexts, has played an important role in encouraging the industrial partners to avoid conflict and find compromises. But at the global (or, for that matter, European) level, this sort of strong state does not exist. As a result, international production is less organized and structured: a context that capital has proven much more effective at exploiting.

The political power of capital is amplified by its ability to exit from national political contexts: the real threat of exit secures owners of more mobile assets a better bargaining position at home. As markets become more integrated across Europe and the globe, owners of more mobile assets (such as finance capital) find themselves able to exploit these advantages. In order to compete on this new international plane, labour must be allowed to exert (and become more comfortable with exerting) its power outside national contexts. Indeed, organized labour needs to overcome the handicaps that have resulted from its commitments to national contexts that have varied significantly. This national variance has made international cooperation especially difficult. For labour to confront capital on this new, global, playing field it needs to develop new, more international, forms of organization. Labor needs to overcome the divergent interests and backgrounds (whether real or perceived) that it inherited from its sundry nationalist settings. Most importantly, labour needs to be freed from its national shackles so that it too can wield the potent threat of exit.

Finally, free human mobility will challenge the power and wealth of one of the ugliest and most pernicious actors in today's global marketplace: people smugglers. Because of national restrictions on immigration, and because nation-states have proven themselves incapable of sealing off their borders completely, there is an enormous illicit market for organized criminals to exploit. The gains from this prohibited trade are now so large that the United Nations Office for Drug Control and Crime Prevention believes that people smuggling has become more lucrative than drug smuggling. Obviously, these unethical traders will find themselves without a market in a world where migration can be a legal, public and regulated activity.

At all levels, there is a remarkable divergence between public attitudes and policy with respect to immigration, on the one hand, and the actual interests that will be negatively and directly affected by it, on the other. While anti-immigration rhetoric and national control policies appears monolithic and uncontroversial, it is obvious that the distribution of costs and benefits within countries, and around the globe, are much more nuanced and varied. It is difficult to explain this gap between attitudes, interests and national policies without reference to conventional wisdom. It is to this last hurdle that we now turn.

8

Questioning Conventional Wisdom

These people were extremely fond of liberty; but seem not to
have understood it very well.

David Hume, *Political Discourses* (1752)

Conventional wisdom is the third significant obstacle along the
path to free human mobility. While social scientists, historians and
philosophers may be willing to entertain the thought of a world
without borders, the average man and/or woman on the street is
not. For most people, the power to admit or exclude aliens is still
seen as an inherent right of state sovereignty, and public opinion
in the developed world remains suspicious of immigrants. Even if
the world's residents came to recognize that their own individual
(or community) interests could be furthered by embracing free
migration, they face an almost monolithic body of conventional
wisdom that defends closed borders.

This chapter confronts some of the most common arguments
used to spoil attempts at broadening the migration discussion:
concerns about the number of anticipated immigrants, the potential
for brain drain, the utopian nature of the proposal, and the effect
of immigration on national culture and security. While the preced-

ing chapter examined the way in which particular interests were affected by (and understood the effects of) migration, this chapter looks at larger issues in the form of conventional wisdom. While conventional wisdom is sometimes aimed at particular interests, it is usually framed in terms that resemble national interests.

The Great Flood of Immigrants

The most insidious argument used to sideline discussions about open borders concerns the potential size of the migrant flows in a world without borders. Although several preceding chapters have addressed this issue on an ad hoc basis, it is such an important and fundamental point of contention – and it has such significant consequences for any interest-based analysis of the effect of free mobility – that it is important to address it directly. One of the main reasons that people fear any discussion about open borders is the implicit threat of hundreds of millions, maybe billions, of poor immigrants knocking at the developed world's door.

When it comes to anticipating the level of migration that we might expect in a world with open borders, the rhetoric itself is an indicator of the underlying biases that cloud the discussion. Although we really have no idea of how many people would choose to migrate if given the opportunity, any discussion of border liberalization is usually framed in terms of tidal gates being opened, allowing a flood of new immigrants, who will swamp domestic welfare policies. Consider a typical letter to the editor of an American newspaper that is soft on immigration:

> We are faced with the fact that some large percentage – and it could be a very large percentage – of the earth's 4 billion non-U.S. inhabitants would opt, if they could, to leave where they now live and come to this country. If that happened, Lifeboat U.S. would quickly sink.[1]

This is obviously a ridiculous claim, but it is one that is embraced by remarkably many people. Across the developed world, residents assume that the demand for entry into their states is almost insatiable. For example, in the run-up to the 1994 referendums on EU membership in Norway, Sweden and Finland there were widespread concerns that membership would induce a flood of poor (e.g. Portuguese) workers to exploit the generous Nordic welfare states. These concerns proved to be completely unfounded. Apparently, it didn't occur to these pundits that spending six months of the year in frozen darkness might not be a very attractive option for Portuguese workers.

Nowhere is this sense of arrogance and national pride stronger than in the United States. As a result of the country's history and isolation, Americans think much more of their country than does the rest of the world. In a recent international poll conducted by several national newscasters, entitled 'What the World Thinks of America', only 18 per cent of the respondents (from countries as diverse as Australia, Indonesia, Canada, Brazil, Jordan, Israel, Russia, Korea, France and the UK) considered America to be a better place to live than their own country. While 89 per cent of the Americans polled thought that the United States was the best place in the world to live, only 19 per cent of the respondents in the other ten countries said they would live in the United States, if given the chance. In stark contrast, 96 per cent of the Americans polled thought that people outside the United States would like to come and live there.[2]

Actually, there are a number of reasons why we might expect relatively few people to leave home. As nearly every critic of immigration has noted, the current system of border controls is very ineffective at stopping highly motivated immigrants. Consequently, today's level of international migration may not be significantly higher than the level we can expect after national controls and restrictions on human mobility are lifted. In other words, given today's social, political and economic inequalities – as described in Chapter 2 – it is truly surprising how few people are actually taking advantage of these 'porous' borders. This, in itself, may be evidence of the relatively limited demand for international migration (as much as it is a statement about the effectiveness of modern control regimes).

In fact, for the vast majority of the world's inhabitants, migration is not a very attractive option: most people would only choose it under extreme circumstances. Generally, people have little inclination to leave their native soil, no matter how onerous their conditions become: family, familiar surroundings and inertia (among other factors) keep the potential migrant at home. After all, as Oscar Handlin reminds us, the essence of migration is alienation.[3] Similarly, to quote a 1916 newspaper editorial, 'Emigration is a form of suicide because it separates a person from all that life gives except the material wants of simple animal pleasure.'[4]

If we are to avoid the exaggerated rhetoric of political pundits, how can we develop more reasoned estimates of the size of migration flows in a world with open borders? After all, one of the reasons for the absence of hard figures is that any perceivable formula for generating these sorts of estimates will be lamed by crippling assumptions. With this caveat in mind, we must begin somewhere, albeit cautiously.

It is possible to conceive of four possible approaches for generating 'guestimates' of free migration. It is necessary to emphasize that each set of estimates depends critically on a number of rather heroic assumptions. More precisely, each estimate depends on a formula derived from parallel movements at different times, levels of analysis or factors. These formulas are then used to make relative projections based on a world population of 6.2 billion. As a baseline, we can compare these projections with the number of people who are potentially mobile today. In particular, from Chapter 2 we learned that a number of estimates could be combined to calculate that roughly 110 million people (some 1.8 per cent of the world's population) are displaced and potential migrants. This figure is based mostly on stock figures (i.e. the total number of people, not the annual flows of people), so it represents a very conservative (read large) estimate for annual international migration flows.[5] Given this baseline figure, how much larger can we expect international migrant flows to grow in the absence of border controls/restrictions?

Historical estimate

By examining the size of migrant flows during the previous period of globalization (i.e. the early twentieth century), we can generate a rough estimate for future emigrant flows. These estimates will probably be biased in one direction (i.e. too small) because it is much easier for people to travel and communicate today; but they may entail biases in the other direction as well (i.e. too large) when one considers that global and political inequalities were smaller then than they are now. It has been estimated that roughly 1.4 million people undertook the Atlantic migration at its peak (*c.* 1908). If we double this figure (2.8 million) to accommodate for other non-Atlantic migrants (where the figures are less certain), and we note that the world's population at the time was about 1.75 billion, then we can estimate that immigrants then made up about 0.16 per cent of the population.[6] This same percentage of today's global population would be almost 10 million people – a mere fraction of the current migration level!

This estimate, of course, is very rough (as are the ones to follow), and depends critically on a number of implausible compatibility assumptions. Nevertheless, it remains remarkably small. Even more surprising is the fact that, from the historical (Atlantic) figures, as many as one-third of the American immigrants eventually left again, mostly to return to their countries of origin. In other areas, the return rate was even higher. Thus the net immigration figures may even be considerably lower than this rough estimate suggests.

Other studies

There are very few explicit estimates of the anticipated size of migrant flows in a world with open borders. One was buried in the *1992 Human Development Report*, described in Chapter 6. This report estimated the expected economic gain from free immigration on the assumption that 2 per cent of the developing world's labour force would choose to leave in the absence of borders.[7] Noting that today's developing-world population is around 4.75 billion, and assuming that the labour force represents 40 per cent of the developing world's population, than we can use the UNDP's formula to generate an estimate of about 38 million potential migrants.[8] While this estimate is nearly four times larger than the historical estimate generated above, it still falls far short of our conservative estimate of the number of annually displaced people!

Migration within federal and supranational states

Another means of estimating what international migration flows might look like in the absence of border controls is to compare the flows in existing federal or supranational states (where inter-state controls have already been lifted). Of course, there are numerous problems with trying to extrapolate world estimates on the basis of experience from existing states. Most important of these is the fact that existing federal and/or supranational states/provinces tend to have smaller cultural/language differences, as well as smaller income and political inequalities, separating them. The first type of differences might lead us to underestimate world migration flows, while the latter differences might lead us to overestimate world migration figures. Still, some back-of-the-envelope calculations are possible for three examples: the USA, Canada and the European Union.

United States

As the United States enjoys a very mobile population, sharing (mostly) a common language/culture, and with relatively small political and economic differences separating the individual states, we might expect interstate immigration rates in the United States to be relatively high. Indeed, in most comparative studies of monetary unions, a high level of labour mobility is one of the main characteristics that distinguishes the American economy from the European (EU). In light of this, the actual figures are not very large. For example, in 1997 only 6,357,000 people moved from one state to another within the United States, or 2.4 per cent of the country's population.[9] If we consider interregional mobility (between the Northeast, Midwest, South and West regions), and not interstate mobility, the figure is even smaller: 3,372,000, or 1.3 per cent.[10] If we use these US percentages to extrapolate from current world population figures, we generate an estimate of potential international migration that varies roughly between 80 and 150 million. These estimates come closest to contemporary migration levels, but they are incredibly low, given our priors.

Canada

Given the significant differences that separate Inuit, English and French-Canadian cultures, the Canadian figures may be more representative of the sort of cultural spread we find internationally. On the other hand, inter-provincial inequalities are probably small, relative to both the United States and the world at large. Figures from *Statistics Canada* suggest that 890,270 people moved from one province to another in 1996. As Canada's population in that year was 26,604,135, these migrants represented 3.3 per cent of the population.[11] Thus, the Canadian extrapolation would lead us to expect world migration flows at the level of about 205 million – about double the figures generated from the US example.

European Union

The European Union arguably provides a better generator of international migration estimates, as the cultural, political and income differentials separating European states are larger than in either the United States or Canada. Indeed, as noted earlier, Northern European fears of Southern migrant invasions were very strong (and quite vocal) prior to the liberalization of migration across the European Economic Area (EEA),[12] and these concerns were again raised as the European Union shifted its borders eastward. Nevertheless, cultural, language and personal barriers continue to limit significantly the number of people who actually take advantage of free mobility. In 1998, only 462,000 people emigrated from one EEA state to another. As the EEA's population in 1998 was 379,305,000, this represents a mere 0.1 per cent![13] The extrapolated figures for world migration would be a mere 7.4 million people.[14]

These figures, in particular the EU figure, are shockingly low. In states where there are no legal restrictions on mobility, and where income and political differentials can be relatively large, we see surprisingly few people migrating each year. The numbers are even more surprising when we consider that each of these sample populations (USA, Canada, EEA) is arguably better endowed to move (in terms of, e.g., money and information) than the world population at large.

Relative to other factor flows

A final estimate can be generated by comparing the relative influence of parallel global factors on a national economy. If we assume that capital and labour function as near economic substitutes (a common, if problematic, assumption among economists), we can use this similarity to generate an expectation of the demand for international labour – based on the size of (deregulated) foreign capital flows. This estimate should wildly overestimate the potential demand for labour in any given country, as it is far easier to move an investment portfolio than it is to move a life. Still, it is a reasonable comparison that may help us balance the strikingly low figures generated above.

In 1999, the United States welcomed $282.5 billion in for-eign direct investment (FDI). This figure, while enormous, only represents about 3.2 per cent of the US gross domestic product (GDP) for that year. In the previous year, the United States had allowed 1.68 million immigrants to enter the country, about 0.6 per cent of its population. If we assume that investment capital is fairly free to move internationally, and that capital and labour can be understood as rough substitutes, then we might expect international labour to enjoy the same sort of influence (relatively speaking) on the US economy as is today enjoyed by international capital, once controls on its movement are lifted. Thus the United States might expect about 8.6 million new immigrants.[15] While this estimate is substantially above the figure now accepted (1.68 million), it is far below the billions often volleyed around in political contests.

These estimates of potential international migration, generated from a number of simple comparisons, vary from 5 million to 205 million potential migrants a year. Nearly every estimate is below our estimate of current migration levels, and the largest estimate (generated from the Canadian example) is only twice as large as the current level estimate. Even the most generous estimate (the one measuring the potential immigrant stream to the United States in light of its demand for international invest-ment) is politically and logistically within that country's capacity for assimilation. From these reasoned estimates – even when we explicitly recognize their many shortcomings – it is difficult to understand the 'immigrant flood' hyperbole usually associated with the idea of open borders.

Brain Drain

While the developed world frets about a future flood of poor immigrants, the developing world fears a brain drain.[16] Much of the initial concern about brain drain was focused on the detrimental effects on the Indian economy. During the 1970s and 1980s, it is said that entire graduating classes from elite Indian institutes of technology emigrated, and that many of them achieved impressive professional and economic success abroad. (Parenthetically, we might note how the boot now seems to be on the other foot, as many technology jobs return to India – at least such is the political rhetoric in American election campaigns.) While India may have been the focus of much initial interest in the brain-drain dilemma, the problem is surely not confined to the subcontinent.

Indeed, Africa may be worst hit by the problem, as it suffers from a very serious shortage of skilled labour. The UN Economic Commission for Africa and the International Organization for Migration (IOM) estimate that 27,000 Africans left the continent for the developed world between 1960 and 1975. From 1975 to 1984 that figure rose to 40,000; since 1990, the estimate is that at least 20,000 people have left the continent annually. One of the most shocking figures is from the UNDP's 1992 *Human Development Report*, which notes that at least 60 per cent of doctors trained in Ghana during the 1980s left the country. Worse, developing countries spend a phenomenal amount of their scarce foreign reserves to attract the foreign nationals necessary to fill the gap created by this skills shortage. The IOM deputy director-general, Ndioro Ndiaye, estimated that African countries spend about $4 billion annually to employ about 100,000 non-African expatriates.[17]

There can be no doubt that poor countries suffer from brain drain. However, it is becoming increasingly common to doubt whether the effects from brain drain are as devastating as conventional wisdom holds. There are many reasons for these doubts. First of all, most of the world's migrants do not take the form of doctors, engineers and physicists in search of a better salary. Brain drain is not even a problem reserved for the developing world – several developed countries (such as Switzerland and Canada) have been actively trying to establish programmes that can dampen brain-drain effects on their own (developed) economies. Nevertheless, the problem is clearly more acute in the developing world, even if it is very difficult to gauge its extent. While the world is awash in global trade and investment statistics, we still do not have a uniform system of statistics for the number and characteristics of international migration! As a result, we have little way of gauging the size or the impact of brain drain: it has proven quite difficult to measure precisely the flow and levels of education of migrants, or the stock of educated workers in each sending country.

It is also unclear whether countries lose more than they gain from sending their high-skilled emigrants abroad. There are several reasons for this. For example, the recent experiences of countries like India and China suggest that short-term brain drain may generate long-term gains to the national economy. Anecdotal evidence suggests that first-generation brain-drain migrants have managed to build technology bridges that span the divide separating developing and developed worlds. Once these bridges are constructed, jobs can return to (once) sending countries to exploit the way in which these countries have invested in education and human capital development. In addition, professional (high-skilled) émigrés can be an important source of foreign currency remittances to the developing world. As we have already learned, remittances have become the most important and stable source of foreign income in the developing world. In many cases, the size of these remittances dwarfs foreign aid, and represents a substantial (and stable) source of development capital in poor countries. Finally, these émigrés can contribute to the local economy in more ways than just sending home money. Many emigrants return home after their stays abroad, and bring with them skills, norms, market contacts, capital, and so on that can be ploughed into the local economy. European experiences from before World War I suggest that returning emigrants can have a significant impact on the home country's economic development and modernization.

Neither is it clear that countries are wasting the money they invest in the education of future emigrants. After all, the prospect of emigration is likely to increase the incentive for individuals in the developing world to acquire more skills and better education. In point of fact, recent scholarship has begun to challenge the way we think about brain drain and social investments in the developing world. New, revisionist, arguments suggest that the incentive to acquire skills may actually be strengthened by the prospect of being able to emigrate.[18] This work suggests that current conditions encourage developing countries to produce a surplus of skilled residents (than would otherwise be the case without the potential for emigration), and this surplus delivers important spillover effects to the local economy. In short, the potential for emigration provides individuals with an incentive to acquire skills that might otherwise be lacking in the developing world.

Finally, there are serious moral and legal problems associated with forcing people to stay in a place where they don't want to be. Brain drain is driven by several complicated factors, such as the lack of employment opportunities, salary differentials, job dissatisfaction, cumbersome employment procedures, abrasive institutional settings, and so forth. These factors will continue to draw potential emigrants abroad, independent of any state's attempt to restrain them forcibly. The solution to brain drain is relatively simple: provide better opportunities for potential emigrants at home. In other words, the brain drain is largely a domestic problem that needs to be resolved by providing incentives for qualified nationals to remain at home. The best motivation for change at home may come from the threat of increased emigration abroad.

Migration's Effect on Culture

While many people are willing to embrace the economic and political gains from globalization, there is a persistent fear that globalization undermines national cultures and identities. In a shrinking world, characterized by fewer and fewer international frontiers, the uniqueness of national identities appears to be challenged by the free flow of goods, services, culture, and now people. This concern, like others in this chapter, is widespread. Indeed, at several points in earlier chapters we have considered how people from different cultures affect local (host) cultures. For example, in Chapter 6 we considered how someone from a different economic culture (e.g. different norms of work, productivity, the role of technology, etc.) might adjust to working in a different economic environment. In Chapters 4, 5 and 7 we contemplated the consequences of someone moving from a more traditional cultural setting into a local culture of democracy. Now is the time to bring these questions together and consider the presumed corrosive effects of cultural mingling.

Our point of departure should be to consider whether immigration has the potential to challenge or undermine traditional notions of culture more than the globalization of other factors (a liberalization that most of the world has already embraced). Indeed, it would seem as though the world's consumers and Internet surfers have accepted the dominance of English, Hollywood and McDonald's (to take just three prominent examples) – and that this type of international exchange presents a far greater threat to cultural and political autonomy (than the threat we can expect from a liberalization of migration flows). Following Jeremy Harding, 'it would take decades of inward migration to bring about the degree of "cultural difference" that a bad patch of international trading, a brisk downsizing or a decision by a large corporation to start "outsourcing" can inject into a social landscape in a year.'[19]

A more fruitful understanding lies in the recognition that identities and cultures are more flexible, accommodating and adaptive than conventional wisdom tends to hold. Consider the fact that French officials sought to ban Coca-Cola in the 1940s; indeed, it was not finally approved for sale in France until 1953. Does anybody really believe that French culinary culture has become less distinct since the invasion of Coca-Cola, over fifty years ago? The answer to this question is an obvious and resounding No. The reason for this is that conventional wisdom about culture (and the effects on it of globalization) rests on three basic flaws.

The first of these flaws is that most cultural autonomy arguments verge on racism, as they apply racial and ethnic stereotypes to differences that are anchored in otherness. 'Cultural integrity' or 'cultural autonomy' are simply new and popular ways of distinguishing between 'us' and 'them' – and it is the threat of this 'otherness' that really lies beneath public concerns about migration. Today the immigrant 'other' is stereotyped in terms of race and culture. But the history of migration is filled with examples of immigrants as 'outsiders' – irrespective of phenotype, religion or culture. For example, Europe's history abounds with examples of migrant labourers moving from one region to another – typically over fairly short distances, often within the same broader ethnic/cultural setting. Frequently, these migrants looked like the locals: they tended to share the same diets, religion, music and rituals, yet were still identified as others or outsiders as they did not come from the immediate (local) community. In short, social identities are not predicated on national, ethnic or cultural building blocks: the distinction between us and them can be (and often is) based on totally arbitrary, temporary and minimalist categories.

This sort of 'outsider' status is clearly visible today within nation-states, even in a place like the United States, where internal migration is relatively common. On the west coast of the United States, just north of Seattle, lies a long thin island named Whidbey in the middle of Puget Sound. Traditionally, this island was a hunting ground for local Indian populations (though none of them lived permanently on the island). Then, at the end of the nineteenth century, a European population settled on the island to fish, cut timber and farm. Today, the offspring of these homesteaders complain loudly about the more recent influx of 'Californians' to the island. Of course, Californians look and act the same as do the locals islanders (although, admittedly, they are wealthier); they are only perceived as different. Indeed, local islanders employ a cultural argument to justify their attempt at excluding Californians. The truth of the matter is that most Californian immigrants to the island (or, for that matter, immigrants whatever their origins) tend to assimilate to and adopt many cultural characteristics on the island. At the same time, many of the new 'cultural attributes' of the immigrants are slowly and subtly being integrated into the local culture.

This sort of experience is shared by migrants everywhere, be it East German emigrants to western Germany, or Nigerian emigrants to Johannesburg. The world is filled with small and large communities that fear and shun migrant outsiders. At the core of this fear lies otherness and difference – references to cultural autonomy are simply a convenient means of hiding that fear. American concerns about 'Latinization' or French references to 'Africanization' or 'Islamification' are little more than new, often racist, names for 'otherness'.

These examples lead us to another reason to question the 'cultural defence' argument for closed borders: this argument rests on a narrow and rather superficial understanding of culture. In this conventional view, culture is understood in terms that are sterile, rigid, standardized, and tightly linked to specific territorial (national) spaces. National cultures are stereotyped images of a romantic and imagined past. Thus, contemporary observers of American culture see it as somehow fast-frozen in the seventeenth century and based on romantic images of America's Anglo-Protestant settlers.[20] Similarly idealized notions lie at the root of most perceptions of European cultures as well. Indeed, most of the cultural attributes that we now associate with nation-states were the direct result of homogenization and nationalization policies from the mid-nineteenth century. What is remarkable (and now mostly forgotten) is that this nationalization project itself was motivated by an effort to stave off the exodus of Europe's surplus labour, at a time when the world was awash with migrants.

Despite their crudeness, we rely on these cultural caricatures as a useful way to generalize (i.e. as rules of thumb): they are accurate enough to provide the cultural observer with simple ways of categorizing vast amounts of information. They also provide relatively firm ground into which individuals (and nations) can anchor their identities. Yet cultural stereotypes of this type fail to realize the degree to which these cultural communities are themselves imagined and constructed.[21]

Perhaps France is the country best known for defending its national culture – and, especially, its language. While great efforts have been extended to defend its purity, the French language – that great standard of cultural integrity – is hardly fixed and dormant. Indeed, today's French is a relatively modern and political creation: we begin to recognize what is now referred to as Modern French only after the seventeenth century, following a period of unification, regulation and purification.[22] In short, the French language was a political construct, and centuries of effort by the French language elite (e.g. the Académie, public education, centuries of official control and the national media) have not been able to hinder France's youth from adopting English or Arabic slang. The French language, like culture generally, does not live (and has never lived) in a vacuum; it grows and thrives by intermixing with other cultural influences.

This notion of a static, fast-frozen, culture is challenged by contemporary theorists of culture. Indeed, one of the great advances of modern cultural theory, to quote Edward Said, 'is the realization, almost universally acknowledged, that cultures are hybrid and heterogeneous, and ... that cultures and civilizations are so interrelated and interdependent as to beggar any unitary or simply delineated description of their individuality.'[23] In contrast to the vision of static culture (or identity) outlined above, modern cultural theory recognizes that culture is a complicated, reflexive process that includes historical, social, intellectual and political processes, as well as the imagined constructions of oppositions, like them and us.

When we take a pliable and reflexive notion of culture as our starting point, it becomes possible to understand reflexive cultural manipulation by the local and new – hybrid – identities: we can speak of American Toyotas, Japanese rap music, Russian democracy, and so on. The new loci of identity are not simply shadows of their former glory, nor simple imprints of global influences. These new identities are a collage, an imaginative blend, of the global and local. Seen from this perspective, migration offers cultural emancipation and assortment, not the threat of dominance or convergence.

Figure 8.1 Sharing customs and tradition

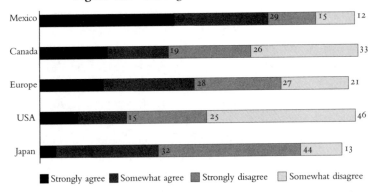

Mexico		29	15	12
Canada	19	26		33
Europe	28	27		21
USA	15	25		46
Japan	32		44	13

■ Strongly agree ■ Somewhat agree ■ Strongly disagree □ Somewhat disagree

Note: Respondents were asked: 'Please tell me if you strongly agree, somewhat agree, somewhat disagree, or strongly disagree with the following statement: It is better for a country if almost everyone shares the same customs and traditions.' 'Europe' includes the UK, Spain, Italy, Germany and France. The graph shows those who expressed an opinion as a percentage. The difference (totalling to 100) are the respondents who were 'not sure'.

Source: IPSOS–Public Affairs and Associated Press (2004).

Public opinion data confirm that most residents of the developed world seem to be aware of how important and desirable it is to live in a place with divergent cultural stimuli. For example, in the Ipsos–Public Affairs and Associated Press poll used in the previous chapter,[24] respondents were asked if they thought their country would be better off if almost everyone shared the same customs and traditions. These responses are illustrated in Figure 8.1. Among the US respondents, only 27 per cent either strongly or somewhat agreed, while 71 per cent somewhat or strongly disagreed. In other words, the vast majority of American respondents felt that their country would be worse off if everyone shared the same customs and traditions. In Canada, where cultural differences have provoked strong secessionist and autonomy movements, 40 per cent agreed (strongly or somewhat), while 59 per cent disagreed. Even in Japan, 37 per cent of the respondents agreed, while 57 per cent disagreed.[25] It is interesting to note how the Mexican respondents – the only respondents in the sample from a developing country – reacted much more strongly about the need to share customs and traditions (71 per cent agreed, only 27 per cent disagreed). Of those sampled from the developed world, Europeans were apparently the most critical of cultural heterogeneity. In the aggregate European sample, opinions were split: 48:48, with 4 per cent unsure.

Finally, this conventional view of cultures is problematic in that it is inherently conflictual. When culture is understood in these static and exclusive terms, and linked to fixed (territorial) entities, it encourages a permanent, irreconcilable division among people. Every culture is seen to be a self-contained, natural entity; each is ethnocentric and fiercely loyal to its own parochial view of the world. It is this parochial view of the world that may be our greatest common threat. Worse, as the relevance of time and space shrinks, these exclusive differences are increasingly challenged. It is this perspective that leads Samuel Huntington to conclude (wrongly) that increased globalization brings a 'Clash of Civilizations'.[26]

It is important to emphasize that this critique of static cultural stereotypes does not question the objective bases of difference. Rather, it suggests that the danger lies in the *perception of difference* that is generated by these static conceptions. By embracing these sorts of traditional carriers of identity, people are encouraged to ignore the plight of their (non-national) neighbours and search out cultural grounds for conflict.

When we recognize culture as fluid, evolving and dynamic it is more difficult to think of it being challenged or undermined by external influences. Local cultures have always been influenced by external forces; today's modern representations simply envelop and embrace them as their own. Today, the boundaries of 'foreignness' are being enlarged because of the ease of access to reproduction, transportation and communications technologies. There is no reason why national cultures cannot and will not be protected and nourished in a world without borders to human mobility. But to use the defence of a particular culture, understood in static terms, as an excuse for limiting human freedom seems rather perverse: culture is not threatened by immigration; it is fed by it.

The Challenge of Political Realism

Much resistance to an argument for open borders comes from a tradition that might be called conservatism or political realism. This resistance can take two (related) forms. The first questions the practicality of a proposed policy; in other words, political decisions should be made on the basis of tried experience, and social (or political) experimentation should be avoided at all costs. The second realist critique aims to sideline moral concerns, and follows what is often called a Machiavellian perspective on politics. From this perspective, actors (usually states) are expected to behave according to narrowly defined interests, not vague conceptions of 'proper' action. Both types of criticism are commonly used to thwart arguments for open borders.

Because of its apparent impracticality, supporters of freer migration often step back from advocating an open-borders position. As immigration controls are here and now, and advocacy of an open-borders policy seems utopian (surely risky and untried), there is a natural tendency to shun the unknown. These conservative concerns are especially strong when we consider core state values such as security and identity.

One response to this sort of criticism is to encourage historical thinking. It is for this reason that this book's positive contribution began with a historical sketch of international migration (Chapter 3). An open-borders policy is not a utopian dream (or nightmare!) with the potential to wreak havoc and destruction on the developed world. As we have already seen, a world with penetrable borders is the normal state of human affairs when we embrace a larger historical perspective. It was only during the course of the twenteieth century that we came to accept and expect states physically to limit and control the movement of people into their territory.

Of course, it is possible to argue that the twentieth century's bounty of social, political and technological developments have changed the needs of the international community, making it difficult to return to a world without borders. But the argument could just as well be turned in the other direction: it is these very changes that provide the opportunities that were unavailable to our ancestors. Rather than keeping us from the liberties enjoyed by those who preceded us (though often out of reach, because of technological and economic barriers), these changes could (and should) empower us. Either way, the resulting discussion is not about the 'realism' of a world without borders, but about the potential costs/benefits associated with it.

Another way of using history to address realist concerns is to consider recent developments in other, related, fields. Most of the arguments used to support controls on migration are familiar to students of globalization in other areas. Arguments about the need to defend cultural and political autonomy, in particular, were employed with great vigour during earlier attempts (now failed) to thwart the liberalization of international goods, services and capital markets.

With the 20:20 hindsight provided by the passing of time, it is not unfair to say that many of these claims were prone to exaggeration. Today it is possible to recognize a remarkable degree of cultural and political autonomy, despite the increased international trade in goods, services and capital. Rather than representing something radical and new, the liberalization of migration controls should be seen as the next step in a series of globalization processes. Indeed, when we consider the degree of internationalization in parallel markets, the lack of free human mobility might be seen as the least 'real' condition. In short, advocacy of an open-borders policy for people is just as 'realistic' and 'practical' as is the advocacy of open borders for goods, services and capital.

This realist emphasis on empirical and practical support draws on a long and respected tradition in political philosophy and social science. Aristotle is often heralded as the father of contemporary science, an honour awarded because of his emphasis on empirical investigation. In a most telling way, Aristotle's magisterial work *Politics* begins with the simple realist mantra: 'Observation shows us...' But Aristotle's dependence on empirical methods was also his bane. By relying on observation as a guide to his actions and analyses, Aristotle was caught in a conservative snare, unable to escape the injustices that surrounded him.

For example, *observation* showed Aristotle that it was natural for women to be subservient to men: the world that surrounded Aristotle provided ample evidence that women and men were not equal. From Aristotle's realist perspective, it was illegitimate to project himself out of surrounding injustices, to imagine a world where observation might show him that women could be equal to men. For all of his intellectual might, Aristotle was unable to escape the biases of his time. Indeed, all realist arguments have difficulty projecting themselves out of the injustices that surround them.

To escape these injustices we need foresight and theory. This was one of the most important lessons of Aristotle's teacher, Plato (to whom, of course, Aristotle was reacting). In the opening book of Plato's *Republic*, Socrates is directly confronted with a full-frontal realist attack in the form of a spirited man named Thrasymachus. For Thrasymachus, *justice is simply the interest of the stronger*; all of Socrates' word games were nothing more than an affront to the simple truth of Thrasymachus' senses. While this is not the place to examine how Socrates turned Thrasymachus' realist argument against itself, Socrates' response to realism is just as powerful today as it was two millennia ago: it is simply not possible to use realism as a means of avoiding difficult moral questions.[27]

Yet Thrasymachus can be used to address the second type of realist argument: the Machiavellian, interest-based, argument against open borders. After all, today's international regime seems to confirm Thrasymachus' position that justice is the power of the stronger. Today's heirs to Thrasymachus still hold that questions of morality are moot, and that policy should be driven by base calculations of interest, not what is right or wrong.

Herein lies our dilemma. Previous chapters have attempted to show how difficult it is to know which interests are best served by a world with closed borders. Indeed, it is particularly difficult to use interest-based arguments to explain the strong resistance – across states, classes and parties – to open borders. If resistance can't be found in the focused opposition of any single group within host countries, or if national and individual interests on both sides of the rich–poor divide can benefit from increased mobility, what explanation remains? Three possible explanations come to mind – although it is doubtful that two of them will satisfy realist critics.

First, it is possible that people are misinformed about or misperceive their best interests. This is the working premiss behind the book before you: to question traditional arguments about the economic and political benefits of closed borders. As we have seen, most people in the developed world assume that border controls are necessary to protect their wealth against a flood of poor immigrants; they see border controls as necessary for protecting self-interest, and they rely on realist arguments to justify their position. It would seem that one of the most respected immigration researchers in political science, Aristide Zolberg, would agree:

Under the conditions of structured spatial inequality that prevail in the world system, it is probably the case that truly free international migrations would on balance effect a radical redistribution of resources and opportunities to the benefit of the peoples originally located in the semi-periphery and the periphery.

This might in the long run benefit humanity as a whole; but it would undoubtedly impose in the short run drastic costs on the population of affluent countries. From this point of view, all classes in the countries of the core become as one bourgeoisie in relation to all classes elsewhere, which become as one proletariat. The imposition of restrictions on entry and incorporation is a necessary condition for the reproduction of the bourgeois state. It contributes to the maintenance of international inequality but serves as well to protect the small island of political freedom mankind has achieved for the time being.[28]

Hopefully, the preceding chapters have revealed that the costs and benefits are not clearly aligned in favour of closed-border regimes, and that it may actually be in the majority's interest to liberalize these borders. More information and debate will only contribute to this realization. For those who are still unconvinced of the interest-based argument for free mobility, a strong (maybe overriding) moral argument remains for dismantling an unjust system that so clearly benefits one group (those lucky enough to be born in rich states), at the expense of the world's majority.

Second, and in a related fashion, it is possible that people are motivated by arguments that are not interest-based. For example, it may be that xenophobia coincides with a (misperceived) conspiracy of interests that turns the wealthy against the poor. Indeed, there is a great deal of rhetorical evidence that suggests xenophobia may be the driving force behind much closed-borders rhetoric. It is in this way that the respected historian of American immigration Brinley Thomas argued that it was not downward pressure on wages, but a fear of foreigners, that explains the first major rise in immigration barriers in the aftermath of World War I:

> there are convincing reasons for thinking that, had it not been for the powerful upsurge of nationalism in the United States as a result of her participation in the First World War, the immigration problem would have been disposed of by the adoption of the literary test in 1917. What happened was one of those sudden changes in public sentiment motivated by fear. Within a few months of the end of the war Europeans began to arrive in large numbers, and shipping companies were quoted in Congress as saying that no less than ten million passengers were waiting for transit. The vision of this formidable host fleeing from a continent in the throes of political upheaval destroyed the optimistic attitudes of the prewar days.[29]

This type of dialogue is not – in any way – unique to the United States. There is, as we have seen, broad public support for restricting immigration, and almost every country in Western Europe now has a right-wing, anti-foreigner, political party or movement – the British National Party, Lega Nord (Italy), Jean-Marie Le Pen's Front National (France), the Liberal Party (Austria), the Republican Party (Germany), the Vlaams Blok (Belgium), and so on.

Worse, this sort of xenophobia is uncomfortably close to the explicit racism of apartheid, as we saw in Chapter 5. In defence of his government's apartheid policy of closing South Africa's cities to black migrants, the (then) National Party leader, Daniel Malan, tried to soothe the concerns of his white followers. The National Party, he explained, 'realises the danger of the flood of Africans moving to the cities and undertakes to protect the white character of our cities and to provide a forceful and effective way for the safety of individuals and property and the peaceful life of the inhabitants.'[30]

While the first two explanations (misperceived interests and xenophobia) may not be appreciated by realists, a third one lies close to the realist's heart: security.

Security Concerns

In the aftermath of 11 September 2001, security concerns have taken centre stage in many discussions about immigration policy. For this reason, it is prudent to discuss how national security might be affected in a world with open borders. While earlier chapters have already addressed several (broadly defined) issues of security (e.g. economic security, securing identities, etc.), there are two specific security concerns that cry out for special attention (and that are not explicitly addressed in the chapters above). Those two concerns are the control of criminal activity, and the question of national security (e.g. terrorist attack, invasion) in a world without borders.

Controlling criminal activity

Many may question the state's ability to control criminal activity in a world without borders. In the absence of stringent border controls and restrictions, can we not expect increased criminal activity? Should we not worry about the increased ease of access by international criminals and criminal organizations? Do we not lose an important instrument in the control of crime when we jettison international border controls? These are all important and legitimate questions, the answers to which might justify the continued use of international border controls.

Any response to these questions should begin by emphasizing that adopting open borders need not affect national criminal systems of justice, or the authorities that support and defend them. Security concerns will remain with us, and local authorities will continue to enforce national (and state) laws and regulations. When criminal activities take place, law-enforcement authorities will respond. In short, free human mobility needn't undermine local legal sovereignty any more than the erosion that has taken place as a result of the free mobility of other factors, goods or services.

The easiest way to imagine how a world with open borders might address international criminality is to think about the way in which legal jurisdictions overlap in today's federal states. There are no border controls between US states aimed at capturing criminals or monitoring criminal activities.[31] Actually, most Americans would probably protest vehemently if such controls were put into place. Worse, it seems like a terribly ineffective way of capturing criminals, who already have an incentive to avoid the law, and who – with limited resources – can easily penetrate otherwise porous state borders.

Instead, US federal authorities have developed important cross-jurisdictional authorities (such as the Federal Bureau of Investigation, the FBI), and sophisticated extradition agreements between states, to ensure that criminals in one jurisdiction are served justice – even if they escape to other jurisdictions. The ease of international transportation, communication and exchange has already increased the demand for greater international cooperation of security, intelligence and policing authorities. Indeed, a growing network of international agreements and institutions already exists, albeit in nascent form. A world without migration controls will simply facilitate its development.

Although it is probably unnecessary, it is possible to conceive of local residency registries – as are common in Europe – where local officials can maintain tally and control over arrivals to, and departures from, the community. Local communities could be free to decide for themselves what sorts of controls are necessary to monitor criminal activity. The point is to allow this type of control to vary at the local level, and to encourage an international system that does not handicap residents in their dealings with states. After all, systems of registration, censuses, identification cards, and so on can continue to exist in the future scenario we are considering.

Like the rising demand for better extradition and international policing cooperation, there is an already unmet demand for better international systems of registration and identification. As the world shrinks for criminals (as it does for businesspeople and tourists), internationally accepted systems of identification will be necessary. These systems are not needed to control movement across space, but to ensure that benefits and obligations are allocated justly, and that justice can be efficiently served across national borders. Free migration will only facilitate these improvements.

National security

The second issue concerns questions of national security. As we saw in the historical chapter (Chapter 3), many of the original constraints on international mobility were first introduced in the name of security and defence during times of war. While this may (or may not) have made sense at a time when states required conscripted soldiers to man their main lines of defence, these concerns are now clearly antiquated. At the time, individuals were forced to fight and protect the interests of their monarch, and migration controls were one effective way of dealing with the flight of unwilling soldiers. Contemporary systems of defence depend less on forced conscription, and more on technology and intelligence – both of which are facilitated by free migration.

Of course, it is possible to imagine situations where open borders might represent a threat to national security. Myron Weiner, for example, asks us to imagine how millions of hard-working Chinese might cross over an unprotected border to settle in Burma. Although Weiner acknowledges that this migration might bring economic prosperity to Burma, he worries that it would come at the expense of Burmese identity: 'the Burmese would no longer be able to control the central cultural symbols of their national life or to maintain political control over their own state.'[32] A similar scenario can be imagined in the Middle East, where millions of Palestinians might move into the state of Israel, and effectively capture the (enemy) state.

While these stories might sell well in Hollywood, they are hardly realistic scenarios. In particular, they ignore the motivation of migrants, and the national laws of existing states. After all, what would a 'Russian' state look like in the absence of border controls? Why would a Georgian want to move to a 'Russian' state, if he or she could live anywhere he or she wanted? If a migrant invasion were the conspiratorial plan of a rogue state, how would that state entice reluctant migrants to join in the campaign? And to what end? Finally, it is difficult to imagine a state that would allow any group of citizens (migrants or others) openly to wield weapons for the purpose of its overthrow. Even if the invasion was political in nature, we might assume that states would require a grace residency period, before new residents were allowed to participate in the political system. During that time, it would be difficult (maybe even impossible) to maintain a unified political voice among the 'invading' migrants.

There are lots of interesting and unexplored scenarios that can be considered in a future borderless world. While it is fun to entertain these thought-experiments, we should remember the realist's concerns about the need to distinguish between realistic and fanciful scenarios. In this light, it seems that the anticipated security threats of realist critics are more fanciful than is the proposal for open borders.

Terrorism

On 11 September 2001, New York's World Trade Center and the US Pentagon were attacked by terrorists. This attack introduced a new series of security concerns, of a kind that didn't seem very pressing just a decade ago. In particular, the attack prompts the question, 'Wouldn't a world without borders make it even easier to realize this type of terrorist activity?'

To be honest, we don't know the answer to this question. How could we? On the surface, if we assume nothing else but the borders change, it would certainly be easier for terrorists to move surreptitiously from state to state. Having said this, it is important to note that the existing border controls were not very effective at repelling the terrorists in question. Indeed, most of the alleged terrorists entered the United States via legal channels, and existing border controls have not been effective at stopping other attempts at terrorist infiltration into the United States, or into other countries.[33]

It is problematic to begin by assuming that nothing will change in a world with free mobility. Much will change, including the calculations of individual terrorists, the power of individual nation-states (both hosting and target states), and the anger that separates the two. It is difficult to speculate about whether (and how) these changes will affect the nature of future terrorist activity. But there is no reason to expect that individual states will be less equipped (than now) to fight terrorism on their own territory.

In the final analysis, terrorist activity falls under the rubric of criminal activity; and, as suggested above, there is little reason to expect that increased human mobility will adversely affect a state's capacity to monitor and enforce its sovereign legislation.

Conclusion

To conclude this section, there are at least three responses to realist concerns. The first is to question their attempt to sideline moral issues altogether. Sometimes moral concerns outweigh more narrowly conceived, interest-based, arguments, and there are good grounds for such in the case for open borders. Yet even if we are unwilling to prioritize moral arguments, the interest-based argument for closed borders is far from clear-cut. We have seen how many of the world's greatest fears are based on rather suspect assumptions about the size and influence of potential migrant flows. Indeed, a majority of the world's residents may actually benefit – in both political and economic terms – by the increased opportunities that would characterize a world without borders. Nor is there any reason to suggest that a world without borders is utopian. There is more than enough historical evidence to suggest that a world with open borders for people is both possible and plausible.

Understood in these terms, some realists may come to recognize, even support, the historical, economic, political and moral arguments for free mobility. Others, undoubtedly, will remain sceptical and/or oppose greater immigration. After all, support for open-borders policies will require significant, and costly, political effort in order to convince sceptical host populations, and to accommodate the hostility and anger they generate among our compatriots. While these costs may be formidable, it would be a shame to give up on the battle before it really starts. In the words of Veit Bader, 'The fact that we cannot know whether better institutions and policies are really impossible or whether our alternatives would worsen things does not justify closing the world more than necessary.'[34]

9

Conclusion and Policy Responses

Male and female are the distinctions of nature, good and bad
the distinctions of heaven; but how a race of men came into
the world so exalted above the rest, and distinguished like
some new species, is worth inquiring into, and whether they
are the means of happiness or of misery to mankind.

Thomas Paine[1]

In a Lombard manumission ceremony of the ninth century, the
slave about to be freed was taken by his owner to a crossroads.
There he was released with the declaration that he now had
'license and power to walk from the crossroads and live where
he may wish.'[2] While the world may be formally freed from the
onus of slavery, today's downtrodden do not enjoy access to an
open crossroad, nor a life where they may wish.

Indeed, the world's poorest individuals face few opportunities
with which they can escape from their impoverished birthright.
The promise of economic liberalization – trade, foreign investment
and domestic economic growth – lies far beyond the grasp of a
poor farmer in Nepal, Laos, Rwanda, or elsewhere. For him the
dream of a responsible, limited democracy (with a vote for his
daughter) is equally distant. The poor can only wait – and hope

– for the best: *maybe* the future will bring a better government; *maybe* the future will bring foreign investment and economic growth; *maybe* the future will bring peace and prosperity. *Maybe.* These opportunities are not within reach for the poor; they are not theirs for the taking. If these opportunities arrive, they will be delivered from afar.

On the other side of the world, denizens of the developed world find themselves – to draw from George Borjas's gripping title – locked behind *Heaven's Door*. By the simple fate of birth, these lucky few benefit from citizenship in countries that have enjoyed economic and political prosperity. In the United States, rather ironically, this prosperity was itself built with the labour and sweat of immigrants and slaves. Yet there, of all places, immigration remains an 'unwelcome debate'.[3]

When the world was filled with distant and unknown places, it was possible to reconcile these differences with a clear conscience. Somehow the poverty of an Afghan farmer didn't need to appear on the developed world's political radar screen; injustices at home demanded more immediate attention. But as the world shrinks for both rich and poor, free and not, the distances that remain become all the more noticeable and difficult to reconcile.

Today's migration debate assumes that territorially confined citizenship is a natural and moral state of affairs. By debating the economic consequences of a marginal change in migration levels, we effectively close off discussion to a host of more pressing (and more difficult) questions. In particular, today's migration debate assumes that political motivation is mostly about securing narrowly defined interests: we oppose greater international migration because it is seen to threaten our political and economic well-being. But interests alone do not animate us; morality and prejudice, though often surreptitiously, play an important role in our motivation. At an earlier time, this sort of narrow dialogue may have sufficed. But the world has changed, and is changing, in ways that make it increasingly difficult to ignore the sort of issues that are sidelined by today's narrow debate.

Moral questions, for example, could always be read as a sub-text (albeit an almost invisible one) to the larger, more public, debates about migration. At times, these questions – because of the eloquence or force of a given critic – may have surfaced in the political discussion, but usually for only brief and fleeting moments. Moral questions, being what they are, are difficult to resolve – they circle around too many disparate rhetorical axes. As long as the potential moral gains were seen to be of limited value, the public could avoid these issues without scarring its own political conscience.

However, the sundry forces of globalization push these moral questions with force onto the screen; the subtexts are increasingly difficult to overlook. When global inequalities remained within reason, or (more importantly) invisible, then the moral subtexts could be ignored. But as these inequalities continue to grow, and residents of both rich and poor countries are increasingly aware of them, these moral questions take centre stage.

There is a burgeoning research on the relationship between globalization and economic inequality: political economists now debate how best to measure inequality, and whether globalization has actually reversed the long-term trend of growing inequalities. In time, we may find that globalization is shrinking some indicators of inequality, if only marginally so. But the larger picture, the one produced daily on television screens around the world, remains: there are phenomenal social, political and economic differences that separate residents of the developed and the developing worlds, and we are all increasingly aware of them. As long as these pictures remain on the public screen, moral questions will not be constrained as subtexts to a narrow, interest-based, debate.

Neither are the developed world's interests clearly in favour of restricted borders (or restricted debate). As we extend the discussion, and find new ways to measure, conceive and operationalize our own interests, we find that these may even coincide with the interests of those on the other side of the globe. In patterns that neatly shadow earlier debates about extending the democratic franchise, our conception of interests is changing in ways that are not sufficiently articulated by the current, narrow, form of debate. In its most blunt formulation, residents of the developed world need to ask themselves, 'Are your interests served by a world where political and economic instability can come to threaten your very existence?'

Finally, changing demographic distributions will force us to reconsider some of these self-imposed constraints, on both migration and the narrow parameters of the migration debate. For a number of reasons, the developed world is ageing rapidly. Foremost in the minds of politicians in the developed world is how to maintain current levels of wealth, given an ageing population: fewer and fewer workers will have to pay for the social security needs of a growing retired population. At the same time, the developing world is brimming with an enormous and mostly untapped supply of younger workers willing to migrate. These two demographic developments can come to complement each other in a world without borders. Immigration is the simplest solution to this problem – but it is a solution that requires us to broaden the way in which we think about and discuss questions of citizenship, identity and migration.

All of these developments – old, new and future – argue for a new debate about open borders. As this vision is new, and its focus is on the distant future, it is bound to contain faults, oversights, and even some exaggeration. The intent of this book has been to collect and present several open-border arguments, with an eye towards encouraging and provoking further discussion.

Policy Responses

The main lesson to be derived from this examination is that the world can expect to reap enormous potential gains by embracing greater freedom of mobility for its residents. We have also learned that several obstacles stand in the way of us harvesting these gains. If the world is ever to reap these significant gains, states will need to embrace policies that ease public concerns, address affected interests, and encourage human freedom.

In the developed world we have seen how public opinion is strongly opposed to increasing immigration, and that there are significant concerns in these populations about the economic, cultural and security effects of immigration. We have also seen that public opinion is not as monolithically opposed to immigration as is often assumed, and that these attitudes are somewhat removed from calculations of individual interest. In particular, we can assume that important and influential interests stand to gain from more international migration, where relatively few people, diffusely scattered in the body politic, are negatively affected by it. Finally, we have seen how trade unions are being forced to rethink radically their opposition to immigration in light of the inability of nation-based regulatory and policy regimes to deliver the goods. Together, these public impressions of the negative costs of international migration constitute the first barrier to free mobility.

One explanation for this discrepancy between interests, influence, opinion and policy is the complicated and controversial nature of the problem at hand. It is entirely conceivable that individual citizens may be unaware of, or uncertain about, how their own interests are affected by migration. Indeed, it seems reasonable to assume that public perceptions on issues related to human mobility are often mistaken and based on inadequate information. As a consequence, resistance to migration may not be as broad, or as deep-seated, as public rhetoric would lead us to believe. The actual interests that are negatively affected by immigration may be so small and so isolated (relative to the overall gains reaped by the community at large) that public support for increased immigration could be expanded with a few targeted policies and educational campaigns.

We can also expect to find that the second barrier to free mobility, perceptions of the omnipotent nation-state, will – on their own – shrink under the pressure of globalization (in its many sundry forms). Public expectations and attitudes about the role of the state will continue to evolve as globalization challenges its exclusionary powers, while influential groups (such as organized labour) find it necessary to defect from nationalist solutions in order better to defend the interests of their members.

The third barrier to free mobility, conventional wisdom, may also become a casualty of a more open dialogue about the history of international migration, the nature of culture, the nature of these diffuse interests, and how they are affected by increased human mobility. In short, the first and third barriers to free mobility might be diminished by a targeted educational campaign that: (1) informs residents about the enormous individual and moral gains that can be reaped from free migration; (2) educates residents about the relatively small impact of migration (across disparate policy areas); and (3) uncovers the enigmatic gap that separates public attitudes, policy and interests. With time, the second barrier will likely erode on its own, as people come to realize that the legitimacy of sovereign states is no longer tied to their ability to isolate themselves from the world beyond.

Unfortunately, these realizations – in themselves – are not enough. Individual perceptions will continue to linger and real interests are indeed threatened by increased migration. Proponents of free migration must be prepared to address these challenges head-on, or risk jeopardizing the political, economic and moral gains that free mobility promises for both rich and poor. While many of these concerns may be irrational and unwarranted, they are real enough to represent a significant constraint on any attempt to liberalize human mobility. To address these concerns, supporters of free mobility can encourage their states to consider the following sorts of policies.

Public education

Many of the developed world's concerns about immigration can be addressed by educational policies that encourage and facilitate the assimilation and integration of new immigrants. For example, immigrants could be encouraged to pass fluency tests in the host-country language(s), or attend basic civic education classes, before being granted access to nation-based citizenship and/or welfare rights. Similarly, communities should continue to emphasize their strong commitments to prosecute illegal activities: nobody should be allowed to stand beyond the law. By employing more of these sorts of education and assimilation policies, developed states can assuage citizen fears about security threats and/or cultural inundation. Indeed, the effects of a well-organized and committed information campaign are clearly seen in the way in which the developed world's political and economic elite have managed to convince a sceptical public about the benefits of free trade.

Developing states tend to lack the resources to commit to wide-ranging information campaigns. Luckily, the resistance to international migration tends to be weaker there. In light of this, it may be sufficient to encourage political and economic elites in these countries to recognize the benefits accrued by developing countries from greater migration. As many of these gains may come at the expense of these very elites, it is important that these sorts of information campaigns receive broad international support.

Rethinking citizen rights and obligations

An alternative, but more radical, approach is for states to rethink the way in which they distribute rights and obligations. Arguably, states will be forced to do this, irrespective of any formal changes in the international migration regime, as existing rights are being undermined by other facets of globalization and by growing levels of illegal immigration. Consequently, states need to consider new ways to distribute the rights and duties that are traditionally tied to nationalist conceptions of sovereignty. These obligations and rights are wide-ranging and include taxation, military service, and other citizenship obligations, on the one hand, and the dispersion of unemployment, social security, health-care benefits, and so on, on the other. There is little reason why these sorts of rights and duties cannot be granted on the basis of residence, rather than by birth or naturalization.

Nevertheless, states tend to change slowly, and only when great effort is exerted from below (or abroad). Embracing a broader conception of citizenship, rights and obligations will allow immigrants to participate more fully in the local community. At the same time, these changes will keep immigrants out of national elections and public office until they are fully assimilated. Indeed, in many European states we have begun to see an extension of local (but not national) voting rights on the basis of residence and participation, not naturalization. In Norway, for example, immigrants and non-citizens are allowed to vote in local elections (but not in Norway's national elections). This sort of solution seems to satisfy immigrant populations, as many are not particularly interested in naturalization, even after a lengthy period of residence. Most immigrants long to return home; they see their stay abroad as a temporary state of affairs.

Grace periods

It is also conceivable that host countries could allow immigrants the right to work, but deny them citizenship and welfare benefits (at least for a certain period of time, while the immigrants assimilate to the local political culture). This convention is already used by many states in the United States and the European Union when dealing with (internal) migration, across their respective unions. By imposing a temporal buffer before rights are extended to immigrants, states could assuage citizen fears that workers are migrating to exploit generous welfare regimes.

These sorts of policies can be implemented in a way that will soothe concerns among the general population in the developed world. In this way, developed-world residents can be confident that immigration, by itself, will not threaten their cultural or civic identities, or the intricate national welfare systems that they have fought so diligently to secure. On the other hand, these residents need to be reminded that sovereign institutions such as these are already being eroded by existing global commitments. Communities need to rethink their traditional reliance on national concepts of citizenship, rights and obligations – independent of any fundamental change in the world's migration regime.

Adjustment policies

With respect to more narrowly defined economic interests, hosting states could provide assistance to those domestic workers whose jobs may be threatened by increased immigration. Indeed, states already employ a plethora of policies to help workers adjust to the threat of changes imposed by free trade. These sorts of adjustment policies were first developed in small open economies: countries that needed to adjust rapidly to changes in the international economy. It is in these countries that we find the most social-democratic regimes taking root, and students of social democracy realize that many tools of national economic management were developed as a response to changes in world markets.[4]

Today's most left-leaning states are those that have learned to adjust rapidly to open and free markets, protecting their denizens from shifts in world demand that are beyond their control. Flexible adjustment policies provide support to workers who benefit from moving to new jobs; education and training to allow workers to retool and exploit new market niches; and a safety net to catch workers who should fall when jumping from one career to the next.

While this sort of left-leaning embrace of markets tends to be found in the smaller developed countries, large countries – like the United States – are no longer immune to its logic. Before the most recent bout of globalization, these states enjoyed the luxury of being relatively isolated from world markets (this was a function of the size of their own home markets). Consequently, large states have not been forced to develop a wider array of adjustment mechanisms (unlike smaller, more open, states). Nevertheless, it was American president John F. Kennedy who introduced a 'Trade Adjustment Assistance' programme to help generate support for free trade among labour groups in the United States. A similar programme might be embraced by a future occupant of the White House, helping workers adjust quickly to the changing labour market conditions that result from increased migration flows.

Sending-state policies

Thus far the policy discussion has been mostly confined to developed states. This is because most resistance to free migration, and its most virulent strains, resides in the developed world. In addition, the developing world often lacks the resources to fund such education programmes. Still, it is possible to conceive of, and promote, policies that can soothe public concerns in the developing world – for example, concerns about brain drain and emigrant mistreatment abroad.

With respect to the brain drain, states have already developed many different ways to encourage émigré workers to return home. These responses might be embraced by an even larger number of sending states. For example, governments have adopted tax instruments that can exploit the potential source of revenue found in the large numbers of citizens living aboard. These taxes range in form from one-time exit taxes to bilateral tax arrangements that require the receiving nation to tax immigrants and remunerate the sending country.

In addition, it is possible to employ more targeted policies that aim to satisfy local demand for professional services. These policies can be of three types: those that (1) encourage domestic professionals to stay; (2) train local substitutes faster than the rate of emigration; and/or (3) exploit international labour markets to import professionals. While all three policy types will grow in importance as human mobility increases in the world, the third (immigration) policy will become especially important in a world with fewer barriers to free mobility. For this reason, we might consider that policy's three main variants.

First, it has become increasingly common for developing states to import professionals from abroad to fill domestic needs. In this way, developing states use the international market to satisfy a demand they are unable to fill on their own. A typical example of this trend is the willingness of many countries to import Cuban doctors to satisfy local needs. This policy variant raises a number of issues related to certification and training requirements, but these tend to be of a more technical (less political) nature.

Second, many developing states are working to encourage the return of expatriated talents. For example, the Republic of Korea encourages the return of skilled emigrants by using intensive recruiting programmes that search out older professionals and scholars, offering them better working conditions and salaries (i.e. that are competitive with overseas incomes), and helping with housing and children's schooling needs. Indeed, the relative success of South Korea in fostering return has been matched in other places, as diverse as China and Ireland. These successes, in turn, have facilitated an opening of their sundry economies and policies to foster domestic investments in innovation as well as research and development.

Third, states are beginning to develop their own networks for émigré populations abroad. 'Scientific diaspora' and 'immigrant entrepreneur' networks can help countries capture benefits and know-how from their emigrant populations abroad. For example, the South African Network of Skills Abroad (SANSA) website invites professional South Africans to promote joint research and training assignments at home. In Thailand, the Reverse Brain Drain (RPD) project aims to use Thai professionals living overseas to help in the country's development (especially in the fields of science and technology).[5] Indian professionals in the USA have been the primary impetus behind knowledge and capital flows to India, while the Indian government has contributed to these private networks by providing legislative and tax benefits that encourage remittances and investments from Indians abroad.

In a world characterized by freer human mobility, poor states will be able to exploit these opportunities in a way that will better satisfy their demand for specialized services and skills at home. Surely this is a better way to meet a country's diverse development needs, rather than forcing people to stay where they don't want to be.

Finally, we should recall that residents of the developing world are rightly concerned that their emigrants face a constant threat of mistreatment and exploitation by callous and largely unregulated labour recruiters. This concern can be addressed by policies that help to protect immigrants as they search for employment and residence abroad. The experience of Sri Lanka is exemplary in this regard; it has adopted a range of policies and institutions that encourage and actively support its labour emigrants.[6] The successful implementation of these policies has, in turn, encouraged a rapid growth in the number of migrants, with a significant increase in international remittances as the nation's reward. Other developing states might follow Sri Lanka's lead in protecting and supporting their expatriate populations abroad as they search (and obtain) work, while maintaining many important links to the home country.

To conclude, it is possible to conceive of a number of policies that can facilitate international exchange, minimize the injustice and hardships that accompany today's international migration regime, and convince sceptical populations in both the developed and the developing worlds of the potential for free mobility. By levelling these barriers to free mobility, and the costs associated with today's (mostly unregulated) migration flows, we can expand the number of opportunities for all of us.

Broadening the Debate

It is now possible to see how the world is approaching an important crossroads. Like freed slaves from the nineteenth century, inhabitants of the world have to choose where they would like to live their future life: in a world with or without borders. Unfortunately, we are in desperate need of more information about the paths that are open to us, and where they might lead.

The first step down the path to free mobility requires that we expand today's migration debate to include broader conceptions of interest. Contrary to the public's perception, there are reasonable economic arguments both for and against closed borders. As the latter arguments are less familiar (at least to the general public), this book has traced the work of several prominent economists to show how it is possible to argue that our (base economic) interests may be best satisfied by encouraging free migration. While there is much dissent and disagreement (as we might expect among economists), it is possible to find significant economic grounds for embracing free mobility, regardless of whether you reside in the developed or the developing world.

In stark contrast to the extensive economic literature, little has been written on the political consequences of open borders. To fill the void, this book has offered a simple framework to suggest that we can expect political voice to increase along with the possibility (threat) of exit. Better still, this threat of exit works for residents of both the developed and the developing worlds. Citizens of exploitative states can simply leave; citizens of more responsive states will have a better means for voicing their discontent and support. Contrary to public fears, liberalizing international barriers to free mobility can amplify resident voices in democratic systems that are increasingly unresponsive to the vote as voice.

As we have seen in the chapters above, both political and economic types of interest-based arguments hinge critically on several important parameters. In particular, the length of the time horizon, the level of analysis, and the potential size of the immigrant flow will all significantly influence our conclusions. Most of these parameters have hardly been examined: they themselves are a result of the restricted nature of today's migration debate.

The first parameter, the length of the time horizon, is allowed to vary in most other analyses, and there is no reason why this parameter should be a hindrance to political debates about (or future) research on international migration. As is common in economic and political analyses, we can expect analysts to evaluate the disparate consequences of a policy over both the short and (with decreasing levels of confidence) the long run. We can also expect that most political rhetoric will be confined to the shortest horizon. What is important is that we continue to recognize that both horizons are legitimate, and that the lessons of analyses conducted at one time horizon may conflict with the lessons from another.

The second parameter requires more attention. The preceding chapter briefly addressed the problem of estimating the potential size of the migration flow in a world without borders. These estimates suggest that the number of potential migrants is perhaps not as large (or as threatening) as contemporary political rhetoric would suggest. Of course, such estimates are very rough, and we should not rely on them uncritically: more work needs to be done on this important parameter. Without more refined estimates, we can never be certain about the potential consequences, both political and economic, of a world without borders.

The last parameter, concerning the disparate levels of analysis, has always interested moral philosophers. Already in 1913, Henry Pratt Fairchild had outlined four moral standpoints from which to consider the consequences of immigration: the host country, the sending country, the immigrants themselves, and humanity in general.[7] The moral debates about immigration and citizenship are rich with references to the various, and conflicting, moral interests of citizens and states, rich and poor. Unfortunately, these debates seldom break out of the narrow halls of academe. A cynic might argue that this is not surprising: the moral argument for free borders is embarrassing for those who frame the larger migration debate. But the moral question, in the very way that it needs to be articulated, reminds us of the challenges (the potential) that are often ignored by interest-based arguments.

In particular, moral philosophers remind us that we need to be more explicit about whose interests we should consider. Like variation in the other parameters of discussion, the choice of a particular level of analysis will affect our conclusion. The narrow, mainstream, debate on the effects of international migration assumes that it is appropriate to consider only the interests of the enfranchised. This is not peculiar: we continue to think about citizenship and sovereignty in terms of mutually exclusive territories, even as globalization undermines these distinctions. But is it appropriate to ignore the interests of the disenfranchised on an issue that transcends the borders of citizenship?

In this light we might return to an important historical parallel: the extension of the democratic franchise. The question, at the time, was whether or not all men (then women, then blacks or indigenous populations, then youths) should be allowed full membership in the political community. For those already en-franchised (white, male, property owners) it was clearly against their immediate (narrow) interests to extend the franchise to include others. Every extension of the franchise was a real limit to their political power.

What is remarkable is that contemporaries of these sundry democratic revolutions managed to frame the political discussion in such a way as to show that it was in everybody's interest to extend the franchise. Those outside the borders of political voice (workers, women, blacks, youths) were successful because they managed to convince the enfranchised minority that equality and desegregation were possible and desirable for the general welfare of the community. When the enfranchised were asked to decide on the future of democracy, they looked beyond their own narrow interests – they calculated at a higher level of aggregation, and considered the interests of the larger community. While there was much resistance at the time, it is probably safe to say that there are few among us today who would wish to return to this earlier arrangement: it is today common (and legitimate) to argue that universal suffrage is in everyone's interest.

The same sort of calculations can be made with the issue of

migration. While some of today's enfranchised may still cling to the idea that their own, selfish, interests are threatened by opening the world's borders, it is possible for others to conceive of their interests in terms of a larger community. There can be little doubt that a world without borders would offer a real increase in opportunities for the vast majority of the world's residents, people who do not today have a formal voice in the question of admission. But a world without borders may bring a shift in identity that will allow us to think of interests in a new, larger, way. By limiting any discussion of interests to those who are already enfranchised, we simply ignore the more difficult moral questions.

While each of us has our own analytical, political and ideological convictions, it is possible to make an argument for free mobility at any number of levels, over a variety of time horizons, and with varying estimates of potential migrant flows. For many of us, the arguments of morality and interest converge to inform a position that embraces a world without borders. From this position, it would appear as though its opposition is informed mostly by ignorance and prejudice. In light of the argument above, the cost of this ignorance and prejudice can represent a significant burden for the world's population.

Readers with different convictions, of course, may arrive at different conclusions. By focusing on a shorter time horizon, or by assuming larger migration flows, or by discounting the interests of the disenfranchised (for example), we can find reasonable grounds for dissent and disagreement. This is, in a sense, the whole point of widening the nature of the current discourse. By allowing these important parameters to vary, we can get a more accurate mapping of the community's interests. Whatever our individual biases, it is possible to conclude that the issue of migration (and any country's 'best interest') is not at all served by the narrow format of today's migration debate.

Notes

Preface

1. The opening paragraph of Thomas Paine's *Common Sense and the Crisis*, Garden City, NY: Anchor Books, 1973), p. 11.

Chaper 1

1. Quoted by Aristide Zolberg, 'Keeping Them Out: Ethical Dilemmas of Immigration Policy', in Robert J. Meyers (ed.), *International Ethics in the Nuclear Age* (Lanham, MD: University Press of America, 1987), p. 293.
2. The vignette of the Mexican women who died in the desert is from the Religious Task Force on Central America and Mexico, www.rtfcam.org/border/deaths061604.pdf, accessed 14 November 2004.
3. 'Out with the New', *The Economist*, 11 December 2004, pp. 51–2. The YouGov poll questioned 1,644 electors throughout Britain (online) on 7 and 8 December 2004.
4. Tom Steinberg, 'Reforming British Immigration Policy', *IEA Working Paper no. 2*, Institute of Economic Affairs, London, October 2000, p.121.
5. Jean-Pierre Garson, 'Zero Immigration Is Pure Fancy', *OECD Observer* (May 2001), online at www.oecdobserver.org/news/print-page.php/aid/436/_Zero_immigration_is_pure_fancy_.html, accessed

14 December 2004.

6. Quoted in Irwin M. Stelzer, 'Immigration in the New Economy', *The Public Interest*, Fall 2000, p. 4; available at www.thepublicinterest. com/archives/2000fall/article1.html, accessed 11 January 2005.

7. See, for example, James F. Hollifield, *Immigrants, Markets and States* (Cambridge, MA: Harvard University Press, 1992); and David Jacobsen, *Rights across Borders: Immigration and the Decline of Citizenship* (Baltimore, MD: Johns Hopkins University Press, 1996).

8. This notion of imagined communities comes from Benedict Anderson's, *Imagined Communities: Reflections on the Origin and Spread of Nationalism*, rev. edn (London: Verso, 1991).

9. Nikita Khrushchev, *Khrushchev Remembers*, trans. and ed. Strobe Talbott (Boston: Little, Brown, 1970), pp. 522, 525.

10. 'President Bush Proposes New Temporary Worker Program', remarks by the US president on immigration policy, The East Room, 7 January 2004; available at www.whitehouse.gov/news/releases/2004/01/20040107-3.html, accessed 19 January 2005.

11. This reference is to Francis Fukuyama's influential book and article: 'The End of History?', *The National Interest* 16 (Summer 1989): 3–18; *The End of History and the Last Man* (New York: Free Press, 1992).

12. Since 1973, the editorial board of the *Wall Street Journal* has frequently supported free migration. See, for example, 'Free Markets except When It Comes to People' (1 June 1983), and 'In Praise of Huddled Masses' (3 July 1984).

13. 'Liberal', here, refers to the traditional, historical and philosophical sense of the term – not the way the term is used in contemporary American political parlance. It is this meaning that is assigned to the word throughout the remainder of the book.

14. 'The Rekindled Flame', *Wall Street Journal*, 3 July 1986, p. A10. The original proposal for a constitutional amendment was made in a 3 July editorial two years earlier, entitled 'In Praise of Huddled Masses'.

Chapter 2

1. http://en.thinkexist.com/quotation/globalization-as_defined_by_rich_people_like_us/212089.html>, accessed 12 January 2005.

2. There is surprisingly little written on international economic inequality, but much on world poverty. Good overviews of this literature are provided in the World Bank's *World Development Report*

2000/1: Attacking Poverty (Washington DC: World Bank, 2000); the
UNDP's *Human Development Report* (New York: UNDP/Oxford
University Press, various years); and the annual UNCTAD *Least
Developed Countries Report* (Geneva: UNCTAD, various years). Most
of these documents (or at least important excerpts from them) are
now available on the Internet. Some examples of the most significant
literature on international economic inequality includes: Roberto
Patricio Korzeniewicz and Timothy Patrick Moran, 'World-Economic
Trends in Distribution of Income', *American Journal of Sociology*, vol.
102, no. 4 (January 1997), pp. 1000–1039; Glenn Firebaugh, 'Empir-
ics of World Income Inequality', *American Journal of Sociology*, vol.
104, no. 6 (May 1999), pp. 1597–1630; Branko Milanovic, 'True
World Income Distribution, 1988 and 1993: First Calculations, Based
on Household Surveys Alone', *World Bank Working Paper no. 2244*
(November 1999); Arne Melchior, Kjetil Telle and Henrik Wiig,
'Globalisation and Inequality: World Income Distribution and Living
Standards, 1960–1998', Royal Norwegian Ministry of Foreign Affairs,
Studies on Foreign Policy Issues Report 6B (Oslo, October 2000);
Brian Goesling, 'Changing Income Inequalities within and between
Nations: New Evidence', *American Sociological Review*, vol. 66, no. 5
(October 2001), pp. 745–61; and X. Sala-i-Martin, 'The Disturbing
"Rise" of Global Income Inequality', NBER Working Paper Series,
no. 8904 (2002). For a discussion of the moral implications, see
Thomas Pogge, *World Poverty and Human Rights* (Cambridge: Polity
Press, 2002). Recently, *The Economist* magazine has begun to address
this issue. See, for example, their Special Report 'Global Economic
Inequality' (13 March 2004), and its supporting papers, at www.
economist.com/inequalitypapers, accessed 20 December 2004.

3. This according to a recent survey by Cap Gemini Ernst & Young,
   the professional services firm. See John Willman, 'Rich Survive
   Market Turmoil to Increase Wealth by 6%', *Financial Times*, 15 May
   2001, p. 16.

4. UNDP, *Human Development Report, 1999: Globalization with a Human
   Face* (Oxford: Oxford University Press, 1999), p. 3.

5. World Bank, *World Development Report 2000/2001: Attacking Poverty*
   (Washington DC: World Bank 2000), p. 3.

6. Ibid., p. 51.

7. UNCTAD, 'Overview', *The Least Developed Countries 1999 Report*
   (Geneva: UNCTAD, 1999), p. 17.

8. Lant Pritchett, 'Divergence, Big Time', *Journal of Economic Perspectives*,
   vol. 11, no. 3 (1997), pp. 3–17. The figures in this paragraph come

from p. 11, Table 2.

9. Dani Rodrik, *Has Globalization Gone Too Far?* (Washington DC: Institute for International Economics, 1997), p. 2.

10. For the American condition, see F. Levy and Richard J. Nurname, 'US Earnings Levels and Earnings Inequality: A Review of Recent Trends and Proposed Explanations', *Journal of Economic Literature* 30 (September 1992), pp. 1333–81. For Europe, see several contributions in Jonathan Michie and John Grieve Smith (eds), *Unemployment in Europe* (London: Academic Press, 1994). The referenced OECD report is Michael F. Förester and Michele Pellizzari, 'Trends and Driving Factors in Income Distribution and Poverty in the OECD Area', Labour Market and Social Policy, OECD Occasional Papers no. 42 (August 2000).

11. United Nations Conference on Trade and Development. UNCTAD was set up to counter the developed world biases inherent to the (then) GATT negotiations.

12. John Williams, *Latin American Adjustment: How Much Has Happened?* (Washington, DC: Institute for International Economics, 1990), ch. 2. A short summary is found in John Williams, 'In Search of a Manual for Technopols', in John Williams (ed.), *The Political Economy of Policy Reform* (Washington, DC: Institute for International Economics, 1994), pp. 9–28.

13. A recent UNCTAD Report has emphasized this by arguing '*the current diagnosis for change which is shaping the new approach to international cooperation is flawed in several crucial respects*' (stress in the original). See UNCTAD, 'Overview', *The Least Developed Countries 2000 Report*, p. 4. See also OECD, *Shaping the 21st Century: The Contribution of Development Cooperation* (Paris: OECD, May 1996).

14. The quotation in the previous paragraph comes from the United Nations Millennium Declaration (September 2000). See www.developmentgoals.org/, accessed 21 December 2004. The Global Monitoring Report is produced jointly by the IMF and the World Bank, in collaboration with other international partners. The first (2004) report is available online at: http://web.worldbank.org/wbsite/external/topics/globalmonitoringext/0,,pagePK:64022007~theSitePK:278515,00.html, accessed 21 December 2004.

15. 'Free' is a descriptive category used by Freedom House; it includes both political and civil rights. For a full list, see Freedom House, 'Comparative Measures of Freedom', www.freedomhouse.org/research/freeworld/2000/table1.htm, accessed 19 January 2005. The number of LDCs comes from UNCTAD, *The Least Developed*

Countries 2000 Report. The nine free countries were Benin, Cape Verde, Kiribati, Mali, Samoa, São Tomé and Príncipe, Solomon Islands, Tuvalu and Vanuatu.

16. For those interested in reading more about the spread of democracy internationally, see Freedom House's website www.freedomhouse.org/. In addition, see Samuel P. Huntington, *The Third Wave: Democratization in the Late Twentieth Century* (Norman and London: University of Oklahoma Press, 1991), and Francis Fukuyama, *The End of History and the Last Man* (New York: Free Press, 1992), which are now standard references in the literature.

17. Freedom House, 'Democracy's Century', www.freedomhouse.org/reports/century.html, accessed 8 January 2005.

18. Ibid.

19. Fareed Zakaria, 'The Rise of Illiberal Democracy', *Foreign Affairs*, vol. 76, no. 2 (November/December 1997), pp. 22–43.

20. Paul Collier, 'Economic Causes of Civil Conflict and their Implications for Policy', Development Research Group, World Bank, 15 June 2000, p. 1.

21. Susan J. Pharr and Robert D. Putnam, *Disaffected Democracies* (Princeton: Princeton University Press, 2000).

22. Ibid., pp. 9–11.

23. Roberta Cohen and Francis M. Deng, *Masses in Flight: The Global Crisis of Internal Displacement* (Washington DC: Brookings Institution, 1998), p. 3.

24. There is a vast literature on migration flows, most of it descriptive. For gripping journalistic accounts of illegal migration, see John Annerion's *Dead in Their Tracks* (New York: Four Walls Eight Windows, 1999) on the US–Mexican border, and Jeremy Harding's *The Uninvited: Refugees at the Rich Man's Gate* (London: Profile Books, 2000) on flows into Europe. For an introduction to the growing IDP dilemma, see Cohen and Deng's *Masses in Flight* and the Norwegian Refugee Council report edited by Janie Hampton, *Internally Displaced People: A Global Survey* (London: Earthscan, 1998). Also, the UNHCR has published an excellent historical overview of humanitarian action: *The State of the World's Refugees 2000: Fifty Years of Humanitarian Action* (New York: Oxford University Press, 2000). Finally, international migration statistics can be found in several annual reports, including the UN's *State of the World's Population*, the IOM's *World Migration Report* and the OECD's *Trends in International Migration*. A useful account of the various (and conflicting) immigration numbers in the American context is provided in Julian

L. Simon, *The Economic Consequences of Immigration* (Oxford: Basil Blackwell, 1989).

25. UNHCR, *The State of the World's Refugees 2000*, p. 280.

26. During the past decade, IDPs have received much more attention, with an increasing number of international conferences and studies dedicated to the issue. In addition to the UNHCR, the Brookings Institution, the Lawyers' Committee for Human Rights, the Refugee Policy Group, the US Committee for Refugees, the IOM, the UNDP, UNICEF, and the Norwegian Refugee Council, have all started programmes to assist them.

27. Cohen and Deng, *Masses in Flight*, p. 31.

28. Parties to the 1951 UN Refugee Convention (or its 1967 Protocol) are obliged not to return refugees to a country where they are likely to face persecution.

29. Figures in this paragraph are from UNHCR, *The State of the World's Refugees 2000*, Annexes 3 and 7.

30. ILO, IOM and UNHCR, *Migrants and International Cooperation: A Joint Contribution to the International Conference on Population and Development – ICPD 1994* (Geneva: ILO, IOM and UNHCR, 1994).

31. UN Population Division, *The World at 6 Billion*, UN: ESA/P/WP.154, 12 October 1999, Table 29. (In this table, the USA is followed by Russia, Saudi Arabia, India and Canada, with the last increasing its net population by 3.3 million over the same period.)

32. Jonathan Coppel, Jean-Christophe Dumont and Ignazio Visco, 'Trends in Immigration and Economic Consequences', OECD Economics Department Working Papers no. 284 (ECO/WKP 2001) 10 (1 February 2001), p. 9. See also Georges Tapinos and Daniel Delaunay, 'Can One Really Talk of the Globalisation of Migration Flows?', in OECD (ed.), *Globalisation, Migration and Development* (Paris: OECD, 2000), pp. 35–58.

33. These figures come from Irwin M. Stelzer, 'Immigration Policy for an Age of Mass Movement', *Policy*, Summer 2001–2002. Stelzer supports his figure with reference to an article from *The Economist* (10 February 2001). In contrast, in 1997 the US authorities estimated that between 700,000 and 2 million women and children were being trafficked each year, and in 2001 the European Commission estimated that about 120,000 women and children were being trafficked into Western Europe each year. These figures would suggest a much lower global figure. See Frank Laczko, 'Human Trafficking: The Need for Better Data', Migration Information Service, 1 November 2002; available at www.migrationinformation.org/Feature/display.cfm?ID=66,

accessed 15 January 2005. In addition, the illegal immigrant flows tend to be much smaller. For example, the US INS estimated that about 500,000 migrants were entering the USA illegally per year (averaged over a ten-year period) – see the IMF's 'Executive Summary: Estimates of the Unauthorized Immigrant Population Residing in the United States: 1990 to 2000' (January 2003), available at http://uscis.gov/graphics/shared/aboutus/statistics/2000ExecSumm. pdf, accessed 15 January 2005.

34. Coppel et al., 'Trends in Immigration', p. 10; and Sharon Stanton Russell, *International Migration in North America, Europe, Central Asia, the Middle East and North Africa* (Geneva: Economic Commission for Europe, 1993).

35. In September 2004, the influential American magazine *Time* dramatically claimed that the USA could expect 3 million illegal immigrants in 2004. This is a dubious figure as it is based on an assumption that three illegal immigrants make it into the USA for every one caught by the US Border Patrol. The problem with using this estimate is that the base number (1 million) represents the number of arrests, not the number of people. As many of those caught are repeat offenders, 1 million arrests do not translate into 1 million different people.

36. The Religious Task Force on Central America and Mexico's homepage: www.rtfcam.org/take_action/water_bottle.htm, accessed 15 November 2004. An organization that tries to create a more just and humane border environment, Humane Borders, estimates that at least 221 border-crossers died in the Arizona desert in 2004. See www.humaneborders.org/index.htm.

37. Jean-Pierre Garson, 'Zero Immigration is Pure Fancy', *OECD Observer* (May 2001), Internet version, www.oecdobserver.org/news/printpage.php/aid/436/_Zero_immigration_is_pure_fancy_.html, accessed 14 December 2004.

38. Roger Cohen, 'Illegal Migration Rises Sharply in European Union', *New York Times*, 25 December 2000, p. A1.

39. UNITED for Intercultural Action, 'The Deadly Consequences of "Fortress Europe" – More than 4500 Deaths', Information leaflet no. 24; see www.united.non-profit.nl/pages/info24.htm#1.2, accessed 21 December 2004.

40. UN Office for the Coordination of Humanitarian Affairs, 'OCHA Senior Advisor on IDPs, Internal Displacement in the Sudan: A Review of UN Strategic Coordination', 28 September 1999.

Chapter 3

1. W. R. Böhning, *Studies in International Labour Migration* (New York: St. Martin's Press, 1984), pp. 12–13.
2. For a legalistic discussion of earlier concepts of nationality and citizenship, see Richard Plender, *International Migration Law*, 2nd rev. edn (Dordrecht: Martinus Nijhoff, 1988 [1972]), pp. 10ff.
3. Alan Dowty, *Closed Borders: The Contemporary Assault on Freedom of Movement* (New Haven: Yale University Press, 1987), p. 21.
4. Plender, *International Migration Law*, p. 62.
5. For a brief introduction to the sort of restrictions that were common in medieval Europe, see John Torpey, *The Invention of the Passport* (Cambridge: Cambridge University Press, 2000), pp. 17–20.
6. Cited in Plender, *International Migration Law*, p. 2.
7. F. de Vitoria, *De Indis et de Jure Belli Reflections*; H. Grotius, *De Jure Belli ac Pacis*; S. Pufendorf, *De Jure Naturæ et Gentium, Libri Octo*; C. Wolff, *Institutiones Juris Naturae et Gentium*; and E. De Vattel, *Le droit de gens*.
8. 'What matters is neither force nor wealth, but men.' Cited in Aristide Zolberg, 'International Migration Policies in a Changing World System', in W.H. McNeill and R.S. Adams (eds), *Human Migration: Patterns and Policies* (Bloomington, IN: Indiana University Press, 1978), p. 246.
9. R. Appleyard, *International Migration: Challenge for the Nineties* (Geneva: International Organization for Migration, 1991), p. 11. For a very thorough and thought-provoking review of forced labour migration, see Lydia Potts, *The World Labour Market: A History of Migration*, trans. Terry Bond (London: Zed Books, 1990).
10. There is an excellent literature on the history of migration to the Americas. First among them is the now classic work by Marcus Lee Hansen: *The Atlantic Migration 1607–1860*, edited with a foreword by Arthur M. Schlesinger (New York: Harper & Row, 1961 [1940]). Two other histories have had a significant impact on subsequent economic analyses of migration, and will be addressed in more detail in a later chapter; these are Dorothy Thomas, *Social and Economic Aspects of Swedish Population Movements: 1750–1933* (New York: Macmillan, 1941); and B. Thomas, *Migration and Economic Growth: A Study of Great Britain and the Atlantic Economy* (Cambridge: Cambridge University Press, 1954).
11. 'coming, staying and going were all on a par'; quoted in Robert E.

Goodin, 'If People Were Money...', in Brian Barry and Robert E. Goodin (eds), *Free Movement* (University Park, PA: Penn State University Press, 1992), p. 13.

12. See Plender, *International Migration Law*, pp. 64–7; and Torpey, *The Invention*, pp. 91–2.

13. Adam McKeown, 'Global Migration, 1846–1940', *Journal of World History*, vol. 15, no. 2 (2004); available at www.historycooperative.org/journals/jwh/15.2/mckeown.html, accessed 8 November 2004.

14. Timothy J. Hatton and Jeffrey Williamson, *The Age of Mass Migration: Causes and Economic Impact* (Oxford: Oxford University Press, 1998), p. 236.

15. Ibid., p. 7.

16. Plender, *International Migration Law,* p. 2.

17. Cited in Thomas, *International Migration and Economic Development*, p.9.

18. Frank George Franklin, *The Legislative History of Naturalization in the United States* (New York: Arno Press, 1969), p. 247.

19. The observer was Werner Bertelsmann, as quoted in Torpey, *The Invention*, p. 111.

20. J.M. Keynes, *The Economic Consequences of the Peace* (1919), Chapter 1; available at socserv2.socsci.mcmaster.ca/~econ/ugcm/3ll3/keynes/peace.htm, accessed 27 September 2004.

21. Torpey, *The Invention*, p. 124.

22. Claudena Skran, *Refugees in Inter-War Europe: The Emergence of a Regime* (Oxford, Clarendon Press, 1995), pp. 104–5.

23. Torpey, *The Invention*, p. 136.

24. This is another UN declaration, approved by the General Assembly. The citation is from Louis B. Sohn and Thomas Buergenthal (eds), *The Movement of Persons Across Borders* (Washington DC: American Society of International Law, 1992), p. 3.

25. For example, the UK allowed freer access to Commonwealth citizens (there were no significant controls placed on their immigration before 1962, and visas were not required before 1985); nationals of other Arab countries were allowed equal legal benefits as Libyan nationals after 1970; the German Democratic Republic allowed nationals from specific other socialist countries, without visas; and Israel permitted Jews of all nationalities to enter and settle in Israel, under the 'Law of the Return'.

Chapter 4

1. Chilton Williamson Jr., *The Immigration Mystique: America's False Conscience* (New York: Basic Books, 1996), p. xii.

2. An abbreviated form of this argument was initially published as 'Two (Short) Moral Arguments for Free Migration', in May Thorseth (ed.), *Anvendt etikk ved NTNU 2* (2003), pp. 25–30.

3. For a wonderful survey of contemporary critics to the modern democratic revolution, see Michael Levin, *The Spectre of Democracy* (London: Macmillan, 1992).

4. Edmund Burke, *Reflections on the Revolution in France* (London: Dent, 1964), p. 76; J.S. Mill, *Autobiography of John Stuart Mill* (New York: Columbia University Press, 1964), p. 168.

5. For two particularly straightforward examples of this argument, see Ann Dummett, 'The Transnational Migration of People Seen from within a Natural Law Tradition', in Brian Barry and Robert E. Goodin (eds), *Free Movement* (University Park, PA: Penn State University Press), pp. 169–80; and Joseph Carens, 'Migration and Morality: A Liberal Egalitarian Perspective', in Barry and Goodin, *Free Movement*, pp. 25–47. There are a variety of definitions of human rights; for an influential introduction, see M. Cranston, *What Are Human Rights?* (NY: Taplinger, 1963). For discussions of rights as they relate to migration and nationalism, see Rosalyn Higgins, 'The Right in International Law of an Individual to Enter, Stay In and Leave a Country', *International Affairs*, vol. 49, no. 3 (July 1973), pp. 341–57; Roger Nett, 'The Civil Right We are Not Ready For: The Right of Free Movement of People on the Face of the Earth', *Ethics* 81 (1971), pp. 212–27; Frederick G. Whelan, 'Citizenship and the Right to Leave', *American Political Science Review* 75 (1981), pp. 636–53; and Myres S. McDougal, Harold D. Lasswell and Luyng-chu Chen, 'Nationality and Human Rights: The Protection of the Individual in External Arenas', *Yale Law Journal* 83 (1974), pp. 900–998.

6. In accepting this principle it is important to recognize an important limitation: that the validity of these rights depend critically on the willingness of a legitimate political authority to secure and defend them.

7. Alan Dowty, *Closed Borders: The Contemporary Assault on Freedom of Movement* (New Haven: Yale University Press, 1987), p. 11.

8. Thomas Hobbes, *De Cive*, ch. 9.

9. Social contract theory is an old and respected tradition in political philosophy, where a person's moral and/or political obligations

are seen as dependent upon a contract or agreement between the composite individuals that form a society. Although social contract theory has deeper historical roots, it is commonly associated with modern moral and political theory (especially the work of Thomas Hobbes, John Locke and Jean-Jacques Rousseau).

10. B. Ackerman, *Social Justice in the Liberal State* (New Haven: Yale University Press, 1980), p. 93.

11. John Locke, *Two Treatises of Government*, II, §118, stress in the original.

12. Quoted in Whelan, 'Citizenship and the Right to Leave', p. 650.

13. For a thoughtful discussion of the liberal biases underlying most theoretical arguments for open borders, see Peter C. Meilaender, *Toward a Theory of Immigration* (New York: Palgrave, 2001).

14. Cranston, *What Are Human Rights?*, p. 31. For two different examinations of the link between contemporary liberal thought and the right to free migration, see Joseph Carens, 'Aliens and Citizens: The Case for Open Borders', *Review of Politics*, vol. 49, no. 2 (1987), pp. 251–73; and Frederick G. Whelan, 'Citizenship and Freedom of Movement: An Open Admission Policy?', in Mark Gibney (ed.), *Open Borders? Closed Societies?* (New York: Greenwood Press, 1988), pp. 3–40.

15. Carens, 'Aliens and Citizens', p. 252.

16. One way to consider this is in terms of Henry George's concept of initial rights to property. George argued that each person was entitled to an equal portion of the value of all the world's natural resources. When the current distribution of ownership is seen to be unjust, owners are obliged to surrender the difference in the form of some sort of tax.

17. Here too (as in n6 above), this question begs another: guaranteed by whom? In the absence of an overarching political authority that is willing and able to defend these universal rights, liberal thinkers tend to retreat to more defendable (and comfortable) ground – where states take responsibility for their territory and its people. In this way, for example, John Rawls argues that '[p]eople must recognize that they cannot make up for failing to regulate their numbers or to care for their land by conquest in war, or by migrating into another people's territory without consent.' John Rawls, *The Law of Peoples* (Cambridge, MA: Harvard University Press, 1999), p. 8. In this framework, wealthier peoples are not seen to have a moral obligation to assist others more than is necessary for them (the other) to have enough potential human resources to realize just institutions (ibid., pp. 113–20).

18. Cited in David C. Hendrickson, 'Migration in Law and Ethics: A Realist Perspective', in Barry and Goodin, *Free Movement*, p. 215.

19. See R.E. Goodin, 'What's So Special about Our Fellow Countrymen?', *Ethics* 98 (1988), pp. 663–86.

20. Ibid., p. 686.

21. My own preference, following the subsidiarity principle in the European Union and the 10th Amendment of the US Constitution, would be to set the default level of sovereignty (with its inherent privileges and obligations) at the lowest level of aggregation. In other words, decisions should be taken as closely as possible to the citizen/individual. But it is not necessary to embrace this position. The point here is simply to argue that there is no reason to prioritize the nation-state.

22. E.g. Michael J. Sandel, *Liberalism and the Limits of Justice* (Cambridge: Cambridge University Press, 1982); Michael Walzer, *Spheres of Justice* (New York: Basic Books, 1983), ch. 2; Will Kymlicka, 'Liberalism and Communitarianism', *Canadian Journal of Philosophy* 18 (1988), pp.181–203; Whelan, 'Citizenship and Freedom of Movement'; and Meilaender, *Toward a Theory of Immigration*.

23. This argument is very familiar from critical discussion of other facets of globalization (e.g. finance capital and goods/services trade). In the end, we have come to recognize that cultural identity can be maintained with open borders for capital, goods and services. Why not people?

24. Eileen N. Hennessy, 'The Heidelberg Manifesto: A German Reaction to Immigration', *Population and Development Review*, vol. 8, no. 3 (September 1982), pp. 636–7.

25. For a critical examination of the relationship between political community (and the welfare state) and the way in which closure is allegedly used to protect it, see Joseph H. Carens, 'Immigration and the Welfare State', in Amy Gutmann (ed.), *Democracy and the Welfare State* (Princeton: Princeton University Press, 1988), pp. 207–30.

26. Carens, 'Immigration and the Welfare State' (pp. 223ff.), provides a brief legal overview of the rights of US states to discriminate between new and old residents.

27. Consider the way in which democratic communities address the biases of minority opinion. In the USA, for example, openly racist groups are not required to commit to the majority's opinions. The 'community' of opinion is varied enough to allow for great intellectual dissent. Instead, minorities are allowed the right to voice their opinion in public; their views are publicly criticized, but they

are not deprived of their status as morally legitimate and equal beings. In short, there is no community of opinion on the most divisive political questions (e.g. racism, the right to life, etc.), only a recognition of moral equality among political participants.

28. Joseph H. Carnes, 'States and Refugees: A Normative Analysis', in Howard Adelman (ed.), *Refugee Policy: Canada and the United States*, Centre for Refugee Studies, York University and Center for Migration Studies, New York (Toronto: York Lanes Press, 1991), pp. 24–5.

29. Hardin has actually weighed in on the migration issue, and his thinking here is clearly swamped when he blames immigration for the fact that 'Traffic problems are being replaced by rush-hour gridlock. Safe drinking water is scarcer every year. Forests are being killed by acid rain.' Cited in Ben J. Wattenberg and Karl Zinsmeister, 'The Case for More Immigration', *Commentary*, vol. 89, no. 4 (April 1990), p. 20.

30. See, for example, James Woodward, 'Commentary: Liberalism and migration', in Barry and Goodin, *Free Movement*, pp. 59–84.

31. E.g. Meilaender, *Toward a Theory of Immigration*.

32. Thomas Pogge, 'Migration and Poverty', in Veit Bader (ed.), *Citizenship and Exclusion* (London: Macmillan, 1997), p. 17.

33. Walzer, *Spheres of Justice*, p. 39.

34. Ibid.

35. Cited in Carens, 'Immigration and the Welfare State', p. 207.

Chapter 5

1. Aristide Zolberg, 'International Migration Policies in a Changing World System', in W.H. McNeill and R.S. Adams (eds), *Human Migration: Patterns and Policies* (Bloomington, IN: Indiana University Press, 1978), p. 271.

2. The reference to the bogus free mobility argument is Veit Bader, 'Fairly Open Borders', in Veit Bader (ed.), *Citizenship and Exclusion*, (London: Macmillan, 1997), pp. 28–60.

3. 'It's just obvious that you can't have free immigration and a welfare state' – Milton Friedman in an interview with Peter Brimelow, 'Milton Friedman at 85', *Forbes*, 29 December 1997, p. 52.

4. In order of presentation, see John Torpey, *The Invention of the Passport* (Cambridge: Cambridge University Press, 2000); Jeannette Money 'No Vacancy: The Political Geography of Immigration Control in

Advanced Industrial Countries', *International Organization* 51 (1998), pp. 685–720, and Jeannette Money, *Fences and Neighbors: The Political Geography of Immigration Control* (Ithaca: Cornell University Press, 1999); James F. Hollifield, *Immigrants, Markets and States* (Cambridge, MA: Harvard University Press, 1992); Zolberg, 'International Migrations', and Myron Weiner, 'On International Migration and International Relations', *Population and Development Review* 11 (1985), pp. 441–55; Saskia Sassen, *Losing Control? Sovereignty in an Age of Globalization* (New York: Columbia University Press, 1996); James Hollifield, 'Migration and International Relations: Conflict and Control in the European Community', *International Migration Review* 25 (1992), pp. 568–95; Virginie Guiraudon and Gallya Lahav, 'A Reappraisal of the State Sovereignty Debate: The Case of Migration Control', *Comparative Political Studies* 33 (2000), pp. 163–95. For a discussion of how different perspectives within the field of International Relations examine migration control issues, see Hollifield, *Immigrants, Markets and States*, ch. 2; and Wayne A. Cornelius, Philip L. Martin and James F. Hollifield, 'Introduction: The Ambivalent Quest for Immigration Control', in Wayne A. Cornelius, Philip L. Martin and James F. Hollifield (eds), *Controlling Immigration: A Global Perspective* (Stanford: Stanford University Press, 1994), p. 4.

5. See, e.g., Stephen Castles and Godula Kosack, *Immigrant Workers and Class Structure in Western Europe* (London: Oxford University Press, 1973); and Michael J. Piore, *Birds of Passage: Migrant Labor in Industrial Societies* (Cambridge: Cambridge University Press, 1979).

6. This view is shared by at least one other. Anthony Richmond argues 'the most economically developed and affluent countries are banding together to protect their privileged position in much the same way that Afrikaners and others of European descent sought to maintain their dominance in South Africa.' See Anthony Richmond, *Global Apartheid: Refugees, Racism, and the New World Order* (New York: Oxford University Press, 1994), p. 216.

7. This is a more popular and common area of study, as scholars and lawyers begin to press the boundaries of national sovereignty when issues such as human rights' abuses are concerned.

8. 'Total strategy' was P.W. Botha's term for describing his government's response to the perceived threat of the 'total onslaught'. Total onslaught was, in turn, the alleged threat posed by the Soviet Union to South Africa (and the Western world). Because of South Africa's location and level of economic development, the country was seen as a target for Soviet-financed revolutionaries, and an attractive

foothold for communist insurgencies in the south of Africa. Thus the apartheid regime sought to be protected by a ring of relatively sympathetic nation-states. This cordon sanitaire of white elitist states protected South Africa from what was considered to be a hostile black Africa to the North: South West Africa (Namibia), Rhodesia (Zimbabwe), Angola and Mozambique (controlled then by Portugal), made it difficult to access South Africa.

Botha's total strategy was designed to defend against just such an attack. This strategy justified a draconian repression of the black population, an enormous propaganda campaign used to convince the white population of the threat, and a policy of actively destabilizing neighbouring states. In short, apartheid's total strategy allowed a regime that served the interests of about 13 per cent of South Africa's population to appear as the sole bastion of Western democracy on the continent of Africa.

9. In this context, 'coloured' is not meant to be derogatory, but refers to a particular legal category of people under the apartheid regime. It is still used in South Africa as a descriptive term for persons of mixed ethnic backgrounds.

10. Like nation-states in the international system, most Bantustans were not ethnically homogeneous. While Zululand and the Transkei, for example, covered relatively homogeneous ethnic areas, this was not always the case. In Bophuthatswana, for instance, there was no clear historical or ethnic heritage to build on, while the Xhosa people were split into two homelands: Ciskei and the Transkei.

11. Albert O. Hirschman, *Exit Voice and Loyalty: Responses to Decline in Firms, Organizations and States* (Cambridge, MA: Harvard University Press, 1970).

12. A more formal presentation of this argument can be found in Jonathon W. Moses, 'Home Alone: Integration and Influence in National Contexts', in Erik Jones and Amy Verdun (eds), *The Political Economy of European Integration: Theory and Analysis* (Oxford and New York: Routledge, 2005), pp. 71–87; and Jonathon W. Moses, 'Exit, Vote and Sovereignty: Migration, States and Globalization', *Review of International Political Economy*, vol. 12, no. 1 (February 2005), pp. 53–77.

13. Actually, some of Hirschman's most recent work suggests that it is not unreasonable to extend the argument in this direction. See, for example, Albert O. Hirschman, 'Abwanderung, Wiederspruch und das Shicksal der Deutschen Demokratischen Republikk', *Leviathan* 20 (1992), pp. 39–58; and his 'Exit, Voice, and the Fate of the German

Democratic Republic: An Essay in Conceptual History', *World Politics* 45 (January 1993), pp. 173–202.

14. This was, after all, the implicit context of the early contract theories described in Chapter 4. How else can we withdraw consent from a contract that is changed in a substantial way?

15. This is the argument made by (among others) Eric Gordy, *The Culture of Power in Serbia: Nationalism and the Destruction of Alternatives* (University Park, PA: Penn State University Press, 1999).

16. Albert O. Hirschman, 'Exit, Voice, and the State', in his *Essays in Trespassing: Economics to Politics and Beyond* (Cambridge: Cambridge University Press, 1981), p. 260; originally published in *World Politics* 31 (1978), pp. 90–107. Hirschman also hinted at the utility of this approach in other studies, referring to John S. MacDonald's work on the effects of outward migration on Italian politics before World War I; and Nicholas R. Burnet's work on postwar Irish policy responses to emigration. For Hirschman's discussion, see Albert O. Hirschman, 'Exit, Voice and Loyalty: Further Reflections and a Survey of Recent Contributions', in *Essays in Trespassing*, p. 226; and Hirschman, 'Exit, Voice and the State', pp. 260–63. Frank Aarebrot and Stein Kuhnle have also applied the exit-voice scheme to historical mobilization in Norway and Sweden. See Frank H. Aarebrot and Stein Kuhnle, 'The Ecology of Exit-Voice: Economic Development and Political Response in an Early Phase of Nationbuilding: 19th Century Norway', paper presented to the Research Committee on Social Ecology, ISA World Congress Toronto, 18–24 August 1976. While the focus is on economic effects, some political effects of earlier emigration are also discussed in Jonathon W. Moses, *Norwegian Catch-Up: Development and Globalization before World War II* (Aldershot: Ashgate Press, 2005). Finally, Stein Kuhnle's argument can be found in his 'Emigration, Democratization, and the Rise of the European Welfare States', in Per Torsvik (ed.), *Mobilization, Center–Periphery Structures and Nation-Building* (Bergen: Universitetsforlaget, 1981), pp. 501–23.

17. Letter to Richard Price of 22 March 1778, in *Oeuvres* (Paris: Delance, 1810), vol. 9, p. 389. Cited in Albert Hirschman, 'Exit, Voice and the State', p. 255 n22.

18. See, for example, Jonathon W. Moses, 'The Social Democratic Predicament and Global Economic Integration: A Capital Dilemma', in William D. Coleman and Geoffrey Underhill (eds), *Regionalism and Global Economic Integration* (London: Routledge, 1998), pp. 122–39.

19. See Adam Przeworski, 'Social Democracy as a Historical Phenom-

enon', *New Left Review* 122 (1980); reprinted in his *Capitalism and Social Democracy* (Cambridge: Cambridge University Press, 1985), pp. 7–46. For background information on the electoral consequences of socialist strategy, see Adam Przeworski and John Sprague, *Paper Stones: A History of Electoral Socialism* (Chicago: University of Chicago Press, 1986). One of the very few threats of significant socialization was in Norway, where the first socialist government (the infamous Hornsrud government) lasted just eighteen days: from 28 January to 15 February 1928.

20. Obviously, this is a terribly simple argument, as capital benefits tremendously from the stability and productivity of workers in modern welfare systems. There are many problems with employing a class analysis to welfare state support; simplicity is its saving grace.

21. In a more economic version of this argument, George Borjas shows that US immigrants appear to be driven by competing welfare state offerings. Immigrant welfare recipients are much more likely to be geographically clustered than immigrants who don't receive welfare, and are also much more clustered than natives. If US immigrants are choosing states of residence because of the policies they offer, it seems that we can extend the same sort of argument for other policy differences. States do have some 'magnet' potential. As such, they compete with one another to attract mobile workers. See George J. Borjas, 'Immigration and Welfare Magnets', NBER Working Paper 6813, November 1998.

22. A forceful representation of this view is Timothy King, who writes: 'If nations fail to impose restrictions on immigration, smaller communities might try to do so. The principles on which these restrictions would be based might be very much less liberal than nationally imposed ones; they might encourage greater segregation by race, income and other individual characteristics.... It is possible that the true alternative to the nation-state as a basis for considering migration choices is not the world as a whole but subnational geographic units, and the nation-state is clearly preferable' (p. 533). King actually suggests that free migration is only realistic under conditions of near equalization of economic conditions, such as in the EU. See Timothy King, 'Immigration from Developing Countries: Some Philosophical Issues', *Ethics* (April 1993), pp. 525–36.

23. Paul Teske, Mark Schneider, Michael Mintrom and Samuel Best, 'Establishing the Micro Foundations of a Macro Theory: Information, Movers, and the Competitive Local Market for Public Goods', *American Political Science Review*, vol. 87, no. 3 (1993), pp. 702–13. In

particular, they argue (p. 710) that: 'perhaps 10% of the population in an average community will have recently entered the community and have high levels of comparative knowledge of local public goods. We believe that this is enough to put pressure on communities to be competitive in their services, especially since these are the residents most important for the continued fiscal viability of communities.'

Chapter 6

1. Julian L. Simon, *The Economic Consequences of Immigration* (Oxford: Basil Blackwell, 1989), p. 299.
2. George J. Borjas, *Heaven's Door: Immigration Policy and the American Economy* (Princeton: Princeton University Press, 1999), p. 181.
3. George Borjas in OECD, *The Changing Course of International Migration* (Paris: OECD, 1993), p. 191.
4. E.g. Borjas, *Heaven's Door*, p. 63.
5. The figure comes from a press account from the *Norsk Folkehjelp*. Kristine Lindberg, 'Der det er penger er det hjerterom', www.folkehjelp.no/presse/hjerterom.htm, accessed 5 October 2001.
6. Although it does not concern itself with open borders, this is the general conclusion of the highly respected (US) National Academy report on immigration. The authors in this study conclude that immigration initially results in an economic burden, but over time the burden becomes a surplus. See James P. Smith and Barry Edmonston (eds), *The New Americans: Economic, Demographic and Fiscal Effects of Immigration* (Washington DC: National Academy Press, 1997).
7. As an enthusiastic supporter of increased immigration, Julian Simon is not always lent a sympathetic ear. For a good counterweight to Julian Simon's argument, see George Borjas's *Heaven's Door*. Other influential studies include the US Department of Labor's *The Effects of Immigration on the US Economy and Labor Market*, Immigration Policy and Research Report 1 (Washington DC: US Department of Labor, 1989); and W.R. Böhning, *Studies in International Labour Migration* (New York: St. Martin's Press, 1984).
8. Consider three other New World examples. For the impact in Canada, see B.R. Swan et al., *Economic and Social Impact of Immigration* (Research Report, Economic Council of Canada, Ottawa, 1991); in Australia, see J. Nevile, 'Immigration and Macro Economic Performance in Australia', *Growth (The Benefits and Costs of Immigration)* (Melbourne: Committee for Economic Development of Australia

(CEDA), September 1991), and G. Withers, 'Migrants and the Labour Market: The Australian Evidence', in OECD, *The Future of Migration* (Paris: OECD, 1987); and in New Zealand, see J. Poot, 'International Migration in the New Zealand Economy of the 1980s', in A.D. Tolim and P. Spoonley (eds), *New Zealand and International Migration: A Digest and Bibliography* no. 2 (Palmerston North: Massey University, 1992). Still, George Borjas disagrees. See his *Heaven's Door*, ch. 2.

9. For a review of the empirical literature on 'permissible illegal immigration', and a new theoretical approach to understanding it, see Arye L. Hillman and Ave Weiss, 'A Theory of Permissible Illegal Immigration', *European Journal of Political Economy* 15 (1999), pp. 585–604.

10. See, e.g., Simon, *The Economic Consequences of Immigration*; George Borjas, *Friends or Strangers: The Impact of Immigrants in the US Economy* (New York: Basic Books, 1990); and R. Friedberg and J. Hunt, 'The Impact of Immigration on Host Country Wages, Employment and Growth', *Journal of Economic Perspectives*, vol. 9, no. 2 (1995), pp. 23–44. For a brief overview of earlier studies, with similar conclusions, see George Borjas, 'Economic Theory and International Migration', *International Migration Review*, vol. 23, no. 3 (1989), p. 481.

11. Jonathan Coppel, Jean-Christophe Dumont and Ignazio Visco, 'Trends in Immigration and Economic Consequences', OECD Economics Department Working Papers no. 284 (ECO/WKP 2001) 10 (1 February 2001).

12. E.g. F.D. Bean, B.L. Lowell and L.J. Taylor, 'Undocumented Mexican Immigrants and the Earnings of Other Workers in the United States', *Demography*, vol. 25, no. 1 (February 1988), pp. 35–52; George Borjas, 'Immigrants, Minorities and Labor Market Competition', *Industrial and Labor Relations Review*, vol. 40, no. 3 (April 1987), pp. 382–92, and his 'The Demographic Determinants of the Demand for Black Labor', in R.B. Freemand and H.J. Holzer (eds), *Black Youth Employment Crisis* (Chicago: University of Chicago Press, 1986); and Jean Baldwin Grossman, 'The Substitutability of Natives and Immigrants in Production', *Review of Economics and Statistics*, vol. 64, no. 5 (November 1982), pp. 593–603.

13. Friedberg and Hunt, 'The Impact of Immigration'.

14. Simon, *The Economic Consequences of Immigration*, p. 7.

15. Jonathon W. Moses and Bjørn Letnes, 'If People Were Money: Estimating the Gains and Scope of Free Migration', in George J. Borjas and Jeffery Crisp (eds), *Poverty, International Migration and Asylum* (New York: Palgrave, 2005): 188–210; p. 198 Table 9.3.

16. CBS/*New York Times*, 14 July 1986, p.1.

17. For an overview of this literature, see the special chapter on immigration and social transfers in OECD, *Trends in International Migration* (Paris: OECD, 1997).

18. Coppel et al., 'Trends in Immigration', p. 20.

19. D. Turner, C. Giorno, A. De Serres, A. Vourc'h and P. Richardson, 'The Macroeconomic Implications of Ageing in a Global Context', *OECD Economics Department Working Paper* no. 193 (1998). For the UN's perspective, see UN Population Division, 'Replacement Migration: Is it a Solution to Declining and Ageing Populations?', ESA/P/WP.160 (21 March 2000).

20. Most of the figures on the USBP in this paragraph and the following paragraphs come from Peter Andreas, 'The Transformation of Migrant Smuggling across the U.S.–Mexican Border', in David Kyle and Rey Koslowski (eds), *Global Human Smuggling* (Baltimore: Johns Hopkins University Press, 2001), pp. 109, 110, 113, 115 and 116. The USBP also has an informative home page: see www.ins. usdoj.gov/graphics/lawenfor/bpatrol/index.htm.

21. The comparative figures are from the OMB homepage, overview of the FY2002 budget.

22. See 'Law to Track Foreigners Entering US Postponed', *New York Times* (West Coast edition), 4 October 1998, p. A4; and 'Agreement Resolved Many Differences over Policy as Well as Money', *New York Times* (West Coast edition), 16 October 1998, p. A17.

23. Philip Martin, 'Bordering on Control: Combating Irregular Migration in North America and Europe', IOM Migration Research Series no. 13 (Geneva: IOM, 2003).

24. Reported in an editorial entitled 'Let the Huddled Masses In', *The Economist*, 29 March 2001.

25. For an overview of classical economic approaches to immigration and economic development, see the first three chapters in B. Thomas, *Migration and Economic Growth: A Study of Great Britain and the Atlantic Economy* (Cambridge: Cambridge University Press, 1954). The reference to Knut Wicksell is his *Om utvandringen: Dess betydelse och orsaker* (Stockholm: Albert Bonniers Forlag, 1882).

26. Harry G. Johnson, *Economic Policies toward Less Developed Countries* (New York: Praeger, 1967), p. 107.

27. For an example of the former, see Robert L. Heilbroner, *The Making of Economic Society*, 7th edn (Englewood Cliffs, NJ: Prentice-Hall, 1985); for an example of the latter, see Paul A. Samuelson, *Economics*, 10th edn (New York: McGraw-Hill, 1976). An important excep-

tion is the work of Arthur Lewis, who formalized a theory where growth and full employment in the more industrialized countries depended on the availability of an abundant supply of labour – as in the USA during the second half of the nineteenth century – and the problems of poor countries could be more easily overcome if they were able to reduce the pressures of their manpower surpluses on their society and economy. Lewis's theory was tested with great success in Charles P. Kindleberger's *Europe's Postwar Growth: The Role of Labor Supply* (Cambridge, MA: Harvard University Press, 1967), discussed below. For a general overview of the literature on migration and development, see Ronald Skeldon, *Migration and Development* (Harlow: Addison Wesley Longman, 1997).

28. The Norwegian example also fits this pattern. See Jonathon W. Moses, *Norwegian Catch-Up: Development and Globalization before World War II* (Aldershot: Ashgate Press, 2005). For more on the economic effects of migration in history, see Sidney Klein, *The Economics of Mass Migration in the Twentieth Century* (New York: Paragon House, 1987). An excellent review of much of this literature can be found in Douglas S. Massey, 'Economic Development and International Migration in Comparative Perspective', *Population and Development Review*, vol. 14, no. 3 (September 1988), pp. 383–413. On the issue of development and migration, generally, see R. Appleyard (ed.), *International Migration Today*, vol. 1: *Trends and Prospects* (Paris: UNESCO, 1989) and his (ed.) *The Impact of International Migration on Developing Countries* (Paris: OECD, 1989); C. Stahl (ed.), *International Migration Today*, vol. 2: *Emerging Issues* (Paris: UNESCO, 1988); and Demetrious G. Papademetrioiu and Philip L. Martin (eds), *The Unsettled Relationship: Labor Migration and Economic Development* (New York: Greenwood Press, 1991).

29. Timothy J. Hatton and Jeffrey Williamson, *The Age of Mass Migration: Causes and Economic Impact* (Oxford: Oxford University Press, 1998), pp. 225ff. This convergence share is so large because some of the convergence effects (in particular, the effects of capital mobility) work in the opposite direction in the aggregate Atlantic economy.

30. Thomas, *Migration and Economic Growth*.

31. Harry Jerome, *Migration and Business Cycles* (New York: NBER, 1926); Dorothy Thomas, *Social and Economic Aspects of Swedish Population Movements: 1750–1933* (New York: Macmillan, 1941).

32. Kindleberger, *Europe's Postwar Growth*.

33. This impact is probably contingent on the relative size of the population vis-à-vis the country's other resources. Thus, we might

expect that highly overpopulated countries will not feel the same threat of exit as do underpopulated countries.

34. For more on remittances, see Fred Arnold, 'The Contribution of Remittances to Economic and Social Development', in Mary M. Kritz, Lin Lean Lim and Hania Zlotnik (eds), *International Migration Systems: A Global Approach* (Oxford: Clarendon Press, 1992), pp. 205–20.

35. This figure includes illegal migrants. If only legal migrants are included, then the annual average remittance was about $700. See Nigel Harris, 'Should Europe End Immigration Controls? A Polemic', *European Journal of Development Research*, vol. 12, no. 1 (June 2000), p. 98.

36. *Migration News*, June 2001, cited in Francis Watkins and Robert Nurick, 'Migration in South Asia in Policy and Practice: A Regional Overview' (2002), p. 68, unpublished manuscript obtained from the authors. Overview available at www.eldis.org/cf/search/disp/docdisplay.cfm?doc=ADOC363&resource=f1, accessed 4 May 2004.

37. Devesh Kapur and John McHale, 'Migration's New Payoff – Globalization at Work', *Foreign Policy*, November–December, 2003, pp. 48–57.

38. IMF, *Balance of Payments Statistics Yearbook*, Part I (Washington DC: IMF, 1999).

39. UNDP, *Global Dimensions of Human Development: Human Development Report 1992* (New York: UNDP, 1992), p. 58.

40. Moses and Letnes, 'If People Were Money', p. 201, Table 9.5.

41. Referred to in UNDP, *Human Development Report 1992*, p. 57.

42. Most of these models can be traced back to an earlier project by Bob Hamilton and John Whalley, 'Efficiency and Distributional Implications of Global Restrictions on Labour Mobility: Calculations of Policy Implications', *Journal of Development Economics* 14 (1984), pp. 61–75.

43. Jonathon W. Moses and Bjørn Letnes, 'The Economic Costs to International Labor Restrictions: Revisiting the Empirical Discussion', *World Development*, vol. 32, no. 10 (October 2004), pp. 1609–26. The figures in this paragraph come from this article.

44. Indeed, in a subsequent study ('If People Were Money'), Moses and Letnes provide the model with some better empirical grounding, from which they could evaluate the reasonableness of their estimates. These (new) estimates were then compared with contemporary migration flows and the findings of studies that analyse their economic impact. In light of these comparisons, the authors concluded

that the original findings were not unreasonable. At the same time, a similar – though completely independent – study was conducted by Ana Maria Iregui at the central bank of Colombia. Her study produced remarkably similar conclusions about the expected international gains from free mobility. Ana María Iregui (2005), 'Efficiency Gains from the Elimination of Global Restrictions on Labour Mobility: An Analysis using a Multiregional CGE Model', in Borjas and Crisp, *Poverty, International Migration and Asylum*, pp. 211–38. See also L.A. Winters, 'The Economic Implications of Liberalising Mode 4 Trade', paper prepared for the Joint WTO–World Bank Symposium on 'The Movement of Natural Persons (Mode 4) under the GATS', Geneva, 11–12 April 2002.

45. World Bank, *World Development Report 2000/1: Attacking Poverty* (Washington DC: World Bank, 2000), p. 76.

Chapter 7

1. 1 June 1984. Cited in Nigel Harris, *The New Untouchables: Immigration and the New World Worker* (London: I.B. Tauris, 1995), p. 187. Chilton Williamson Jr. attributes the quote to French Smith, Reagan's attorney general. See Chilton Williamson Jr., *The Immigration Mystique: America's False Conscience* (New York: Basic Books, 1996), p. 4.

2. For more information about his survey, see www.issp.org/. The analysis that follows draws from the work of Anna Maria Mayda, who uses both the ISSP–NI data (1995) and data from the third wave of the World Value Survey (1995–1997). Anna Maria Mayda, 'Who is Against Immigration? A Cross-country Investigation of Individual Attitudes toward Immigrants', IZA Discussion Paper No. 1115 (April 2004).

3. West Germany, East Germany, Great Britain, the USA, Austria, Hungry, Italy, Ireland, the Netherlands, Norway, Sweden, the Czech Republic, Slovenia, Bulgaria, Russia, New Zealand, Canada, the Philippines, Japan, Spain, Latvia and the Slovak Republic. The sample mean of respondents from these countries (who thought immigration policies should increase a little or a lot) was 6.4 per cent.

4. For the statistically astute, some clarification is in order. The 54 per cent figure is the sample mean, across states. References to 'reducing' immigration are aggregate responses (combined score of those wishing to reduce immigration by either 'a little' or 'a lot'), unless otherwise noted.

5. Curiously, individual skill level is positively correlated with pro-immigration attitudes in the richest countries, but negatively correlated with pro-immigration attitudes in countries with a lower per capita GDP. For example, in a country like the United States, college-educated people tend to have more positive attitudes towards immigration than do high-school graduates and/or those respondents with some secondary education. In a poorer country such as Nigeria, however, the trend is the reverse: respondents with some secondary education hold pro-immigration attitudes, while those with a high-school or college education tend to hold less positive attitudes with respect to immigration.

6. Racism was operationalized in terms of a response to a question about the race of potential neighbours. 'A respondent who would rather not have as neighbours individuals of a different race is more than eight percentage points less likely to be in favor of an increase in immigration' (Mayda, 'Who is Against Immigration?', p. 23). The gender effect actually did appear in Mayda's ISSP–NI sample, but disappeared again when she controlled for individual occupation. Finally, it should be noted that Mayda did find relative income to have a positive effect on immigration attitudes when she ran the analysis on the World Value Survey sample of countries. See ibid., p. 8.

7. IPSOS–Public Affairs and Associated Press, 'Globus: International Affairs Poll'; interviews were conducted 7–17 May 2004. See www. ipsos-na.com/news/pdf/media/mr040527–2chart.pdf, accessed 23 October 2004.

8. Julian L. Simon, *The Economic Consequences of Immigration* (Oxford: Basil Blackwell, 1989), p. 11.

9. Irwin M. Stelzer, 'Immigration Policy for an Age of Mass Movement', *Policy*, Summer 2001–2002, p. 4.

10. Mode 4 refers to the temporary movement of service providers across WTO signatory states. Technically, it is defined in Article I.2(d) of GATS as being 'the supply of a service … by a service supplier of one Member, through presence of natural persons of a Member in the territory of another Member.' At a more general level, discussions about Mode 4 are mostly motivated by labour and skills shortages in the developed world, as well as the need of multinational corporations to move staff around the world at short notice. In other words, the WTO is interested in facilitating short-term labour migration – and is explicitly not interested in a general liberalization of migration.

11. The figures from this paragraph come from Table 9.3 in Jonathon W. Moses and Bjørn Letnes, 'If People Were Money: Estimating the Gains and Scope of Free Migration', in George J. Borjas and Jeffery Crisp (eds), *Poverty, International Migration and Asylum* (New York: Palgrave, 2005). See also Jonathon W. Moses and Bjørn Letnes, 'The Economic Costs to International Labor Restrictions: Revisiting the Empirical Discussion', *World Development*, vol. 32, no. 10 (October 2004).

12. George J. Borjas, *Heaven's Door: Immigration Policy and the American Economy* (Princeton: Princeton University Press, 1999), p. 87. See also p. 103: 'The immigration debate is best viewed as a political struggle between those who win and those who lose. Simply put, immigration changes the way the economic pie is split – and this undeniable fact goes a long way toward explaining why some segments of society favor the entry of large numbers of immigrants, while other segments want to curtail or cut off the immigrant flow.'

13. It is important to emphasize that the starting assumption of this argument is strongly contested in the literature. See the discussion in Chapter 6.

14. Borjas provides one of the cleanest depictions of this sort of argument: 'To get an idea of how large this redistribution can be, recall that 70 percent of GDP goes to workers (with the rest going to the owners of the firms), and that natives make up 90 percent of the population. Therefore, native workers take home about 63 percent of GDP in the form of wages and salaries. If immigration reduces natives' wages by 3%, the share of GDP accruing to native workers falls by 1.9 percentage points (or .63 times .03). In an \$8 trillion economy, native earnings would drop by about \$152 billion' (*Heaven's Door*, p. 91).

15. The relationship is slightly negative, as we would expect from the model, but the model explains little of the variation ($R2 = 0.0325$). Similarly weak relationships were found between other indicators of labour strength (e.g. percentage of left party vote, degree of union centralization, bargaining centralization, etc.).

16. This point is made hesitantly, in the interest of fairness. There is, after all, little evidence to suggest that migrants are attracted to generous welfare states more than other places, or that migration undermines welfare state policies more than any other sort of international engagements. Indeed, European states are beginning to realize that many aspects of the welfare state itself are threatened by domestic demographic trends: without immigrant workers to pay

the bill, there will be little welfare state money left to redistribute. Still, perceptions of the negative effects of migration on the welfare state remain strong, and need to be addressed.

17. See, for example, the introduction to C. Lis, J. Lucassen and H. Soly, 'Before the Unions: Wage Earners and Collective Action in Europe, 1300–1850', Supplement 2, *International Review of Social History* 1994, pp. 1–11.

18. See, for example, Vernon M. Briggs, Jr., *Immigration and American Unionism* (Ithaca: Cornell University Press, 2001).

19. See 'The AFL–CIO Policy on Immigration', available online at: www.aflcio.org/issuespolitics/immigration/upload/AFLCIOPO.pdf, accessed 14 January 2005.

20. This was the situation in many European countries before World War I. For an introduction to the Norwegian experience, see Jonathon W. Moses, *Norwegian Catch-Up: Development and Globalization before World War II* (Aldershot: Ashgate Press, 2005).

21. For further elaboration of this argument, see Jonathon W. Moses, 'Home Alone: Integration and Influence in National Contexts', in Erik Jones and Amy Verdun (eds), *The Political Economy of European Integration: Theory and Analysis* (Oxford and New York: Routledge, 2005), pp. 71–87; and Jonathon W. Moses, 'Exit, Vote and Sovereignty: Migration, States and Globalization', *Review of International Political Economy*, vol. 12, no. 1 (February 2005), pp. 53–77.

Chapter 8

1. Letter to the editor of the *Wall Street Journal* from Roger Lewis, 30 November 1981, p. 23, referenced in Julian L. Simon, *The Economic Consequences of Immigration* (Oxford: Basil Blackwell, 1989), p. 49.

2. ICM Research poll conducted for the BBC (and other broadcasters) in the course of 2003. For example, the Canadian sample was taken between 16 May and 1 June 2003. See www.cbc.ca/news/america/finaldata.pdf, accessed 30 November 2004.

3. Oscar Handlin, *The Uprooted*, 2nd edn (Boston: Little, Brown, 1973).

4. This is a quotation from an Ausburg newspaper editorial expressing amazement at the numbers emigrating to the New World in 1916: *Allgemeine Zeitung*, 9 December 1916. Cited in Marcus Lee Hansen, *The Atlantic Migration 1607–1860* (New York: Harper & Row, 1961 [1940]), p. 3.

5. In particular: 30 million IDPs + 10 million refugees + 30 million migrants with their 40 million dependents = 110,000,000 potentially mobile.

6. The Atlantic migration figure (1.4 million) comes from Timothy J. Hatton and Jeffrey Williamson, *The Age of Mass Migration: Causes and Economic Impact* (Oxford: Oxford University Press, 1998), p. 8. The world population figure is for 1910, and comes from the Population Division, Department for Economic and Social Information and Policy Analysis, 'World Population Growth from Year 0 to Stabilization' (New York: United Nations), mimeo, 6 July 1994.

7. UNDP, *Global Dimensions of Human Development: Human Development Report 1992* (New York: UNDP, 1992), p. 58. From their calculations, it would appear the UNDP assumed 44 million people would take advantage of free migration.

8. The developing-world population figure comes from the US Census Bureau, *Official Statistics*, Table A-4: Population by Region and Country: 1950 to 2025 (1 March 1999); the 40 per cent assumption is the same used by Hamilton and Whaley in their study. See Bob Hamilton and John Whalley, 'Efficiency and Distributional Implications of Global Restrictions on Labour Mobility: Calculations of Policy Implications', *Journal of Development Economics* 14 (1984), p. 70.

9. The mobility figures are for the period March 1997–March 1998, and come from the US Bureau of Census, 'Geographic Mobility: March 1997–March 1998', Congressional Information Service, January 2000 (ASI 2000 2546–1.516). The US population in July 1997 was 267,784,000, according to the Resident Population Estimates of the United States (US Census Bureau).

10. This is close to Barry Eichengreen's estimate of 1.3 per cent. See SOPEMI, *Trends in International Migration* (Paris: OECD, 2001), p.34.

11. Statistics Canada, 'Population 5 years and over by mobility status, 1991 and 1996 Censuses', www.statcan.ca/english/Pgdb/People/Population/demo42a.htm, accessed 19 December 2001.

12. The EEA includes the (then) fifteen member states of the European Union, plus Iceland, Liechtenstein and Norway.

13. Both the EEA immigration and population figures come from the *EUROSTAT Yearbook 2001*, pp. 9 and 3, respectively. The OECD's figure for internal EU mobility is 0.2 per cent. See SOPEMI, *Trends in International Migration*, p. 34.

14. Of course developed welfare states and significant redistribution

schemes within and across Europe can explain some of this reluctance to migrate. In addition, the mobility of workers from the poorest new member states has traditionally been limited by temporary restrictions during a given transition period.

15. 3.2 per cent of 270,200,000 is 8,646,400. The FDI figures are from OECD, *Financial Market Trends*, no. 76 (June 2000); the 1999 US GDP was $8,848.2 billion, according to the US Department of Commerce, Bureau of Economic Analysis, *Survey of Current Business*. The immigrant figures come from OECD, *Trends in International Migration* (Paris: OECD), p. 12; the population figure (270.2 million) is from the US Bureau of the Census, State Population Estimates, 29 December 1999.

16. For a brief (if somewhat polemical) review of 'the brain drain refrain', see Alan Dowty, *Closed Borders: The Contemporary Assault on Freedom of Movement* (New Haven: Yale University Press, 1987), pp. 147–66.

17. The figures in this paragraph come from Gumisai Mutume, 'Reversing Africa's "brain drain"', *Africa Recovery*, vol. 17, no. 2 (July 2003), available at www.un.org/ecosocdev/geninfo/afrec/vol17no2/172brain.htm, accessed 2 November 2004.

18. For an overview of these revisionist arguments, see Riccardo Faini, 'Migration, Remittances, and Growth', in George J. Borjas and Jeffery Crisp (eds), *Poverty, International Migration and Asylum* (New York: Palgrave, 2005), pp. 171–87.

19. Jeremy Harding, *The Uninvited: Refugees at the Rich Man's Gate* (London: Profile Books, 2000), p. 9.

20. An influential example of this sort of argument is Samuel Huntington, *Who Are We?* (New York: Simon & Schuster, 2004).

21. As noted in the introduction, this notion of imagined communities comes from Benedict Anderson's *Imagined Communities: Reflections on the Origin and Spread of Nationalism*, rev. edn (London: Verso, 1991).

22. In 1634 Cardinal Richelieu created an official body, the Académie française, whose goal was the purification and preservation of the French language. This group of forty members (the 'immortals') is chosen for life and still exists today for the policing of French and the adaptation of foreign words and expressions. Despite the efforts of Cardinal Richelieu, as many as one-half of the French population did not speak or understand French in the late 1790s, and many other languages continued to be spoken in France at the end of that century.

23. Edward Said, *Orientalism: Western Conceptions of the Orient* (London: Penguin 1995 [1978]), pp. 348–9.

24. IPSOS–Public Affairs and Associated Press poll conducted in May of 2004.

25. The same sort of open-mindedness is evidenced in the developed world's attitude towards alternative religions. When asked if their country benefited by a variety of religions, a remarkable 90 per cent of the American respondents agreed, while only 8 per cent disagreed (either strongly or somewhat). In Canada the celebration of religious diversity was only a little more muted (83 per cent agreed, while only 15 per cent disagreed). In this sample, the Canadians were followed by the Europeans (in aggregate, 66 per cent agreed, while 30 per cent disagreed) and the Japanese (58 per cent agreed, 34 per cent disagreed).

26. Samuel Huntington, 'The Clash of Civilizations?', *Foreign Affairs*, Summer 1993, p. 25: 'the world is becoming a smaller place. The interactions between peoples of different civilizations are increasing; these increasing interactions intensify civilization consciousness and awareness of differences between civilizations and commonalities within civilizations.'

27. For a contemporary critique of the realist position on morality, see Michael Walzer, *Just and Unjust Wars: A Moral Argument with Historical Illustrations* (New York: Basic Books, 1977), pp. 2–30.

28. Aristide Zolberg, 'International Migration Policies in a Changing World System', in W.H. McNeill and R.S. Adams (eds), *Human Migration: Patterns and Policies* (Bloomington, IN: Indiana University Press, 1978), p. 280.

29. B. Thomas, *Migration and Economic Growth: A Study of Great Britain and the Atlantic Economy* (Cambridge: Cambridge University Press, 1954), p. 191. Nor are racism and xenophobia restricted to the post-World War I period. Whenever immigration levels rose in the USA, it was possible to find segments of American society that denounced so-called alien invaders. For example, in the 1850s, the 'Order of the Star Spangled Banner' whipped up public sentiment against Irish and German immigrants; in the 1880s, Catholics were the brunt of a similar movement (the American Protective Association), and in 1915 the Ku Klux Klan began its 'hundred per cent Americanism' offensive against Jews, Catholics, blacks and foreigners.

30. Cited in Dougie Oakes, *Illustrated History of South Africa: The Real Story*, 3rd rev. edn (Pleasantville, NY: Readers Digest, May 1995), p. 373.

31. Of course, some states do maintain border controls in order to deter the spread of disease to important food industries (agriculture and

animal husbandry), and there is no reason why these sorts of controls shouldn't continue, when necessary, between states.

32. Myron Weiner, *The Global Migration Crisis* (New York: HarperCollins, 1995), p. 13.

33. The Port Angeles (Washington) arrest and later conviction of an Algerian, Ahmed Ressam, is one noticeable exception that seems to prove the rule. Ressam was arrested in December 1999 for trying to smuggle bomb-making materials across the Canadian/US border in an apparent attempt to disrupt millennium celebrations on the west coast of the United States. Most suspected terrorist arrests are made by local police authorities, not border guards.

34. Veit Bader, 'Fairly Open Borders', in Veit Bader (ed.), *Citizenship and Exclusion* (London: Macmillan, 1997), p. 52 n4.

Chapter 9

1. Thomas Paine, *Common Sense and the Crisis* (Garden City, NY: Anchor Book, 1973), p. 19.

2. William Linn Westermann, 'Between Slavery and Freedom', *American Historical Review* 50 (January 1945), p. 223.

3. This is the title to the first chapter in Chilton Williamson Jr., *The Immigration Mystique: America's False Conscience* (New York: Basic Books, 1996).

4. Indeed, it needs to be said that there is nothing inherently conservative about embracing international markets. Socialists and other labour representatives at the turn of the last century were fully aware of this, but this lesson seems to be lost on labour and leftist groups that cut their political teeth in local or national struggles. Progressive politics should be about embracing changes that have the potential to transform the world radically and the opportunities available to its most desperate residents. (By contrast, it is conservativism's defining characteristic to seek the return to a glorified past.) In this light, the left needs to stop trying to put the globalization genie back in its bottle.

5. The SANSA website is located at http://sansa.nrf.ac.za/; Thailand's RDP project can be found at http://rbd.nstda.or.th/.

6. Established in 1985, the Sri Lanka Bureau of Foreign Employment (SLBFE) promotes and organizes the supply of Sri Lankan labour abroad. Indeed, the Sri Lankan government actively searches for new migrant labour markets in the Middle East and elsewhere (e.g.

Singapore, South Korea, Cyprus). In addition, the SLBFE regulates the private recruiting industry to ensure that emigrants (and their families in Sri Lanka) enjoy adequate welfare facilities. With the revenues from fees paid by the recruitment agencies, the SLBFE can provide insurance to all migrants, train women leaving to work as housemaids abroad, and implement a wide range of worker welfare programmes (both locally and in host countries) to ensure the protection of migrant workers during the entire migration process (prior to departure, during their stay in the host country, and after returning).

7. Henry Pratt Fairchild, *Immigration: A World Movement and its American Significance* (New York: Macmillan, 1913).

Suggested Reading

Interested readers might trawl the individual chapter endnotes to find references for a particular area of interest. The following list of readings is suggested for readers who are looking for general introductions to broader migration topics.

General sources on migration

Castles, Stephen, and Mark J. Miller, *The Age of Migration*, 3rd edn (New York: Palgrave, 2003).

Dowty, Alan, *Closed Borders: The Contemporary Assault on Freedom of Movement* (New Haven: Yale University Press, 1987).

Harris, Nigel, *Thinking the Unthinkable: The Immigration Myth Exposed* (London: I.B. Tauris, 2002).

Hayter, Teresa, Open *Borders: The Case against Immigration Controls*, 2nd edn (London: Pluto, 2004).

IOM, *World Migration Report* (annual).

Meilaender, Peter C., *Toward a Theory of Immigration* (New York: Palgrave, 2001).

OECD's *Trends in International Migration* (annual).

Sasken, Saskia, *Guests and Aliens* (New York: New Press, 1999).

Stalker, Peter, *Workers without Frontiers* (Bolder CO and Geneva: Lynne Rienner/ILO, 2000).

History of migration

Hatton, Timothy J., and Jeffrey Williamson, *The Age of Mass Migration: Causes and Economic Impact* (Oxford: Oxford University Press, 1998).

McKeown, Adam, 'Global Migration, 1846–1940', *Journal of World History*, vol. 15, no. 2 (2004).

Potts, Lydia, *The World Labour Market: A History of Migration*, trans. Terry Bond (London: Zed Books, 1990).

Torpey, John, *The Invention of the Passport* (Cambridge: Cambridge University Press, 2000).

Migration and development

Massey, Douglas S., 'Economic Development and International Migration in Comparative Perspective', *Population and Development Review*, vol. 14, no. 3 (September 1988), pp. 383–413.

Skeldon, Ronald, *Migration and Development* (Harlow: Addison Wesley Longman, 1997).

Kapur, Devesh, and John McHale, 'Migration's New Payoff', *Foreign Policy* (November/December 2003), pp. 48–57.

Illegal immigration, refugees and asylum-seekers

Annerion, John, *Dead in Their Tracks* (New York: Four Walls Eight Windows, 1999).

Harding, Jeremy, *The Uninvited: Refugees at the Rich Man's Gate* (London: Profile Books, 2000).

Harris, Nigel, *The New Untouchables: Immigration and the New World Worker* (London: I.B. Tauris, 1995).

Moorehead, Caroline, *Human Cargo: A Journey among Refugees* (New York: Henry Holt, 2005).

UNHCR, *The State of the World's Refugees: Fifty Years of Humanitarian Action* (New York: Oxford University Press, 2000).

Internally displaced peoples

Cohen, Roberta, and Francis M. Deng, *Masses in Flight: The Global Crisis of Internal Displacement* (Washington DC: Brookings Institution, 1998).

Hampton, Janie (ed.), *Internally Displaced People: A Global Survey* (London: Earthscan, 1998).

Norwegian Refugee Council, *Internal Displacement: Global Overview of Trends and Developments in 2004*; available at www.idpproject.org/global_overview.htm.

Websites

In addition, readers can learn more about the different facets of international migration by visiting the following (very diverse) set of links:

The Brookings-Bern Project on Internal Displacement: www.brook.edu/fp/projects/idp/idp.htm.

Global Commission on International Migration (GCIM): www.gcim.org/en/links.html.

Humane Borders: www.humaneborders.org/index.htm.

International Organization for Migration (IOM): www.iom.int/.

ILO's International Labor Migration site: www.ilo.org/public/english/protection/migrant/.

Norwegian Refugee Council's Global IDP project: www.idpproject.org/.

OECD's Trends in International Migration and in Migration Policies site: www.oecd.org/department/0,2688,en_2649_33931_1_1_1_1_1,00.html.

Peter Stalker's guide to international migration: http://pstalker.com/migration/.

UNITED for Intercultural Action: www.united.non-profit.nl/.

Index

A BRAVE NEW SERIES

Global Issues
in a Changing World

This new series of short, accessible think-pieces deals with leading global issues of relevance to humanity today. Intended for the enquiring reader and social activists in the North and the South, as well as students, the books explain what is at stake and question conventional ideas and policies. Drawn from many different parts of the world, the series' authors pay particular attention to the needs and interests of ordinary people, whether living in the rich industrial or the developing countries. They all share a common objective – to help stimulate new thinking and social action in the opening years of the new century.

Global Issues in a Changing World is a joint initiative by Zed Books in collaboration with a number of partner publishers and non-governmental organizations around the world. By working together, we intend to maximize the relevance and availability of the books published in the series.

Participating NGOs

Both ENDS, Amsterdam
Catholic Institute for International Relations, London
Corner House, Sturminster Newton
Council on International and Public Affairs, New York
Dag Hammarskjöld Foundation, Uppsala
Development GAP, Washington DC
Focus on the Global South, Bangkok
IBON, Manila
Inter Pares, Ottawa
Public Interest Research Centre, Delhi
Third World Network, Penang
Third World Network–Africa, Accra
World Development Movement, London

About this series

'Communities in the South are facing great difficulties in coping with global trends. I hope this brave new series will throw much needed light on the issues ahead and help us choose the right options.'

MARTIN KHOR, *Director,*
Third World Network, Penang

'There is no more important campaign than our struggle to bring the global economy under democratic control. But the issues are fearsomely complex. This Global Issues series is a valuable resource for the committed campaigner and the educated citizen.'

BARRY COATES,
Director, Oxfam New Zealand

'Zed Books has long provided an inspiring list about the issues that touch and change people's lives. The Global Issues series is another dimension of Zed's fine record, allowing access to a range of subjects and authors that, to my knowledge, very few publishers have tried. I strongly recommend these new, powerful titles and this exciting series.'

JOHN PILGER, *author*

'We are all part of a generation that actually has the means to eliminate extreme poverty world-wide. Our task is to harness the forces of globalization for the benefit of working people, their families and their communities – that is our collective duty. The Global Issues series makes a powerful contribution to the global campaign for justice, sustainable and equitable development, and peaceful progress.'

GLENYS KINNOCK, *MEP*

The Global Issues series

Already available

Peggy Antrobus, *The Global Women's Movement: Origins, Issues and Strategies*

Walden Bello, *Deglobalization: Ideas for a New World Economy*

Robert Ali Brac de la Perrière and Franck Seuret, *Brave New Seeds: The Threat of GM Crops to Farmers*

Greg Buckman, *Globalization: Tame it or Scrap It?*

Greg Buckman, *Global Trade: Past Mistakes, Future Choices*

Ha-Joon Chang and Ilene Grabel, *Reclaiming Development: An Alternative Economic Policy Manual*

Koen De Feyter, *Human Rights: Social Justice in the Age of the Market*

Oswaldo de Rivero, *The Myth of Development: The Non-viable Economies of the 21st Century*

Graham Dunkley, *Free Trade: Myth, Reality and Alternatives*

Joyeeta Gupta, *Our Simmering Planet: What to Do about Global Warming?*

Nicholas Guyatt, *Another American Century? The United States and the World since 9/11*

Ann-Christin Sjölander Holland, *Water for Sale? Corporations against People*

Martin Khor, *Rethinking Globalization: Critical Issues and Policy Choices*

John Madeley, *Food for All: The Need for a New Agriculture*

John Madeley, *Hungry for Trade: How the Poor Pay for Free Trade*

Damien Millet and Eric Toussaint, *Who Owes Who? 50 Questions About World Debt*

Paola Monzini, *Sex Traffic: Prostitution, Crime and Exploitation*

Jonathon W. Moses, *International Migration: Globalization's Last Frontier*

A.G. Noorani, *Islam and Jihad: Prejudice versus Reality*

Riccardo Petrella, *The Water Manifesto: Arguments for a World Water Contract*

Peter Robbins, *Stolen Fruit: The Tropical Commodities Disaster*

Toby Shelley, *Oil: Politics, Poverty and the Planet*

Vandana Shiva, *Protect or Plunder? Understanding Intellectual Property Rights*

Harry Shutt, *A New Democracy: Alternatives to a Bankrupt World Order*

David Sogge, *Give and Take: What's the Matter with Foreign Aid?*

Paul Todd and Jonathan Bloch, *Global Intelligence: The World's Secret Services Today*

In preparation

Liz Kelly, *Violence against Women*

Alan Marshall, *A New Nuclear Age? The Case for Nuclear Power Revisited*

Roger Moody, *Digging the Dirt: The Modern World of Global Mining*

Edgar Pieterse, *City Futures: Confronting the Crisis of Urban Development*

Peter M. Rosset, *Food is Not Just Another Commodity: Why the WTO Should Get Out of Agriculture*

Toby Shelley, *Nanotechnology: New Promises, New Dangers*

Vivien Stern, *Creating Criminals: Prisons and People in a Market Society*

For full details of this list and Zed's other subject and general catalogues, please write to: The Marketing Department, Zed Books, 7 Cynthia Street, London N1 9JF, UK or email Sales@zedbooks.net

Visit our website at: www.zedbooks.co.uk

Participating organizations

Both ENDS   A service and advocacy organization which collaborates with environment and indigenous organizations, both in the South and in the North, with the aim of helping to create and sustain a vigilant and effective environmental movement.

> Nieuwe Keizersgracht 45, 1018 VC Amsterdam, The Netherlands
> Phone: +31 20 623 0823   Fax: +31 20 620 8049
> Email: info@bothends.org   Website: www.bothends.org

Catholic Institute for International Relations (CIIR)   CIIR aims to contribute to the eradication of poverty through a programme that combines advocacy at national and international level with community-based development.

> Unit 3, Canonbury Yard, 190a New North Road, London N1 7BJ, UK
> Phone +44 (0)20 7354 0883   Fax +44 (0)20 7359 0017
> Email: ciir@ciir.org   Website: www.ciir.org

Corner House   The Corner House is a UK-based research and solidarity group working on social and environmental justice issues in North and South.

> PO Box 3137, Station Road, Sturminster Newton, Dorset DT10 1YJ, UK
> Tel.: +44 (0)1258 473795   Fax: +44 (0)1258 473748
> Email: cornerhouse@gn.apc.org   Website: www.cornerhouse.icaap.org

Council on International and Public Affairs (CIPA)   CIPA is a human rights research, education and advocacy group, with a particular focus on economic and social rights in the USA and elsewhere around the world. Emphasis in recent years has been given to resistance to corporate domination.

> 777 United Nations Plaza, Suite 3C, New York, NY 10017, USA
> Tel. +1 212 972 9877   Fax +1 212 972 9878
> Email: cipany@igc.org   Website: www.cipa-apex.org

Dag Hammarskjöld Foundation   The Dag Hammarskjöld Foundation, established 1962, organises seminars and workshops on social, economic and cultural issues facing developing countries with a particular focus on alternative and innovative solutions. Results are published in its journal *Develpment Dialogue*.

> Övre Slottsgatan 2, 753 10 Uppsala, Sweden.
> Tel.: +46 18 102772   Fax: +46 18 122072
> Email: secretariat@dhf.uu.se   Website: www.dhf.uu.se

Development GAP The Development Group for Alternative Policies is a Non-Profit Development Resource Organization working with popular organizations in the South and their Northern partners in support of a development that is truly sustainable and that advances social justice.

927 15th Street NW, 4th Floor, Washington, DC, 20005, USA
Tel.: +1 202 898 1566   Fax: +1 202 898 1612
E-mail: dgap@igc.org   Website: www.developmentgap.org

Focus on the Global South Focus is dedicated to regional and global policy analysis and advocacy work. It works to strengthen the capacity of organizations of the poor and marginalized people of the South and to better analyse and understand the impacts of the globalization process on their daily lives.

C/o CUSRI, Chulalongkorn University, Bangkok 10330, Thailand
Tel.: +66 2 218 7363 Fax: +66 2 255 9976
Email: Admin@focusweb.org   Website: www.focusweb.org

IBON IBON Foundation is a research, education and information institution that provides publications and services on socio-economic issues as support to advocacy in the Philippines and abroad. Through its research and databank, formal and non-formal education programmes, media work and international networking, IBON aims to build the capacity of both Philippine and international organizations.

Room 303 SCC Bldg, 4427 Int. Old Sta. Mesa, Manila 1008, Philippines
Phone +632 7132729   Fax +632 7160108
Email: editors@ibon.org   Website: www.ibon.org

Inter Pares Inter Pares, a Canadian social justice organization, has been active since 1975 in building relationships with Third World development groups and providing support for community-based development programmes. Inter Pares is also involved in education and advocacy in Canada, promoting understanding about the causes, effects and solutions to poverty.

221 Laurier Avenue East, Ottawa, Ontario, KIN 6PI Canada
Phone +1 613 563 4801   Fax +1 613 594 4704
Email: info@interpares.ca   Website: www.interpares.ca

Public Interest Research Centre PIRC is a research and campaigning group based in Delhi which seeks to serve the information needs of activists and organizations working on macro-economic issues concerning finance, trade and development.

142 Maitri Apartments, Plot No. 28, Patparganj, Delhi 110092, India
Phone: +91 11 2221081/2432054   Fax: +91 11 2224233
Email: kaval@nde.vsnl.net.in

Third World Network TWN is an international network of groups and individuals involved in efforts to bring about a greater articulation of the needs and rights of peoples in the Third World; a fair distribution of the world's resources; and forms of development which are ecologically sustainable and fulfil human needs. Its international secretariat is based in Penang, Malaysia.

> 121-S Jalan Utama, 10450 Penang, Malaysia
> Tel.: +60 4 226 6159   Fax: +60 4 226 4505
> Email: twnet@po.jaring.my   Website: www.twnside.org.sg

Third World Network–Africa TWN–Africa is engaged in research and advocacy on economic, environmental and gender issues. In relation to its current particular interest in globalization and Africa, its work focuses on trade and investment, the extractive sectors and gender and economic reform.

> 2 Ollenu Street, East Legon, PO Box AN19452, Accra-North, Ghana.
> Tel.: +233 21 511189/503669/500419   Fax: +233 21 511188
> Email: twnafrica@ghana.com

World Development Movement (WDM) The World Development Movement campaigns to tackle the causes of poverty and injustice. It is a democratic membership movement that works with partners in the South to cancel unpayable debt and break the ties of IMF conditionality, for fairer trade and investment rules, and for strong international rules on multinationals.

> 25 Beehive Place, London SW9 7QR, UK
> Tel.: +44 (0)20 7737 6215   Fax: +44 (0)20 7274 8232
> Email: wdm@wdm.org.uk   Website: www.wdm.org.uk

This book is also available
in the following countries

CARIBBEAN

Arawak Publications
17 Kensington Crescent
Apt 5
Kingston 5, Jamaica
Tel: 876 960 7538
Fax: 876 960 9219

EGYPT

MERIC
2 Bahgat Ali Street,
Tower D/Apt. 24
Zamalek, Cairo
Tel: 20 2 735 3818/3824
Fax: 20 2 736 9355

FIJI

University Book Centre,
University of South Pacific
Suva
Tel: 679 313 900
Fax: 679 303 265

GUYANA

Austin's Book Services
190 Church St
Cummingsburg
Georgetown
austins@guyana.net.gy
Tel: 592 227 7395
Fax: 592 227 7396

IRAN

Book City
743 North Hafez Avenue
15977 Tehran
Tel: 98 21 889 7875
Fax: 98 21 889 7785
bookcity@neda.net

MAURITIUS

Editions Le Printemps
4 Club Rd, Vacoas

NAMIBIA

Book Den
PO Box 3469, Shop 4
Frans Indongo Gardens
Windhoek
Tel: 264 61 239976
Fax: 264 61 234248

NEPAL

Everest Media Services,
GPO Box 5443
Dillibazar
Putalisadak Chowk
Kathmandu
Tel: 977 1 416026
Fax: 977 1 250176

NIGERIA

Mosuro Publishers
52 Magazine Road
Jericho, Ibadan
Tel: 234 2 241 3375
Fax: 234 2 241 3374

PAKISTAN

Vanguard Books
45 The Mall, Lahore
Tel: 92 42 735 5079
Fax: 92 42 735 5197

PAPUA NEW GUINEA

Unisearch PNG Pty Ltd
Box 320, University
National Capital District
Tel: 675 326 0130
Fax: 675 326 0127

RWANDA

Librairie Ikirezi
PO Box 443, Kigali
Tel/Fax: 250 71314

SUDAN

The Nile Bookshop
New Extension Street 41
PO Box 8036, Khartoum
Tel: 249 11 463 749

UGANDA

Aristoc Booklex Ltd
PO Box 5130, Kampala Rd
Diamond Trust Building
Kampala
Tel/Fax: 256 41 254867

ZAMBIA

UNZA Press
PO Box 32379, Lusaka
Tel: 260 1 290409
Fax: 260 1 253952